EIBAR THE BRAVE

First published by Pitch Publishing, 2015

Pitch Publishing
A2 Yeoman Gate
Yeoman Way
Durrington
BN13 3QZ
www.pitchpublishing.co.uk

© Euan McTear, 2015
Edited by Dan Tester

All rights reserved. No part of this book may be reproduced, sold or utilised in any form or transmitted in any form or by any means, electronic or mechanical, including photocopying, recording or by any information storage and retrieval system, without prior permission in writing from the Publisher.

A CIP catalogue record is available for this book from the British Library.

ISBN 978 178531-036-2

Typesetting and origination by Pitch Publishing
Printed Nutech Print Services - India

EIBAR THE BRAVE

THE EXTRAORDINARY RISE OF LA LIGA'S SMALLEST TEAM

EUAN MCTEAR

Contents

Acknowledgements 6

Foreword 7

Introduction 9

   1. A Fairytale Season: Act 1 11

   2. Modelo 32

   3. A Fairytale Season: Act 2 48

   4. Ipurua 66

   5. A Fairytale Season: Act 3 89

   6. Ascenso 105

   7. A Fairytale Season: Act 4 128

   8. Ánimo 143

   9. A Fairytale Season: Act 5 160

   10. Justicia 186

Acknowledgements

I am extremely thankful for the input and advice of so many people for this, my first book.

I'd like to thank my girlfriend Rebecca and parents David and Petrina for allowing me to lock myself away from real life for so long to focus on this work, while also dragging me away from my desk often enough to keep me sane.

All of the staff I have come across at SD Eibar for their help, particularly president Álex Aranzábal, Iñaki Duque and Patricia Rodriguez Barrios. I'd also like to thank Colin at the press office of Derby County for allowing me to speak with their new signing Raúl Albentosa.

Those who took the time to speak to me about Eibar, in alphabetical order: Raúl Albentosa, Guillem Balague, Andrés Basurto, Henry Boguslavsky, Chris Clements, Joseba Combarro, Verónica Díez, Jose Enrique, Unai Eraso, Alba Garin-Muga, Sid Lowe, Mikel Mandinabeita, Javier Ortiz de Lazcano, Jason Pettigrove, Paul Reidy and John Sager.

Revista Líbero, Diario Vasco and *El Correo* for granting me the rights to some of their exclusive interviews to be featured in this work.

Félix Morquecho, who has been photographing Eibar since 1999 and whose excellent and iconic images can be found in the centre of this book.

Paul and Jane at Pitch Publishing for giving me the chance to write this remarkable story, Dan Tester for editing, and also to Duncan Olner who used Félix's photos to design the beautiful cover.

And finally, I'd like to thank SD Eibar, their players and coaching staff for providing me with a wonderful story to write about. No work of fiction could have come up with a tale so interesting, which is a testament to the monumental achievement of this plucky underdog.

Living On A Roller Coaster

A Foreword by Eibar President Álex Aranzábal

The past 16 months – from February 2014 to July 2015 – have been for me, as president of Sociedad Deportiva Eibar, a vertiginous experience; it has been a continuous roller coaster of valleys and peaks, of climbs and falls.

In February 2014, when we found ourselves in prime position to try to achieve the greatest sporting success in the history of our club – a first promotion to the *Primera* division – our foundations were shaken by a legal requirement from the sport's ministry which was as absurd as it was unfair.

Despite being a healthy club with no debts and zero deficit, the country's sports law obliged us to undertake a raising of our social capital by almost €2million and we had to do so in a period of six months. Failing to achieve the target would not only have meant forfeiting the possible promotion to the *Primera*, but would have ended up with the club being relegated to the *Segunda* B.

After passing from amazement to incredulity and from incredulity to fear, we got to work and, conscious that we would not be able to achieve the objective on our own, we launched an international marketing campaign that quickly went viral and which allowed us to achieve success in the middle of July, before the deadline.

The end result was that we had a massive group of shareholders, with more than 10,000 shareholders from more than 70 countries and from all corners of the world.

To reach that moment, the team had secured a spectacular sporting success which was practically unheard of in the history of Spanish football; they won two consecutive promotions to reach the very top at meteoric speed, with a stadium capacity of hardly 5,000 and from a town of fewer than 28,000 residents.

The beginning of our *Primera* division debut was spectacular, with an excellent first round of fixtures leaving us in eighth position in the league standings and as the best Basque team. The dream was not ending.

However, nothing has ever been easy in the town of Eibar. The results started to turn against us, the team's form collapsed and, after picking up just eight points in the second half of the season and after a cruel final day in which the team fell from heaven to hell in hardly ten minutes, Eibar was relegated to the *Segunda* division.

We still hadn't fully recovered from the tremendous disappointment when a window of hope was opened to us because of the disastrous financial situation of Elche, a club with debts on all fronts and at serious risk of administrative relegation because of its repeated non-payments to *Hacienda*, the Spanish taxman, and to its players.

At the beginning of June, the Spanish Football League relegated Elche and just over a month later the Court of Sporting Discipline confirmed this ruling, one which returned Eibar to the *Primera*. The final ruling lay in the hands of the ordinary courts, to which Elche then turned in an attempt to save their position in the top division.

In reality, all of this, that which has occurred in the last year and a half, is a summary of the whole history of Eibar. It is a history full of great successes and deep disappointments and one which is, above all, characterised by the same spirit of resilience with which the city of Eibar was able to literally rise from its ashes after lying devastated at the time of the Spanish Civil War following a long and bloody siege.

Ten years have already passed since I became a director at Eibar, six of them as president. They have probably been the most exciting and enriching years of my life and they have helped me to understand the significance of a quote from the Nobel Prize in Literature winner Albert Camus which seemed to me a great exaggeration when I heard it for the first time: "Everything I know about morality and the obligations of men, I owe it to football."

Eibar is a football club, but above all it is an expression of the identity of a town. For that reason, as president I have tried to ensure that the football becomes more than just football and that it permeates all of society, at the same time spreading all of the positive values that this noble sport is capable of passing on.

I firmly believe that football is more than just football and I strive each day to instil a fairer and more democratic management model in which all, even the very smallest, have a place and are respected.

Each little step in this journey is a great triumph for everyone.

Álex Aranzábal,
Eibar,
July 2015

Introduction

I first came across Sociedad Deportiva Eibar in Tom Shields's sports diary in *The Glasgow Herald* in 2005. I was just a teenager at the time and I'm sure I was only attracted to the piece because of the pictures, but the links between Eibar and Scotland were immediately laid out and over the next decade – particularly as my interest in Spanish football grew with a move to Barcelona – I took pleasure in fleeting glimpses of lower league Spanish football scores whenever Eibar's name popped up in the wins column.

Then, in 2014, Eibar's story escalated and I began to seriously investigate this amazing football club.

This book tells Eibar's fairytale, a story for football's frog princes, beanstalk scalers and sleeping beauties. It is a Cinderella story in which our protagonist is the ugly sister of Spanish football and was never supposed to go to the La Liga ball. That was indeed the case until a footballing miracle elevated this modest and tiny club to the heights of La Liga in 2014. In the club's very own words: 'To celebrate the 75th anniversary of the club by playing in stadiums like the Camp Nou, Bernabéu or San Mamés was not even in our wildest dreams.'

It is a tale that Hollywood script writers would discard for being too far-fetched. Thankfully, however, the footballing gods have allowed Spanish football's most extraordinary story to be told; a story that is greater than a Messi dribble, greater than *la décima* and greater than *that* night in Soccer City.

This is no Middle East oil or American sugar daddy-backed fairytale. The scene of the heroics is Ipurua, a stadium which does not carry the name of any airline or energy drink. The closest the fans get to the players is not a life-size cardboard cutout in the club megastore; rather the players meet with and know the fans by name.

Eibar's story may not generate the 'good traffic' that some modern journalists strive for and that a story about Neymar's new tattoo or Ronaldo's romances might. However, this is a story actually worth telling.

EIBAR THE BRAVE

In my research for this book, my understanding of Eibar's history and values has increased infinityfold from that Sunday afternoon reading Tom Shields's sports diary. I aim to share that insight with you through the following series of tales.

1

A Fairytale Season: *Act 1*

"We have a lot of respect for the game and for Eibar. It's not easy to play on this pitch."

Carlo Ancelotti

Saturday, 22nd November 2014. Ipurua Stadium, Eibar.
It is 133 days since Toni Kroos cradled the World Cup on the confetti-laden pitch of the Maracanã in Rio de Janeiro, in front of almost 75,000 people. Today, the German superstar is playing in front of another sell-out crowd, yet today's record attendance figure won't even reach 6,000. This is Ipurua Municipal Stadium, home of Sociedad Deportiva Eibar and La Liga's smallest ever club.

Joining Kroos in European champions – and soon to be world champions – Real Madrid's starting XI are seven other players who represented their country in the summer's carnival of football in Brazil, including 2010 winners Sergio Ramos and the captain of that triumphant 2010 Spanish *La Roja* side, Iker Casillas. As if that wasn't enough glitz to bring on the roadshow to La Liga's tiniest stadium, this starting XI also includes the star of the World Cup, James Rodríguez, and the world's most expensive player, Gareth Bale. And joining them up front? Yes, that's Cristiano Ronaldo warming up.

There's a Harlem Globetrotters-esque sense of inevitability about the visit of this star-studded Real Madrid side, on a 13-match winning run in Spain's top division. However, there is a hugely significant league fixture to be played this Saturday evening and declaring an away win before a ball is kicked would be arrogant in the extreme.

Eibar come into this fixture, the twelfth of the 2014/15 Spanish La Liga season, in ninth place. The minnows are, at this point, the highest Basque club in the table – no mean feat given that Athletic Club de Bilbao and Real Sociedad both qualified for European competition the previous season – and it would be understandable for the club hailing from a town of just 27,000 people to be suffering from La Liga altitude sickness. Eibar is comparable in size to the likes of Elgin, Morecambe, Fleetwood or Glossop North End, which with a population of 30,000 is the smallest town to have ever produced a top division football club in England – although it is difficult to compare that achievement with this given the Hillmen's last top-flight appearance came in the 1899/1900 season.

The ever-articulate Real Madrid coach Carlo Ancelotti has shown no signs of getting carried away ahead of this match, telling the media: "We have a lot of respect for the game and for Eibar. It's not easy to play on this pitch." The odds, however, are firmly in his side's favour and the locals flocking up the town's outdoor escalators towards Ipurua for the match, while hopeful, understand which outcome is most likely. The fact Cristiano Ronaldo, with his pay packet of almost €17million per year, earns more than SD Eibar's entire annual €15.9million budget is just one of those unbelievable comparisons normally reserved for cup ties contested between clubs several divisions apart.

Think David versus Goliath, but imagine David doesn't even get to use a slingshot because Goliath has already bought it from him. Yes, the difference between these two clubs is that vast.

Another example… In the summer of 2009 Real Madrid spent a then-record fee of €93million to bring Ronaldo to the Bernabéu, a figure Eibar could only ever dream of and likely wouldn't even bother to. To celebrate the signing, Real staged a presentation in front of a near-capacity crowd of 80,000 fans. In contrast, over the whole of the 2013/14 season Eibar's total aggregate attendance after 21 home league fixtures was 63,440, still thousands short of the figure that watched Ronaldo perform a few keepy-uppies that summer evening in 2009.

And that €100million fee Real Madrid paid when they made Gareth Bale the world's most expensive player? Yes, that was slightly larger than Eibar's record transfer fee, paid when Dani Nieto signed from Barcelona in the 2014 summer; his €200,000 fee was a massive 500 times smaller.

In the end, the little hope given to Eibar is justified. Real Madrid coolly dispatch of the *Primera* newcomers and depart Ipurua with a 4-0 victory and the three points they have visited this Basque valley town for.

To lose by four is unfair on Eibar, with James Rodríguez's first goal – a header from a yard out – featuring a touch from an offside Karim Benzema in its build-up. The goal stands and Eibar are behind on 23 minutes, just after they appear to be settling into the game and not long after local boy Jon Errasti – the only *eibarrés*, the only player actually from the town, in the Eibar squad – nutmegs Rodríguez, the €80million star of the World Cup and – although he doesn't know it yet – winner of the FIFA Puskás Award for goal of the year.

A FAIRYTALE SEASON: ACT 1

Having exacted his revenge for that humiliation, Rodríguez and his team-mates lead, but things could be so different had Eibar's Manu del Moral converted a clear chance. Unfortunately, for the home crowd, he fluffs his lines and instead scuffs a powder-puff shot towards Casillas's goal. That proves even more costly when, just before the break, Ronaldo nudges a shot into the top corner from just inside the box, prompting his normally reserved manager Carlo Ancelotti to show his whimsical side, mimicking his star forward's celebration. There's something in the Eibar air that makes even the coolest of us act a little differently.

So Eibar retreat at the break two goals down despite having matched the league leaders across the pitch and already the blue and claret balloons of the home support are beginning to deflate as the result appears confirmed.

The second half fails to provide any miraculous comeback; luck again deserts Eibar when Karim Benzema scores in the 70th minute after James Rodríguez crosses a ball that had appeared to cross the chalk line at the end of the ground where Eibar's famous and lively fan group *Eskozia La Brava* – translated as 'Scotland the Brave' – sit just a couple of metres behind the goal. Having been in a much better position to see the ball cross the line than the referee, the passionate fan group very 'politely' offer their advice to the man in the middle. Unsurprisingly, they don't receive much change from the referee and the goal stands to make the score 3-0. The fourth follows shortly afterwards when a Ronaldo free kick strikes hero centre-back Raúl Albentosa on the arm and a penalty is given. The Portuguese nets his 20th goal of the season from the spot, in just the 11th week.

And that's that – Second division champions 0. European champions 4.

Despite losing by four goals, the 5,859 crowd at Ipurua – a stadium record which doesn't even take into account the hundreds more watching from the apartments which overlook the pitch – is not as distraught as one might expect. Today has been a heady day, not just thanks to the beer and cider drank in the main square along with a full kilometre of sausages and a meringue the size of a bus. Just two seasons previously, this club was playing in Spain's third tier and fantasies of Saturday night encounters with Real Madrid were exactly that: fantasies. Now Eibar have made it to Spain's top division and they will still be in the top half by the end of this weekend – a cause for a *fiesta*.

There's a Basque proverb which says; *'Dantzatu nahi ez dana, ez doala dantzara.'* It translates as; 'If you don't want to dance, don't go to a dance.' Two years ago, Eibar dreamed of dancing with the giants like Real Madrid. Now they are finally here partying with the big boys, the fans aren't going to let a 4-0 loss ruin their night. They are here for a party, a party which began three months earlier with the first La Liga match in Eibar's history.

Sunday, 24th August 2014. Ipurua Stadium, Eibar.

The 2014/15 La Liga season begins with a Basque derby in the opening *jornada*, the word for each round of fixtures. Yet both San Mamés stadium in Bilbao and Anoeta in San Sebastián lie empty.

Where is this Basque derby being held then? The answer: almost exactly halfway between the largest two cities of the Basque Country, in little Eibar. Sociedad Deportiva Eibar is about to face Real Sociedad as an equal in Spain's *Primera* division, a match that no amount of tea leaf reading could ever have predicted.

For Eibar, competing against Real Sociedad, or Athletic Club de Bilbao, is in many ways like lining up against a big brother. Over the decades since the club was formed in 1940, both their Basque neighbours have taken turns to 'look out for' Eibar by being *convenido*, linked, to the Ipurua club.

As Javier Ortiz de Lazcano, a football correspondent for Basque newspaper *El Correo*, explains to me: "Right now, there is an agreement with Real Sociedad, by which I mean they loan out players to Eibar and in return Eibar gives preference to Real when selling their own players if Real can match the offers of other clubs. In other periods there have been similar agreements with Athletic Club. It's swung from club to club naturally over time."

"Eibar knows the help from Real has been key to reaching the top," Javier also points out.

There is no rule to impede two teams in the same division having such a *convenido* agreement and, as such, one Real Sociedad loanee this season is Raúl Navas; the player starts for Eibar today, as he has done for the past two seasons. Having been bought by Real in the summer, the Andalusian has been loaned back to Eibar for one further campaign. As well as discussing Navas, the Eibar fans making the procession towards this derby run the rule over the rest of their newly-assembled top-flight squad of loanees and journeymen. Unanimous opinion is that Navas's centre-back partner Raúl Albentosa is one of the most talented players in the team and that the two Raúls will dominate the centre of defence in place of the 35-but-going-on-50 club captain and legend Txema Añibarro, who will be the oldest player to ever debut in the *Primera* and who is expected to content himself with the odd cameo appearance. Like Añibarro, ex-Athletic youth teamer Borja Ekiza will be an adequate stand-in when required.

The rest of the defence is also highly regarded, with keeper Irureta an obvious fan favourite having won the Zamora Award for his efforts in defending his goalposts like the most agile of Russian gymnasts during the promotion campaign. Eneko Bóveda, the right-back and Telecommunications Engineering student who arrived in 2011 after turning down a contract at Athletic Club, deserves his chance too. Less obvious is who will win the left-back role, with Abraham – on loan from Real Zaragoza – starting today and Dídac Vilà set to sign on a year's loan from AC Milan in the coming days.

In midfield, Dani García has arrived from Real Sociedad on a permanent deal after a loan spell and there is no doubt that he and local hero Jon Errasti will form a formidable partnership in central midfield. Eibar youth product Ander Capa has impressed over the previous promotions and those around Ipurua believe he has earned his spot on the right wing, while Javi Lara will line up on the opposite flank. Although nobody is quite sure what to make of this new arrival from Ponferradina, the fans here will be singing Javi Lara's praises before the sun falls behind those mountains in the distance.

Despite the fact he won't start today, the last-minute arrival of former Ghana international defensive midfielder Derek Boateng is an excitingly intriguing one, while there are also high hopes for the two ex-Barcelona B wingers, Dani Nieto and Saúl Berjón.

The most polemic position among the fans concerns who should accompany legendary striker and all-time Eibar top goalscorer, Mikel Arruabarrena, up front, a traditional poacher with the bolt-on of outstanding technical skill and the ability to effectively hold up the ball. Free agent Ángel gets the chance to start alongside him ahead of Manu del Moral today, but the loan deal to bring Sampdoria striker Federico Piovaccari – a man with a reputation for getting both goals and bookings in roughly equal measure – is the one which appears to have attracted the most excitement. The serial loanee – as a quick glance at his Wikipedia page will make clear – is as exotic a signing as they come for Eibar fans, having just helped Steaua București to the Romanian league title with ten goals in 25 appearances the previous season.

It is a decent squad, but unquestionably the worst in the division. If anyone can get a tune out of this group, however, it is current manager and miracle worker Gaizka Garitano, the brains behind the club's double promotion. Once again, Garitano will have to work with a new group of loanees and free signings, some of whom haven't even learned their team-mates' names yet. While not an ideal way to build a team for Spain's top tier, Eibar's sporting director Fran Garagarza is forever grateful to the loan arrangements in place with clubs like Real Sociedad.

The fact that such agreements have always been able to exist between Eibar and its Basque neighbours stems from the fact they have very rarely played in the same division and, consequently, have never been direct rivals. Eibar met Athletic in the 2012/13 *Copa del*

Rey – in fact knocking their big brother out of the tournament – while Real Sociedad and Eibar met competitively four times in Spain's second division, the *Segunda*, between 2007 and 2009 when the San Sebastián club was relegated from La Liga. Having spent all of their existence until today in the lower tiers of Spanish football, Eibar have much more frequently met the B teams of their neighbours – on 32 occasions – than they have met the first teams. That will begin to change today, however, in the Gipuzkoa – the region of the Basque Country that Eibar and Real Sociedad call home – derby.

As the 22 players, all of them Spaniards – this is the first La Liga match since Sporting Gijón versus Athletic Club in 2010 to feature no foreigners – and 13 of them Basque, take to the rugged Ipurua pitch for a first division match, the Eibar and Real fans alike understand the poignancy of the occasion.

It has not been at all easy to make this dream a reality for Eibar, with the club having had to jump through a series of hoops in order to comply with an absurd 1999 Spanish law which required an increase in their social capital of €1.7million. Nor was it easy for Eibar on the football pitch, having had to work extra hard to win the 2013/14 second division – the *Segunda* – title with the smallest budget in the division. We'll discuss that later on, but for now the only thing that matters to Eibar is being here.

Correction: two things matter to Eibar this Sunday afternoon. Yes, being here in La Liga is one but also clear once the match kicks off is that getting the three points also matters to Garitano's team. There had been a lot of chatter in the Spanish press – there is always a lot of chatter in the Spanish press, to be fair, without particularly much ever being said – before Eibar's top-flight debut on just how uncompetitive *los armeros* – the gunners as they are nicknamed – would be. Would they perform even worse than the 1997/98 Sporting Gijón team which collected La Liga's record fewest points tally – since three points for a win was introduced – of 13? Many thought they would.

After their first 90 minutes of the season, the minnows are already just ten points away from equalling Gijón's record.

The home side dominate 'big brother' Real in the first 45 minutes, nearly taking the lead twice from close-range headers. First, Raúl Navas has a crack; he heads inches wide from a seventh-minute corner. Ángel then sends another header off target minutes later.

The crowd has been excited since the early hours of the morning when the town centre was already a sea of blue and claret, referred to as *azulgrana*. Scarves, flags and replica shirts – the 2014/15 version sold out within days – were the backdrop for the singing, chanting and fireworks show which began in earnest at midday, but the locals are even more encouraged now by the way Eibar open the match. That

Real's goalkeeper Zubikarai has to make a tremendous double save from Javi Lara and Mikel Arruabarrena only adds to the growing sense that Eibar could win this match, and possibly do so comfortably. Javi Lara turns expectation into celebration just before the stroke of half-time with an incredible free kick from the tightest of angles. Just a few metres out from the corner flag, he lofts the ball beautifully into the far top corner via the post, sending his team-mates wild and the Ipurua decibel levels soaring anew.

The euphoria lasts throughout the break and beyond, only slightly dampened during a second half in which Real Sociedad finally appear to wake up from their summer slumber. Wave after wave of coherent attack flows towards Xabi Irureta's goal, but former Eibar full-back Yuri Berchiche shoots wide, as does substitute Carlos Vela, while Imanol Agirretxe's drilled effort finds Irureta in its way. Several more chances, many from set pieces, fall the visitors' way, but the match is drawing to a close.

Were there a clock in the stadium it would tell you that the 90 minutes are up, but there is little need for one given it is easily read from the anxious faces in the stands that stoppage time has arrived. The pressure and tension build without any clear chances being carved out and as soon as Irureta falls on Chory Castro's long-range bullet in the fourth minute of additional time, the result is confirmed. Eibar become the only side in history with a 100% record in Spain's top division, while Garitano is – on this August day – only the second permanent manager to boast a personal 100% winning record; the other, remarkably, is his uncle Ander.

'*Unsta habiatu den lana, erdi akabirik,*' as they say in the Basque Country. 'Well begun is half done.' In terms of achieving the ultimate goal of avoiding a bottom-three finish, and thus avoiding relegation in this 20-team league, Eibar have started as well as they possibly could. thirty-seven matches remain, but this has been the most moralising of victories.

Monday, 25th August 2014. Times Square, New York City.

Times Square has turned purple. Prince is set to release two new albums – hence the purple – and ABC's *Good Morning America* programme is here to see it. Prince himself hasn't joined the gathering, but has kindly sent his backing band 3rdeyegirl – yes, that is a name – to announce the new releases to the world. Guitarist Donna Grantis makes the big announcement that the *Purple Rain* artist is to release his first new material since 2010 in front of a sea of purple flags, purple banners and purple T-shirts. The centre of New York has gone full purple. Well, almost.

As well as the purple there is a little bit of *azulgrana* present in Times Square this Monday morning. As 3rdeyegirl reveal the big news to America, the blue and claret stripes of a flag with the words '*Aupa Eibar*', basically saying 'Come on Eibar', slowly rises above the purple-clothed-and-now-slightly-confused crowd in the shot's background; the flag immediately takes up over half the TV screen as the camera zooms in on the band.

As big a deal as Prince's new album releases are for Prince fans, Eibar's achievement against Real Sociedad yesterday was even bigger for fans of the club and that fanbase is now a global one. Eibar mania has even infected Times Square, perhaps the most iconic global location on the planet.

While Eibar's fanbase is extending to foreign and exotic locations, news of the club's victory appears in similarly foreign territory: the front pages of the Spanish press. It may only be in the Basque press that Eibar actually make the front page headlines – Barcelona also played the night before and Real Madrid are to play on the Monday evening so the pair dominate the headlines elsewhere – but for their result to even appear on the front page of *Marca* is unheard of for Eibar. This morning's *Diario Vasco* shouts 'Eibar Keeps Dreaming' on its front page, while *Mundo Deportivo* announces that 'Eibar Debuts In Style', albeit not until page 30 after countless column inches of Messi worship.

Eibar will again make it on to the front pages of the press the following weekend; they face reigning La Liga champions Atlético Madrid in a Saturday night showdown in the capital. Following the unbelievable situation at the end of the previous season in which Spanish Football Federation president Ángel María Villar couldn't attend the most important match of the season as Barcelona faced Atlético in a head-to-head duel for the title on the final day, Atlético have still not been presented with their La Liga trophy. Now two weeks into the following season, Diego Simeone's title-winning squad – or what remains of it – will finally be able to lift their tenth league trophy ahead of their first home match of the season against Eibar.

The three Atlético captains Gabi, Raúl García and Diego Godín collect the trophy in front of a packed Vicente Calderón Stadium before bringing it down to the pitch to march through a guard of honour performed by the Eibar team.

Usually following a trophy presentation it is time to go home, but this presentation is instead the warm-up for an important match, particularly so for the hosts who have already dropped points at Rayo Vallecano in their season opener. Receiving the trophy certainly warms Atlético Madrid up and it takes only 12 minutes for João Miranda to open the scoring with a typical Atlético goal from a corner. If Eibar hadn't realised by then that set pieces are where this Atlético team is at its most dangerous then their hosts oblige with a further schooling another 12 minutes later when Mario Mandžukić heads home from Gabi's free kick.

The game should be over there and then, but this Eibar team is both plucky and talented, from the players on the pitch to their medic Ostaiska Egia – who bravely scolds some abusive Atlético fans who dare make sexist comments towards her. On the pitch, the players are just as prepared to stand up for themselves and defend Atlético's crosses into the box, as well as working their way up the park on the counter attack. A flash of the talent this Eibar squad possesses then shines through in the 33rd minute with an absolute *golazo,* a wonder goal. Javi Lara picks up the ball just past the halfway line on the left-hand side of the pitch and picks out left-back Abraham on the wing who jinks inside and knocks the ball through Gabi's legs to Ángel, who has already spotted the run of Arruabarrena into the box. A neat back-heel from Arruabarrena sets the ball up cleanly for Abraham, but there is still no way this lovely move is going to finish in a goal from Abraham, a player who has picked up four red cards since his last goal two years and five months ago. Surely not…

This is Eibar, remember. Expect the unexpected. They achieve the unachievable. And Abraham does indeed score that unscorable goal, curling the ball teed-up for him so perfectly by Arruabarrena into the far top corner from just outside the box. Game on.

Atlético are too good to panic and continue to pressure the Eibar defence. They find a defiant Irureta in goal and Eibar soon discover a new lease of life, breaking into the large spaces left behind every Atlético charge forward. In the second half, Mario Suárez could, but doesn't, see a second yellow card for swiping out at Eibar's Dani García. Just as worrying for the hosts is the fact that Eibar are grasping more and more control in the match. Javi Lara loops a 74th-minute free kick into the box which right-back Eneko Bóveda really should knock into the net – instead it bounces a yard wide. Bóveda's isn't to be Eibar's last or best chance. That falls to Ángel, whose poked shot picks up enough of a touch from Atlético stopper Moyá's fingernails to roll past the post. Two minutes later the final whistle echoes around the Vicente Calderón, as does a collective sigh of relief.

It finishes *Primera* champions 2. *Segunda* champions 1.

It is Abraham's goal that will stick in the memory – and rightly so, for it is ridiculously good – but the overall graft, grit and determination of this performance is what should impress Eibar fans most. The team's heroics will again receive plenty of attention in the following day's press, although the world-class team goal of Eibar's AAA – Abraham, Arruabarrena and Ángel – won't quite knock Real Madrid's BBC – Benzema, Bale and Cristiano – from the back pages. Hidden a little deeper in the Sunday sports papers will be the praise Eibar deserves.

The main photos of the match justifiably show Atlético players, coaches and directors parading the La Liga trophy, but a snap of Abraham's *golazo* would be just as worthy of a full-page spread.

Saturday, 27th September 2014. Somera Kalea, Bilbao.

'Somera es azulgrana. ¡Es azulgrana! Somera es azulgrana.'
So rings out the chant on Somera Kalea, a street which runs through the old town Casco Viejo area of Bilbao like a vein. It certainly looks like a vein today, with a stream of blue and a tint of claret winding its way along the whole street. It is only midday, but the fans of SD Eibar have already taken over. Today, on derby day, Somera Street is most definitely blue and claret.

Only 1,200 Eibar fans have tickets for this evening's match in the new San Mamés stadium, but with the town of Eibar just 50 kilometres and 40 minutes away, double that number have made the short trip to Bilbao to soak up the feel-good atmosphere of this gloriously sunny September afternoon. The first buses arrived at 11am and disgorged a tide of fans – a true wave of blue, claret and skin – towards their first stop of Somera, a street packed with bars and draped in the red and white colours of Athletic Club. It is soon packed with supporters of Eibar and promptly declared occupied by the famous *Eskozia La Brava* fan group.

There is certainly a party atmosphere here as *pintxos* – popular Basque snacks of meat stapled to bread by a cocktail stick – are shared, glasses of beer are toasted, games are played and old friends are reunited. The blue and claret of Eibar is eventually matched by the red and white of Athletic fans – who were not quite as punctual but who now arrive in numbers – and the two sets of fans mix amicably without any hint of trouble whatsoever. The children are kept occupied by pop-up games of 'Beat the Goalie' and the lion mascots of Athletic, while the adults move from bar to bar drinking *copa* after *copa* of beer. The barkeepers are also out and about criss-crossing Somera as they return the stacks of glasses that fans have brought with them from one bar to the next, much like the swash and backwash of sand moving along a shoreline.

This evening's match is a grand occasion for both teams and is the first-ever time Athletic and Eibar will meet in the league; Athletic, on one hand, have never been relegated from the top tier of Spanish football, while Eibar is enjoying its maiden season in the *Primera*.

And, enjoying it they most definitely are. After five rounds of matches, Eibar find themselves in the top half of the league table in a lofty ninth position, while Athletic find themselves in the relegation zone after picking up just three points from their first weeks of the season. Real Sociedad have thus far not fared much better, making Eibar the highest-placed Basque team ahead of this derby.

A FAIRYTALE SEASON: ACT 1

The 1-0 win against Real Sociedad kick-started Eibar's cause, while the defeat away to Atlético Madrid was not too costly and the fact that they never gave up even won the gunners many admirers. Next up for Gaizka Garitano's side was the visit of Deportivo La Coruña the following Monday and this was a match which would again end in defeat, though quite how Deportivo managed to take all three points remains a mystery. Eibar started with the same 11 players as had lined up against Real and Atlético and by the end of the match had 14 shots on goal to Deportivo's four. Despite their limited chances it was Deportivo that managed to find the back of the net; Juan Domínguez's 13th-minute strike was among the luckiest goals of the season as a Juanfran cross from the right wing fell, like manna from heaven, to Domínguez just five yards from goal, thanks to a generous ricochet off Eibar's Bóveda. Deportivo's number ten didn't pass up the opportunity and the team that Eibar pipped to the second division title the previous season led.

Eibar quickly set about correcting the scoreline and would create enough chances to reverse the deficit, but could not capitalise on a single one of them. The second period continued in the same vein with chances for Dani Nieto, Saúl Berjón and Javi Lara. It wasn't to be and, although the opponents were a fellow newly-promoted side, the match certainly taught Eibar how costly not being clinical could be in La Liga. In his post-match press conference, Garitano commented on the difference between life in the first and second divisions: "We played well for many minutes. They, with a few good minutes, have won by just the one goal. We dominated but we lacked that good pass or good move in the final third. This is the difference between the *Primera* and the *Segunda*."

Luckily for Garitano's squad, they would get the opportunity to put things right just four days later in the week's Friday night game away to Elche. And put things right they did.

For the first time since December 2013, Elche lost a home match. Eibar took the lead in the third minute with a sweet long-range effort from Dani García that pinged into the back of the net via the left upright. After diffusing a brief period of pressure from the locals in the first half, Eibar were able to add to their lead three minutes before the break to round off the first half in palindromic style. Raúl Albentosa, the ex-Elche centre-back who had until then dominated all action in his own penalty box, proved key at the other end of the pitch as he leapt to nod the corner sent in by Saúl Berjón – the only change to the starting line-up from the first three matches – into the empty net after Elche's Polish keeper Tyton had fortuitously found himself caught up in traffic. It would remain 2-0 and the impressive win saw Eibar double their points tally for the season, a tally that would again be added to the following Wednesday.

Despite playing three weekday matches in a row, it should be noted that midweek games are not, in fact, all that common in the Spanish league. Each round or fixtures, called a *jornada*, has at most two weekday matches on a Friday and Monday night, while there tend to be only a couple of full *jornadas* per season held on a Tuesday and Wednesday. One such midweek round was to follow the Elche trip as Eibar welcomed Villarreal to Ipurua for Garitano's 100th match in charge. The 'Yellow Submarine' was an opponent to be wary of and was the third opponent from Eibar's first five La Liga matches that had qualified for Europe the previous season, making Eibar's decent opening run of results all the more impressive.

As they had done the previous Friday night at Elche's Martínez Valero Stadium, Eibar would start as brightly as Villarreal's kit was yellow. It may have taken Eibar's star striker Mikel Arruabarrena five matches to grab his first goal of the season, but it only took the man from neighbouring Tolosa eight minutes of this particular match to find the back of the net. Saúl Berjón started the move with an intelligent one-two free kick that allowed him to take the ball down the left flank before lofting a cross into the centre. It fell to Borja, who made the visiting keeper save down low, but Villarreal couldn't clear and after some frantic attempts at doing so, the ball fell for Borja's defensive partner Albentosa, who squared it for captain Arruabarrena to crossbow the ball into the net like Robin Hood stealing from the rich and giving to Eibar.

Shortly afterwards, Saúl Berjón would again send a dangerous ball in from the left wing, this time aiming for goal from 30 yards out and nearly finding the net; Asenjo in the visiting goal had to be at full stretch to tip it over. Villarreal would hit the top of the Eibar crossbar, but the first 45 minutes belonged to the home side and they were given a standing ovation as they headed for the tunnel at the break. The second half would see a complete role-reversal and the fans in Ipurua's West Stand – also known as the stand of *las monjas*, of the nuns, due to its proximity to the old convent – saw all the action take place at their end once again. Those fans would have seen the ball strike the arm of Abraham in the Eibar box, but the referee failed to see it himself so Eibar escaped the punishment of a penalty. Villarreal would soon score regardless; Gerard Moreno appeared just inside the box to curl the ball around Irureta with only 20 minutes remaining.

That was how Eibar picked up a seventh point from five matches and the reason they find themselves above neighbours Athletic Club – who have only picked up three – ahead of today's late September derby. Even a defeat for the visiting minnows would see them remain ahead of Athletic in the league table, but Eibar's fans are dreaming of an even more memorable result, such as the one in the 2012/13 *Copa del Rey* when a 1-1 draw in the old San Mamés knocked the Basque giants out on away goals. The locals are keen to avoid a repeat, while the guests are even keener to force one.

As the match approaches, it's time for the hundreds of Eibar fans to leave Somera and to head westwards towards the brand new San Mamés stadium.

"How are we getting to the stadium?" I ask the immediately-likable head of the *Eskozia La Brava* fan group Joseba Combarro, curious as to whether we'll be walking, getting a bus or taking the underground. I certainly don't expect his reply.

"*Barco,*" he says.

I must look confused because he switches to English.

"Boat," he repeats.

It isn't the Spanish that causes my confusion, but I'm surprised nonetheless. "Boat?!" I think to myself. What kind of a fan group travels to the match by boat?! I should know by now that *Eskozia La Brava* is no ordinary fan group.

Sure enough, as we reach the banks of the Nervión River, there is a boat awaiting us and the members of the group quickly set about attaching banners and flags to the side of the vessel as if this is a routine journey they are performing for the thousandth time. We soon set sail – after some beers are cracked open – and it's only a matter of moments before the flares are distributed and a red mist descends over the whole boat. As we approach Bilbao's fascinatingly-shaped Guggenheim Museum, crowds of tourists begin to appear on the banks of the river cheering the boat onwards towards the stadium. Never mind the fact the majority are Athletic fans, the arrival of a team such as Eibar to San Mamés is a special event and the locals are genuinely pleased for their neighbours. So long as they don't go on to cause an upset in the match, of course.

A few beers and a few songs later, the boat docks just a couple of hundred metres from the stadium. The banners and flags are unattached and carried on to their next exhibition: Poza Lizentziatuaren Kalea.

Pozas, as the street is better known, runs through Bilbao from the city centre to the stadium, whose red glow stares down the street. This is where Athletic fans meet pre-match for a drink or three and cars know better than to try to part the sea of red and white in the hours before a big game. Today, the Eibar faithful have joined their Athletic counterparts and every type of supporter is present. The fan groups are here, young people are here, couples are here, families are here. Even the Eibar club president Álex Aranzábal is here on the streets with the fans before the match. There are few other La Liga presidents who would do likewise, though that's because there are few other La Liga presidents like Aranzábal – but more on him later.

The sun starts to set after a few friendly rounds of drinks, emphasising the red glow from the stadium, and it's time to enter. The away section of the brand new arena is on the Pozas side, tucked away in the top corner, and the Eibar fans hook out their valuable tickets – that required up to three hours of queuing on Thursday morning – as they approach the turnstiles. The banners and flags of *Eskozia La Brava* are quickly given prime position.

It is settings like these that make promotion worth it. From playing in *Segunda B* division stadiums that sometimes had only two stands, just two seasons before, to taking to the field here at San Mamés, it has been a long journey for Eibar – much longer than today's 40-minute drive along the AP-8 motorway. This is the story of the match: the fact that Eibar have finally earned the chance after 74 years of existence to face Athletic Club in a league match.

The other story of the match is one of great goalkeeping and daft finishing. Both Eibar's Xabi Irureta and Bilbao's Gorka Iraizoz – once of Eibar himself – have good games and both earn a clean sheet in a match that lacks both goals and entertainment. This doesn't stop the travelling support from making their voices heard, though, and a subdued home support makes it even easier. The biggest cheer of the night celebrates the full-time whistle, with the *azulgrana* support celebrating it like a goal; it is a very valuable point and, therefore, worth cherishing. Despite their rivals' early season troubles, this is an impressive point for Eibar and one which the fans on the buses back to Eibar hope will make a repeat of this fixture possible the following season.

Saturday, 18th October 2014. Camp Nou, Barcelona.

This is the Camp Nou, the largest club stadium in Europe, host of European Cup finals, European Championship matches, World Cup matches, more *Clásicos* than is healthy for the average human heart rate, the Olympic Games and a visit of the Pope. Nothing happens at the Camp Nou that has not already happened before.

Except today. Today's 'Category C' match is history in the making.

For the first time, FC Barcelona will play SD Eibar. The two have never met, yet these two clubs already share history despite having never played each other.

Immediately, there is one overt similarity: the colours of their home kits. Following SD Eibar's foundation in 1940, the club initially played in red and white striped shirts and black shorts, mimicking neighbouring Athletic Club. Those colours would only last until the 1943/44 season when, short of a kit to play in, the regional federation gifted the club enough Barcelona shirts to get by – this, of course, in the days before logos, badges and numbers were plastered all over them. The blue and claret stripes the club 'borrowed' have stuck to this day and it was in blue and claret that winger José Ignacio Peleteiro Ramallo, better known as Jota – remember that name – would score the memorable goal that sealed Eibar's promotion to La Liga and made today's encounter with Barcelona possible.

Although both clubs now wear the same colours, there still exist marked differences between the two sets of kits. While FC Barcelona provide their players with as many as 130 shirts each over the course of a season, Eibar's squad are given just eight to last the whole campaign and any exchanged with other players must be paid for, albeit at the discounted price the club offers them. It's therefore rare to see any of Eibar's players exchanging shirts after a match, not least because it may not even be a fair trade if swapping a 2014/15 season Eibar shirt with the high-tech Barcelona equivalent. Barcelona's 2014/15 shirts include, for example, Nike Dri-Fit technology, which apparently draws sweat to the exterior of the shirts, as well as laser-cut ventilation holes to aid cooling. Eibar may have upgraded their shirt manufacturer to Hummel after 22 years with Astore – nope, I hadn't heard of them either – but their fancy new shirts don't contain anything like the 'technology' of Barcelona's, nor are they made from an average of 18 recycled plastic bottles as each Barcelona shirt is. It's safe to assume that the 1943 Barcelona kits gifted to Eibar were a lot less advanced. They were a lot less disposable too, but the colours have certainly endured.

At least that is how the story commonly goes, but not according to late *Diario Vasco* journalist Tomás Zubizarreta who maintained that: "It is totally false that the Gipuzkoa Football Federation or Barcelona gave us blue and claret shirts." Instead, argued Zubizarreta, the colours were selected "to match the colours of the town's shield."

While it is true that the Eibar town crest contains both blue and claret, the truth behind the origin of Eibar's home kit likely lies somewhere in the middle of the two glib stories. Although there is evidence that the Gipuzkoa Football Federation did gift Eibar those Barcelona kits back in the 1940s, the directors of the club could well have allowed the blue and claret stripes to remain having realised the gifted kits matched well with the Eibar town crest. What's important is that the colours did indeed remain and Eibar has, over the years, become as synonymous with blue and claret as Barcelona – at least in the Basque valleys.

One other team in La Liga that wears blue and claret stripes is Valencian side Levante, the team Eibar most recently met before their Camp Nou excursion. Following the draws against Villarreal and Athletic Club, Eibar picked up a third straight point as José Luis Mendilibar – who previously managed Eibar in the 2004/05 season when a side captained by current manager Gaizka Garitano, and featuring a young David Silva, so very nearly achieved promotion to the first division – brought his struggling Levante to Ipurua in his penultimate game before being sacked. In a match that was much more exciting than the goalless draw of San Mamés, Eibar held Levante to a 3-3 draw with a stoppage time *golazo* from Italian striker Piovaccari. Ex-Eibar hero José Morales – who had played 36 games on the wing for the Basques in the promotion-winning 2013/14 season – had opened the scoring for Levante as early as Piovaccari's equaliser was late, with a second-minute strike from outside the box. Piovaccari's late equaliser kept Eibar's accumulation of points going and only time would tell whether the moment would be enough to take anything away from the Camp Nou.

It does indeed take quite some time to tell, some sixty minutes to be exact. Eibar acquitted themselves more than admirably and treasure a 0-0 scoreline at the interval. Eibar displayed a ton of desire, if not the technical ability, to match these megastars in the first half, yet even matching Barcelona for desire is always going to be difficult considering they are fielding Javier Mascherano, a player who literally tore his anus to win a place in the World Cup Final.

In actual fact, it is Eibar who could and should be ahead at half-time. For this match, the toughest they have faced yet, Garitano has dispensed with his usual 4-2-3-1 formation and his extra-defensive 5-3-2 has worked well in the first period, particularly with Dani García playing further up the park than usual and Javi Lara and Jon Errasti effectively protecting the back five. It is a particularly proud day for Errasti as he captains his local side for the first time as a *Primera* player. What better setting to do so than the Camp Nou?

Barcelona have struggled to find the space they thrive on and Irureta has made a couple of decent stops from Leo Messi, but has been otherwise untroubled. At the other end, Eibar should have taken the lead before the break when Ander Capa did all the hard work in rounding Claudio Bravo in the Barcelona goal before shooting wide at an open target from, to be fair, a fairly tight angle. Regardless, the Camp Nou was, understandably, stunned and Eibar finished that first half thriving on the audible silence; their half culminated with an equally good opportunity for Saúl Berjón who found himself one-on-one with Bravo, but the Chilean was able to parry the shot. Eibar have seen two decent, but difficult, chances pass them by. Such wastefulness tends to be punished at the Camp Nou, and indeed it will be in the second period.

The introduction of Andrés Iniesta on 55 minutes is followed by the first goal just five minutes later when Messi slips a ball through to Xavi, who slots past Irureta to score Barcelona's first-ever goal against Eibar. It may have taken 74 years for the first, but the second arrives just 12 minutes later when Dani Alves chips a cross towards his Brazilian team-mate Neymar, who duly obliges and doubles the Barcelona lead. Eibar quickly fall apart and Messi is able to score two minutes later with what looks to be a great *tiki-taka* goal, but made all too easy by some slack defending. The Argentine is permitted two more great opportunities before the game's end, but Irureta is equal to both to keep the scoreline from becoming embarrassing.

There aren't many teams that take anything from a match at Barcelona and Eibar would have been well aware their survival hopes were never going to be decided at the Camp Nou; rather, their fate will be decided at the more modest stadiums of the league, including the most modest. Their own.

Monday, 3rd November 2014. Vallecas, Madrid.

It is one of the great mysteries of this planet Earth, up there with Stonehenge, the Loch Ness Monster and the Bermuda Triangle: what are Homer Simpson and family watching when they gather around the famous purple TV set in the opening sequence of the cartoon series?

Well, it turns out it might be some La Liga football.

Faced with yet another Monday night fixture, Rayo Vallecano's wonderfully creative fan group *Los Bukaneros* decide it's time to take a stand. Of their nine fixtures before this November 3rd match-up, both Eibar and Rayo have already played once on a Monday and once on a Friday and are now facing yet another game on a weekday. Before the season's end, Eibar would play ten Monday or Friday matches while Rayo would play nine – only Getafe, with 11, would play more.

"It's inevitable that the smaller clubs get the Friday and Monday night kick-off times," explains Paul Reidy of *Diario AS*, himself a Rayo Vallecano fan. "Modern football is all about numbers and, as much as it's a kick in the teeth, clubs like Rayo or Eibar are not major box office."

Rayo and Eibar may not draw the prime-time numbers the TV channels are after, but both sets of fans are frustrated because Monday and Friday night matches are logistically a pain for the supporter who attends games. For those with jobs, away matches are virtually impossible to make, while even home matches involve a rush to the stadium. The fact fixture dates and times are rarely announced more than a few weeks in advance usually rules out taking time off work as an option.

Spanish football expert, and author of the brilliant *Fear and Loathing in La Liga*, Sid Lowe reveals his frustration to me with this short-notice approach to scheduling. "One thing, which I think is really significant, is the timing of it. Alright, so you say to a fan group or the collective fans of a club, in this case Eibar: 'Right, you're going to play Elche, for example, on a Monday night.' Okay, fine, if you're telling me this now and I'm playing Elche on a Monday night in three months' time, but not if you're telling me it now and I'm playing them in two weeks. How do I get the time off work? How do I get a hotel? How do I get the travel? In my opinion, this all feeds in to a general sense that there is a total lack of respect for the football fan who goes to the stadium. It's all about TV. It's a bit shambolic."

Besides Monday and Friday night matches being a logistical nightmare for fans, Sid thinks there is another just as important 'emotional' problem with only moving the smaller teams' matches to the Monday and Friday slots – and it does tend to be the smaller teams like Eibar and Rayo Vallecano that suffer from this, with it almost unheard of for Barcelona or Real Madrid to play then. He tells me: "There's a bit of me that thinks in a way it's as if the reward for getting to the first division is not being allowed to participate in the first division because the Monday night and the Friday night games feel like they don't form part of the *jornada*, the weekend's matches.

"And I'll give you a very basic example," he continues. "I write a La Liga column based on what happened over the weekend on a Monday, and that Monday game is never in it. Now obviously I'm not the definition of what counts as La Liga, but the same thing happens in *Diario AS*. *AS*'s Monday wrap of the league games of the weekend ignores the Monday night game and the Friday night game feels like it's stuck out and is kind of like a game before it [the *jornada*] all happens. And the fact there are never any of the big teams also creates a mindset where you almost don't count Mondays and Fridays."

So on this Monday night, *Los Bukaneros* – with the support of the travelling Eibar fans – take a stand with one of the strangest protests ever likely to be witnessed in a football stadium.

Before the match kicks off, *Los Bukaneros* set up a scene behind the goal of their *Fondo* stand to the north-west of the stadium. A group of fans dress up as Homer, Marge, Bart, Lisa and Maggie in front of a TV set prop. In front of them sits a banner which demands, 'No to football on a Monday', as well as one which reads, 'More TV rights means more money in the pockets', portraying the league president Javier Tebas as the money-grabbing Montgomery Burns. Eibar's fans also take part in the protests, unveiling a banner in the away section which features *The Simpsons'* famous long-haired stoner bus driver Otto saying: "With these time slots we don't even fill one bus, man!"

The scene is set up in the area where *Los Bukaneros* normally sit, but for the first 24 minutes tonight they cede the rows to the protest before arriving in minute 25 to tidy away the props – minus the 'No to football on a Monday' banner, which remains – and to support their team for the remainder of the match.

With the scores still at 0-0 the home fans haven't missed much and return just in time for 65 minutes so exciting they'll make stag weekends in Vegas look boring. The drama begins when Eibar take a controversial lead. As a corner flies into the Rayo penalty area, Eibar's Bóveda falls to the ground after very slight contact from home left-back Nacho. Captain Arruabarrena duly steps up to fire home the resulting spot kick, his first but not last goal of the evening.

Arruabarrena's penalty is Eibar's tenth goal of the campaign, but the captain's penalty makes him the first repeat scorer for the *armeros*. The week before this trip to Vallecas, following their 3-0 reverse in the Camp Nou, Eibar had welcomed Granada to Ipurua. An early goal from Allan Nyom gave Granada a lead, but Eneko Bóveda's wonderful strike – set up by a marvellous diving chested pass by Piovaccari, as amazing as it sounds – equalled the scores before a dull and eventless second half. Scoring the club's ninth goal of the season not only earned Eibar a 1-1 draw, but also made Bóveda their ninth different scorer, proving that Eibar's early season successes were down to collective effort rather than one free-scoring soloist. Before Bóveda, Eibar had found the back of the net thanks to – in this order – Javi Lara, Abraham, Dani García, Albentosa, Arruabarrena, an own goal from Levante's Pedro López, Saúl Berjón and Piovaccari. Ander Capa could have made Bóveda the tenth unique scorer of the season, remember, had he slotted into that open goal in the Camp Nou.

Boasting nine different scorers of their first nine La Liga goals – the next best such record was Málaga's seven – was certainly a fine record to have, but the Eibar faithful are content to see the run end when Arruabarrena becomes their first repeat scorer here in Vallecas. Tonight's captain would go on to score his third of the season just an hour later, but three more goals are to be added to the scoresheet before then.

The first of those lengthens the Eibar lead; Italian striker Piovaccari doubles his own tally for the season just minutes after the restart, converting a delightful 40-yard through ball from the outside of Saúl Berjón's right boot. Rather than seal the result for the visitors, Piovaccari's goal only inspires the Rayo Vallecano of Paco Jémez – motivating his troops from the sideline in his customary suit and scarf combo – and the Madrid outfit almost pull one back immediately, only to be denied by a double stop; first Irureta parries a shot from Licá before Bóveda clears the rebound off the line.

Piovaccari then finds himself one on one with David Cobeño – who replaced the injured Toño in the Rayo goal – but the Italian skies his shot. That looks like it will prove costly when Léo Baptistão pulls not one but two goals back for the home team to level the scores. The Brazilian home hero first heads in Licá's cross in the 67th minute before he taps Kakuta's cross past Irureta just seconds after the restart – one of those goals scored so quickly the TV replay begins with the kick-off.

Those hopes of an impressive away victory for Eibar appear to have been dashed in a flash, but Arruabarrena restores them with just five minutes remaining. He rounds off the evening's scoring by volleying Dani García's cross from the left flank into the net in front of the *Fondo* stand where *Los Bukaneros'* protest had taken place at the beginning of this wild contest.

So Eibar come out on top in this fascinating encounter that deserves the headlines as much for the play on the field as for the protest off of it. The three points lift them above Rayo but fortunes will have turned for both clubs by the return fixture at Ipurua the following April. A fixture that will be held on – you guessed it – a Friday night.

Saturday, 8th November 2014. La Rosaleda, Málaga

Already Eibar have proven they don't need a hand from anyone; in fact, this Saturday evening in Málaga they could have done with less of a hand. The hand in question belongs to Raúl Navas, in a match which comes down to fine margins as Eibar visit La Rosaleda Stadium in Málaga in their 11th La Liga match, a game that proves just how cruel the *Primera* can be.

The first fine margin comes just two minutes into the contest, when Navas's headed goal from a Saúl Berjón free kick is ruled out for offside. The visiting defender's arm may be offside but the rest of his body appears to be in line with the Málaga defence. Referees and linesmen often get a hard time, but when incidents like this remain unclear after a dozen viewings of the replay perhaps a little consideration for the difficulty of the job is due. Still, this is the tightest of margins and Eibar, understandably, feel aggrieved.

Raúl Navas's stray left arm costs Eibar once again, just two minutes before full-time. A Mikel Arruabarrena strike – his fourth of the season following his brace at Rayo Vallecano – had given Eibar a first-half lead that Juanmi cancelled out as he tidied up a rebound from a Samuel shot. Chances followed for both sides but with just a couple of minutes remaining, Eibar appear to be heading towards an impressive point against a Málaga team that has won four matches on the bounce. This will become five thanks to a late penalty, awarded to the hosts after Sergi Darder's ball pops up to hit Navas's arm from two yards despite the defender's best attempts to pull his limb out of the way. Navas is a split second too slow in doing so and referee Martínez Munuera awards the controversial penalty. To rub salt in the wounds, Navas picks up the double punishment of a second yellow card and so misses Nordin Amrabat slotting the spot kick into Irureta's bottom left corner and earning the hosts a fortunate 2-1 victory.

The width of Navas's left arm is the fine margin by which Eibar leave La Rosaleda with no points instead of all three.

A FAIRYTALE SEASON: ACT 1

Despite that defeat, Garitano's squad remain in the top half of the table. Few had given Eibar any chance of staying up when the season kicked off in August, but with some bravery, skill and dedicated support they have started the campaign brilliantly to take 13 points from their first 11 matches and already equal Gijón's record worst-point haul – the one which sceptics proclaimed would better Eibar's efforts. The consensus after these first 11 outings is that the club's early season mission is being met and even surpassed: to deposit as many early La Liga points in the piggy bank of survival as possible ahead of judgement day the following May when the time would come to cash them in.

Even the 4-0 home defeat to Real Madrid the following week would fail to take the shine off this impressive start. Rather than a blow, the arrival of the Spanish giants to Ipurua would be a cause for celebration. It wasn't ever going to be the matches against Real Madrid that would determine the course of Eibar's season. The next seven matches will do exactly that.

La Liga standings after *jornada* 12

#	Team	Matches Played	Matches Won	Matches Drawn	Matches Lost	Points
12	Eibar	12	3	4	5	13
16	Real Sociedad	12	2	4	6	10
17	Almería	12	2	4	6	10
18	Deportivo	12	2	4	6	10
19	Elche	12	2	4	6	10
20	Córdoba	12	0	7	5	7

2
Modelo

"We don't even contemplate making significant cash payments to sign the big stars, like other clubs do."

Patricia Rodriguez Barrios

Monday, 7th April 2014. Escuela De Armería, Eibar.
There are few followers of Spanish football who agree with anything league president Javier Tebas has to say. It's worth remembering, though, even a broken clock is correct twice a day and the laws of chance dictate that occasionally even Tebas will say the right thing.

One such rare occasion came when Tebas visited Ipurua in October 2013 and praised the *Modelo Eibar*, the 'Eibar Model' of managing finances. Tebas spoke of how proud he was to have a club like Eibar in the *Segunda* division and how 'their model makes football sustainable'. There was still time for a further compliment before Tebas headed back along the AP-8 motorway to somewhere a little more comfortable. "We need the 'Eibar Model' to become commonplace," he announced; high praise for this little club tucked away from civilisation in the Basque mountains.

That was all very well, yet six months later the *Modelo Eibar* has yet to take off and Eibar remains one of a handful of clubs in Spanish professional football with zero – yes, completely zero – debt, while the rest of Spain's first and second division clubs persist with their myopic shaky finances and owe a combined €1billion to *Hacienda*, the Spanish tax man. Furthermore, 19 of the 42 clubs in the top two divisions have declared bankruptcy in the last decade – and many more could be said to be morally bankrupt. In the often back-to-front world of modern football, haemorrhaging red ink does appear to pay off. Think about it, when was the last time you saw an open-top bus parade through the town centre to celebrate the submission of debt-free accounts for the year? No, splashing out on superstars, embracing modern football's endemic greed and sticking the middle finger up at Financial Fair Play is what wins the trophies that justify such celebrations and it's becoming harder and harder for small sensibly-run clubs like Eibar to compete. It's like having to run faster just to stand still.

Now, though, not only has Eibar's example of running a football club failed to catch on, but the club could actually be punished for it. Yes, you read that right.

Thanks to a bizarre line in a Spanish law, the *Real Decreto 1251/1999*, every team in professional football must have a social capital which equates to 25% of the average expenses of all other teams in the *Segunda* division, minus the two clubs with the largest expenditures and the two clubs with the smallest. The professional divisions in Spain are the top two, meaning that Eibar's promotion from the *Segunda B* third tier to the *Segunda A* (second tier) – typically just referred to as the *Segunda* – following the 2012/13 season has seen them classified as a professional club and therefore subject to this law just 11 years after Eibar made the switch from part-time to full-time football. Failure to comply with this *Real Decreto* would see Eibar administratively relegated back to the *Segunda B*, a punishment made even more severe by the fact that on this April night Eibar occupies the second automatic promotion spot for a place in Spain's top flight.

Yes, Eibar could win promotion and be rewarded with relegation. Welcome to Spain.

The law has been called bizarre, absurd, ridiculous... Sid Low explains to me that the biggest problem is how the law wasn't prepared for a case such as Eibar's.

"[The Eibar case has] highlighted how badly thought-out the law was because it seems to me that there was one really fundamental flaw, which was to prevent clubs from putting themselves in trouble you didn't measure them by their own capabilities, you measured them against the capabilities of other clubs." Sid continues: "I mean it is ridiculous, really, to try and impose a series of restrictions or criteria on a club like Eibar on the basis of the financial capacity to generate money of a club like, Real Betis, for example."

It is precisely because of this flawed law that SD Eibar's directors and *socios* – its members – have gathered here at Eibar's Escuela De Armería School at 7.30 this Monday evening for an Extraordinary General Meeting. Despite regularly communicating with the *Consejo Superior de Deportes,* the Sports Ministry, since November and despite petitions from across the political parties of the Basque Country to change the law, Eibar president Álex Aranzábal announces the news no exceptions will be made and that Eibar must raise its social capital.

Sid proposes the authorities might have been more willing to make an exception or change the law had this situation arisen in previous years. "I think six or seven years ago, or maybe even two or three, they would have found a solution for Eibar. Now, I'm not so sure because

Tebas – who I've been extremely critical of for lots of things – is doing some things right and one of them – although he's coming up against all sorts of resistance – is financial control."

"So," says Sid, "I think there's a reasonable chance this year that they'd have said, 'We're really sorry, but tough luck.'"

There is no exception, therefore, for Eibar and the club has no choice but to raise the required capital by 6th August 2014. Once the calculations had been done and the law applied, it was revealed on 5th February that the capital value Eibar must achieve is €2,146,525 and 95 cents. Eibar's current capital value sits at just €422,253. Remember, though, this is a club in the black not the red.

Eibar must, as a result, quadruple their social capital in four months, somehow finding €1,724,272 – and don't forget those pesky 95 cents – in new share value. As it stands, this April evening, the club has 1,800 shareholders, stemming from the 1992 share issue when they became a *Sociedad Anónima Deportiva*, a public limited sports company, in order to comply with a new law obliging professional clubs – minus Athletic Club, Barcelona, Real Madrid and Osasuna because they had shown positive capital balances since the 1985/86 season – to become joint-stock companies with limited liability rather than member-owned clubs. For this reason, Eibar's official name is Sociedad Deportiva Eibar S.A.D. or Eibar Kirol Elkartea S.A.D. in the Basque language *euskara*. The idea behind this change in the structure of football clubs was that by running the clubs in the same way as businesses, complete with shareholders and boards of directors, financial accountability would improve. It has not, to absolutely nobody's surprise.

Álex Aranzábal was one of those early shareholders; he bought some shares while studying at university. Now he is tasked with the new much more ambitious *ampliación de capital*, or share issue. In a city of just 27,000 people – which has a high unemployment rate of 13% – achieving the target by 6th August appears impossible. Given that Eibar's season ticket holders are 23% children, 16% young people and 15% retired, disabled or unemployed, the €490 the club's 3,500 members would have to pay each is beyond comprehension. Despite the Sports Minister Miguel Cardenal's less-than-reassuring reassurance it should be "fairly simple" to find the required capital, few here in Eibar are as confident.

So what is the plan? Well, that's what Eibar's *socios* are gathered here tonight to find out.

In order to triumph over what he calls "a great injustice" president Aranzábal has announced a plan to sell shares of €60 and ten cents, each of which will be sold at a discounted €50 with the club making up the €10.10 difference; the kicker for Eibar is that they do have cash reserves, just not social capital. There will be two phases: firstly, the *socios* will be able to purchase shares from Wednesday onwards before the purchase of shares will be made public exactly one month later on 9th May. If that sounds simple, it is not. Eibar barely registers on a national, never mind international, level. Raising awareness will be an onerous task.

Importantly, the club is 100% unwilling to entertain the idea of an oligarch or sugar daddy taking the reins so there will be a cap of €100,000 on the value of shares any one individual can purchase. Aranzábal explains: "One of the keys to our model is that people feel close to the club. Eibar has always been more or less for everyone and there has never been a major investor, a sheikh or a big business which has controlled the club." Such an approach, says Aranzábal, "wouldn't work here".

The president wants to keep it that way and insists everyone at the club would rather suffer the relegation than sell the *alma* of the club – its soul. "We don't want to reach the target through any means," Aranzábal continues. "We'd rather take the punishment and get demoted than share the soul of what SD Eibar is as a football club." Eibar will never be the plaything of a millionaire.

Such commitment to the club's values is admirable, but it certainly won't make the task any easier.

And so, while Eibar remains Spanish football's 'model club' and the only professional club to receive the UNE-EN-ISO 9001 Award for excellent business management, it is the one which now has a fight on its hands to keep its *Segunda* division place and earn the right to a potential place in the *Primera*. Like a gentlemen's club, it seems one can only enter the *Primera* if their bank account is large enough. Rather than forcing the rest of Spain's clubs to base themselves on Eibar's business model as Tebas desires, it is Eibar which must base their social capital on 25% of exactly the kind of reckless spending this club avoids.

The capital-raising 'marathon' which Aranzábal has just outlined is unanimously approved tonight at the school. Here we go…

Tuesday, 20th May 2014. Hogar Vasco, Madrid.

SD Eibar has two very important fixtures this week if they are to earn promotion to Spain's top flight – and become the smallest club and smallest town to ever do so.

One is at Ipurua on Sunday evening; against Basque rivals and relegation-fighting Alavés which could see Eibar mathematically clinch promotion, depending on other results.

The other fixture also requires some number crunching and is being held this Tuesday afternoon in the Spanish capital. Today's battle won't be won on any turf, however, but it is more significant to Eibar's chances of competing in La Liga. This PR event being held at the Hogar Vasco in Madrid – literally the Basque House – is the promotion decider.

There may not be any football on show, but the quality of footballers in attendance is inspiring. Ex-Eibar man Xabi Alonso is here to lend his support, and has brought his Real Madrid team-mate and fellow Basque Asier Illarramendi with him. The great José Eulogio Gárate, Atlético Madrid's all-time fourth leading goalscorer, is here to back the club where he began his career, while Rafa of Getafe has come along to support the club where he spent a season on loan. Other important figures have turned up too, such as San Sebastián's mayor of 20 years Odón Elorza and MPs from the Basque Nationalist Party, the *Partido Nacionalista Vasco*. All have come with the same objective, to raise awareness of Eibar's crowd-funding share issue.

The process has now reached its second phase, where shares are available to anyone from any country. The Eibar *socios* forked out an impressive €153,450 in the first phase on 3,069 shares which, combined with the club's existing capital, means the club has reached 28% of its €2,146,525 and 95 cents target.

The *socios* alone were never going to raise the full amount required and that they have raised more than expected is an inspiration for the second phase which the club hopes will receive a boost from the appearance of stars such as Alonso and Illarramendi, not least because these players have reached into their own back pockets to support the cause – even if the limit on shares means the likes of Alonso can 'only' put one week's wages towards the cause.

Even more important than Alonso, however, is Álex Aranzábal, the man speaking to the assembled Madrid and global media as he launches Eibar's marketing campaign for raising the required capital. An army of Eibar fans on Twitter bashing out the hashtag #defiendealeibar, #defendeibar in English, are already backing up everything Aranzábal has to say, adding that final human and persuasive element to the campaign's slick graphics and its *Akziometro,* a meter measuring the summation of shares on the dedicated campaign website.

It is a very professional marketing campaign, not altogether surprising given that Aranzábal's day job is as a marketing director for an energy company. It is the human element that will prove crucial. To have real fans of the club rattling away on their smartphones and laptops to plead with the world in as many languages as they know is that magic ingredient that can sway fans of football, soccer, *sokker, calico, fútbol, futebol, Fußball, fótbolti* or whatever the sport may be called in their country to part with €50 to help the real people of this real club.

"Social media was important," explains one such fan and campaigner Unai Eraso, president of the club's Madrid-based fan group. "I think it makes sense that with this story and the reputation Eibar has for being a small team punching above its weight with the chance to go up to the *Primera*, combined with the fact so many people are online on social media across so many countries, lots of people would support the cause.

"It's a bit like the American Dream, for a team so small to rise through the ranks," Unai adds. That Eibar's hard work might go unrewarded because of what Unai calls an "absurd law" is likely to resonate with those from the States. Outlining just how ridiculous the law is, Unai draws on his experience working in finance: "I work in the banking sector and imagine asking a bank like Caja Laboral, which is a very small bank, to have a capital in line with that of Santander Bank. It's not possible."

Unai's point about the ideology of the American Dream striking a chord with football fans stateside is an interesting one. To get an even better understanding of the American mindset with respect to Eibar, I spoke to US shareholder, Henry Boguslavsky.

"Eibar is the ultimate underdog story and we Americans love supporting an underdog Cinderella-type story," Henry explains. "The fact Eibar earned its first-ever promotion by winning the *Segunda* yet were going to be denied over a technicality which wasn't supported by sense or reason, didn't sit well with fans who consider themselves to be purists of the sport. Seeing megaclubs in Europe spending astronomical sums of money, but operating with heavy losses, while Eibar remained a financially sound club operating in the black from their humble means, and being punished for it, didn't add up to us. To me it felt like a local mom-and-pop shop losing its business to the big generic corporate bully like Wal-Mart."

So Unai's theory that Americans would be appalled at the idea of a hard-working organisation – whether a small US shop, Spanish bank or Basque football team – being denied their moment as punishment for its limited size holds up?

It would appear so, according to Henry. "Eibar earned their time in the sun and once we fans heard their tale and the call for help, we wanted to do what we could to see this feel-good underdog story told to the world."

It is this idea of supporting the underdog that Aranzábal appeals to in his speech today at the Hogar Vasco. Again he speaks of the 'Eibar Model' which so many are happy to praise, but which is under threat. "For some time, people have said that Eibar is a model of economic and sporting management, especially the economic part. People speak of the 'Eibar Model' as a way of understanding football," he says.

Aranzábal pleads for people to act, to buy one share if they can to support what *El Correo*'s Javier Ortiz de Lazcano calls, "the healthiest, the most modest and the most honourable club in professional football in Spain". Asked why he thinks people would want to contribute to Eibar's share issue, Javier tells me: "The view of the club is that people want to contribute to just causes like this."

This will prove to be the case. People want to contribute to a just cause, but they will be even more inclined to contribute to a just cause which forms part of the best league in the world. Winning the week's second battle and securing promotion would strengthen the Eibar cause no end.

Tuesday, 15th July 2014. Ipurua Stadium, Eibar.
There are some goals in football that are priceless; you simply cannot put a valuation on them. Jota's strike to send Eibar into Spain's *Primera* division on that rainy night in May 2014 had all the required ingredients: it was a match-winner, won promotion and was bloody well fantastic. But it wasn't priceless. It was worth shares.

The Friday before Eibar's win against Alavés christened them a La Liga side, the capital raised stood at €646,450 – 30% of the total. Thanks to confirming promotion to Spain's top flight, the club broke the €1million barrier the following Friday, passing the halfway milestone in the process. The *armeros* may have acquired sufficient league points to call themselves a La Liga club – and they certainly did call themselves a La Liga club, tweeting the likes of Neymar and Cristiano Ronaldo from the official club account just in case the superstars weren't aware amidst all their World Cup preparations – but the sufficient shares hadn't yet been sold and all attentions turned to the process.

As well as encouraging individuals to purchase shares, local businesses were urged to contribute what they could. Even the mayor of Eibar got his wallet out. The securing of promotion caused the shares to sell and sell and sell; the process snowballed. By 7th June, 71% of the required capital had been raised, by 11th June that was up to 76%, by 15th June it reached 80%, before breaking 90% on 26th June. By 10th July there were less than 1,000 shares still needing to be sold. Four days later, it was down to just 30. There was no doubt now that Eibar was on course to meet its target and claim its rightful place amongst Spain's elite.

Which brings us to today, 15th July 2015, at the reception of Ipurua. There remains just one share left to pass the total required: share number 46,200. Here to claim it is Eibar's oldest supporter: 90-year-old Luis María Cendoya has been a *socio* of the club since 1945. For Señor Cendoya to have coincidentally been the last shareholder is miles too glib; rather the club had asked him some time ago if he would like to claim the symbolic final share, making for a special photo opportunity. While Jota scored the dream goal to secure promotion on the pitch, history will remind us it was Luis María Cendoya who really sealed

Eibar's place in the *Primera* division. It is time to crack open the bubbly, which Aranzábal duly does, and celebrate.

"*Zorionak!! Hemos conseguido el objetivo,*" declares the club's website. "Well done!! We've achieved the objective."

It may have taken one simple signature from the club's oldest fan to kick off the celebrations, but it has been an exhausting journey to get to this point, one which required 700 articles across the global media plus ten press conferences, such as the event at Madrid's Hogar Vasco, and similar ones at the San Sebastián Aquarium and Bilbao Maritime Museum. The support of politicians from a range of parties had also been secured, while the share issue had been a trending topic on Twitter on several occasions.

Seventy agreements with local businesses were agreed, while 8,000 international shareholders pledged their €50 from no fewer than 50 different countries, such as the UK, USA, Australia, Canada, China, Italy, France, Portugal, Oman and many more. The USA's 400-strong contingent of investors was the largest from abroad, while China was second largest. Those fans would be honoured with a thank you message before kick-off against Real Sociedad on the opening day of the season, unveiled around the pitch in a series of different languages.

Meanwhile, a heartening 36% of shareholders are from Eibar. This town suffering more than most from the recession may have needed a little help from its new international friends to raise the required capital, but to have contributed over a third of the capital itself is more than impressive. The *alma* of the club will certainly remain in this Basque valley.

The share issue doesn't stop here. The club will keep the issuing of shares going until the following Monday because, Aranzábal explains, "We don't want anyone who wants to be a part of this to be left on the outside." By then, €1,980,000 will have been raised – surpassing the required figure and with a fortnight to spare – by 10,094 unique shareholders. Each of them will be celebrated on *El Muro de la Defensa*, The Wall of Defence, on the wall of the North Stand of Ipurua. There, the names of each shareholder, both individuals and businesses, are to be listed along with their location, with representatives from Eibar to Ireland to Australia and back again.

Just over a month later, the club will take to the field as a La Liga outfit and, now their place is secure, preparations and changes must be made.

Yes, Jota's promotion-winning goal was worth a lot of shares. And two divisions.

Monday, 11th August 2014. Ipurua Stadium, Eibar.
Today is Patricia Rodriguez Barrios's first day at her new job.

Sure, people start new roles every Monday morning, but few start at Sociedad Deportiva Eibar. In fact, until this summer very few people started jobs at Eibar. Barrios is the club's new finance manager, one of eight new additions to an administration team which needed significant reinforcements to carry out the paperwork required at a top-flight club.

Before this summer's recruitment drive, the club employed just three in its office, plus the then-unpaid president Álex Aranzábal, but that team has now increased to 11, with Barrios among the new recruits. The following table shows just how unequivocally the club has increased its admin team for the 2014/15 season.

Role	Staff In Role 2013/14	Staff In Role 2014/15
Administration	1	1
Finance and Shareholder Liaison	0	1
Marketing	0	2
Customer Service	1	2
Communication	1	3
Works and Installations	0	1
President/Director General	1	1

Never before has the position of president been a full-time job, always occupied in a part-time capacity as was the case in the years since Aranzábal took over in 2009. The club has, this season, departed from that norm to entice Aranzábal away from his marketing position with a full-time salary.

In the club's search for a full-time president to manage the new and expanded 46-member team of administration, coaching and playing staff, the key specifications were to find someone with knowledge of the football industry, experience in business management and who was 'rooted in the ethos and values of Eibar'. There was only ever going to be one man for the job.

Given many football club presidents are not very popular, it is worth explicitly outlining that Álex Aranzábal is an absolute hero in Eibar. A local boy who became a club director in 2005 at just 31 years old, Aranzábal was promoted to the club presidency following the departure of Jaime Barriuso in January 2009, making him younger than some members of the playing staff and the youngest president in Spanish professional football. As well as having an economics PhD, Aranzábal has taught for 12 years at the University of Deusto, on top of teaching on the FIFA-approved Sports Management course run by Madrid's University of King Juan Carlos. Oh, and he has been a marketing director for one of the country's largest energy firms. To put it lightly, he's a smart bloke.

And he is Eibar's smart bloke. The fans adore him. He may not have ever worn the number ten shirt, coached the team or been club captain – and his goal tally for Eibar is zero – yet Aranzábal has achieved legendary status at Eibar and fans owe as much to him as Barcelona fans owe to Leo Messi, or Manchester United fans owe to Sir Alex Ferguson. In Eibar, he is Sir Álex.

Besides overseeing the best period of on-field success in Eibar's history, including two successive promotions and knocking their big brother from Bilbao out of the *Copa del Rey* in 2012, Aranzábal was also the brains behind the *Defiende al Eibar* campaign which has secured Eibar's La Liga slice of glory. There was never going to be another candidate for the full-time director general role.

The contract as director general is not a lengthy one, however. In line with the 'Eibar Model', all of the club's new staff have been hired in the knowledge relegation from the *Primera* would require a disbanding of this newly-formed administration team. Given how likely such relegation is, those in Eibar's new team have taken a major gamble by leaving secure jobs for an annual rolling contract based on the club with the smallest budget remaining in the top flight. Which brings us back to Patricia Rodriguez Barrios.

Eibar's new finance manager is convinced the risky move she has taken is the right choice. She explains: "In my case I decided to leave PwC, where I had a secure job, a good career and a very likely promotion to senior auditing manager within a year. I didn't think that two years more at PwC were going to bring me the professional growth and new experiences that switching to Eibar would bring.

"At this moment in time I am completely convinced the decision and risk I took were worth it, and it really was a risk since the survival of the current management team is subject to the team staying in the *Primera*. Every day is a challenge, but a new and highly enriching experience."

Given how much is at stake for the management team, as well as the playing staff, how then do Barrios and her colleagues aim to ensure a further season of top-flight football?

"In my opinion, the key to things going well in all aspects – both in sporting and management terms – is the hard work, the commitment, the enthusiasm and the great ambition we all have; the continuing desire to better ourselves." Barrios continues; "We don't even contemplate making significant cash payments to sign the big stars, like other clubs do. In Eibar we work like we're in a private company whose objective is profitability. That's to say that *la Dirección Deportiva*, the sporting arm of the club, knows it has a certain budget to make up the team and it's simply not possible to exceed that figure. They decide how to spend it."

The limited budget is in the control of sporting director Fran Garagarza.

Negotiating transfer fees barely features on Garagarza's to-do list as Eibar have always relied on free agents, loan deals and been a club which prefers to trade in blood, sweat and tears. Securing these 'free' players is hard enough work given that Eibar barely pay above the minimum salary required by their division; most players earn the same pay packet besides differences of one or two thousand here or there.

With promotion to the *Primera*, the minimum salary stipulated by the league has increased to €128,000 – more than Eibar's entire sponsorship deal from their local ironmonger shirt sponsors Hierros Servando the previous season. This has required a rewriting of the players' *Segunda* contracts as they only contained clauses for how wages would change should the club suffer relegation, while promotion to the *Primera* was so unlikely clauses for this scenario were not included. Fortunately, featuring in the top flight has increased the club's revenues and Garagarza has a budget of €8,906,000 – 56% of the club's total annual budget – available to make up the 2014/15 season's playing staff. It may be the largest budget he has ever had to work with, yet it is a mile behind the €210,000,000 and €205,000,000 budgets of Real Madrid and Barcelona, respectively, and would only be enough to pay Cristiano Ronaldo alone for half a season.

Also problematic is the fact Eibar's scouting network has, until now, barely stretched beyond the borders of the peninsula. Now, the club will have to compete in the search for first-team players with the *Primera* clubs which boast scouting tentacles that reach all corners of the globe, even able to afford the occasional check-in to see which Eskimos are promisingly kicking snowballs around the North Pole.

Garagarza must, therefore, employ his finest negotiating skills to sign players up for a full season at a wage much lower than the league average of €1.2million, as calculated by the Association of Spanish Footballers, and even lower than the salary offered by some teams in the division below. He does, though, have one tried-and-tested trick up the sleeve of his many check shirts: the fact Eibar can pay players on time. As 86-year-old former journalist and SD Eibar anorak Mateo Guilabert explains, "Eibar have never promised more than it can give, but whatever it has promised to give it has given."

It may not sound like a massive advantage for the modern footballer to have wages arriving on the day they are supposed to, but at the level at which Eibar operates Garagarza explains the club's reputation for paying all staff on time has enticed several players in the past. One of those players was star centre-back Raúl Albentosa, who moved to Eibar for a lower wage following issues while at former club Cádiz where he was frequently owed money and often concerned about whether his – albeit larger – wages would arrive before the bills were due.

Albentosa conveys the mindset of a footballer better than I ever could so here is what he said about the attraction of Eibar's financial model: "I had been playing in Spain at various clubs and the only club which has paid me the full wage without delays has been Eibar. This, for footballers, when it comes to deciding [whether to sign or not] is always going to be favourable."

It's not only the security Eibar offers, but the chance to audition for a big pay-day elsewhere that can entice players to sign for Garagarza. *Sky Sports* resident Spanish football expert Guillem Balague explains to me his interpretation of 'the Eibar concept'. Essentially, he tells me, the model is: "That we don't spend more than we have, everybody earns very little, but [players] know if they're doing well within the idea of the football [Eibar] want to play then they will get picked by bigger teams and manage to make a life out of football.

"In the *Segunda B* division," Guillem continues, "now players are either not getting paid or not getting paid enough so only *Segunda* and *Primera* [players] become professionals and obviously what happens then is that from the pool of players – which is huge – the ones earning a living from [football] is becoming smaller. So, if you have the opportunity to work in a team, as I'm saying, with a good coach and with the right idea, then you give 120% and if it works as a team it works for you as an individual."

Players value both the security of the 'Eibar Model' and the chance to use the club as a stepping stone to bigger things, as Guillem has just explained and as Albentosa was able to eventually do in – deservedly – moving on to Derby County for a salary 12 times his Eibar pay packet, the kind of increase that might even make a payday lender blush. In fact, insists Garagarza, because players realise Eibar offers both of the above some have even been happy to pay part of their professional license fee themselves when Eibar could not afford it. Still, there are few players willing to take a pay cut to join Eibar so what else does Garagarza look for in his signings?

Workers. That is the key requirement both he and current manager Gaizka Garitano look for in players and their success rate, so far, would make even Midas jealous; new recruit after new recruit seems to turn to gold.

Eibar cannot afford to carry those players not willing to put in the effort, or those who cause controversies by kicking bottles on sidelines when substituted, or who arrive late for training. Every signing must pass three levels of review and a player with a reputation for slacking has more chance of captaining Scotland to World Cup glory than passing those three analyses. You might think Eibar can't afford to be picky with the players available to them, but the club will stay true to its hard-working ethos; they simply abhors slackers. The town may lie halfway up the valley of the River Ego, but there is no room for egos in the Ipurua dressing room. That is simply not in Eibar's DNA.

The club is 'an example against modern football', argues midfielder Jon Errasti who, after home matches, doesn't drive home in a Ferrari or Lamborghini. Instead, this local lad born in Eibar walks home, clutching his kitbag underneath his arm, often stopping to have a quick chat with the fans drinking outside Bar Xania or Borda Bar on Sostoa-Tarren Kalea, a street just outside the stadium. As for those players who don't stay in the town, again there are no flash cars or mansions. The players collect their cars – parked not in a secure car park but in the street alongside the stadium, bumped up on to the kerb like everyone else's – before heading to their modest homes, such as Mikel Arruabarrena, who still lives in the family home in nearby Tolosa.

These are the kinds of players Eibar want in the dressing room, those without egos and happy to eschew the limelight. By the end of his recruitment for the 2014/15 season, Garagarza will have brought in 12 such players, 11 of whom will be free or loan signings. The one paid-for player would hardly break the bank either; Dani Nieto signs from Barcelona for €200,000, a fee that would cover under 1% of what the Catalans shelled out on Luis Suárez.

Along with Dani Nieto, Garagarza would be able to attract a couple of internationals – the minimum requirement for the likes of Barcelona and Real Madrid but a welcome bonus for a club like Eibar. Striker Dejan Lekić, capped ten times by Serbia, would arrive following a 12-goal season with Sporting Gijón; while Derek Boateng, capped 46 times by Ghana, would make Eibar his second new club of the summer after having signed for Rayo Vallecano in June. He was released days before the start of the season and picked up by Garagarza the very same day.

The core of this Eibar team, however, is to be the same group of players that have carried them to this biggest stage. Garagarza's limited budget forces him to rely on this core group, but he's also more than happy to do so.

It would be little use for Eibar to raise their sporting budget more than necessary for a season in which the club is expected to go down, instead preferring to funnel some of the *Primera* profits into freezing season tickets prices between €209 and €297 for loyal fans in a country with the highest ticket prices in Europe's top five leagues. In the Basque Country, they say: *"Etxean gatza ugari dagoela eta, ez dezazula bazkaria gehiegi gazita."* Just because there is a lot of salt in the house, they say, you shouldn't make your food too salty. Those running the club certainly don't want to blow the La Liga income on a short-termist gung-ho approach when saving for a rainier *Segunda* division day makes more sense.

Whenever that inevitable day comes, Aranzábal will still be content. The interesting thing is that Aranzábal maintains the 'Eibar Model' deserves no more praise now than in previous seasons given the model itself has not changed and, therefore, is not the sole variable explaining Eibar's rise to the top. All that has changed in recent times has been the performance of the sensibly-acquired squad, but he insists that Eibar's fans and directors are just as proud of the club's sustainable model when results are poor as when they are exceptional.

Guillem Balague agrees. "I don't think it is a club thing," he tells me before elaborating. "I don't think [winning promotion to the *Primera*] is the consequence of a club very well-run – as in eventually it was going to happen and eventually they've been [running the club] so well that they were going to get into the first division – because if that was the case then why hasn't it happened in 60 years? What it is, is that, number one, the financial difficulties [of other clubs] make it easier to go up the divisions and, number two, the work of Garitano.

"If you are well-organised, keep an idea and stick to it, and get players that believe in it, then you go up the places and up the divisions, as Eibar have been doing," Guillem concludes. He doesn't deny, therefore, that Eibar's organised and sensible model has been an advantage, but for both Guillem and for Álex Aranzábal it's the 'work of Garitano' and the 'players that believe' which have been the keys to Eibar's success, two factors which have more to do with recent good fortune than Eibar's sensible financial model. So does this mean Eibar's model is not sustainable, in terms of maintaining top division status, in the long run? In short, yes, it probably does.

Less successful times are almost certainly on the horizon and Aranzábal admits avoiding relegation would be, 'near impossible' for Eibar. Yet even finishing bottom would count as an overachievement for a club whose natural place is in the *Segunda B*, but which aspires to merely punch above its weight in the *Segunda*. The very worst that could happen for Eibar would be beginning the 2015/16 season in the *Segunda*, normally considered a great achievement.

Survival would be as great a success as promotion to La Liga was, but maintaining the 'Eibar Model' comes first. There are now thousands of new shareholders across the world, the long-term stability of the club has become an even greater priority and the *'Tanto tengo, tanto gasto'* model of spending only as much as one has will remain the Eibar way. As Barrios explains: "We understand that the money we spend isn't our own. It's the money of more than 10,000 shareholders who have placed their trust in us through the board of directors, so for that reason we must be careful and responsible in the decisions we take."

All associated with the club have a hope that Barrios and her fellow new colleagues will still be there making those decisions ahead of the 2015/16 season.

Sunday, 24th August 2014. Ipurua Stadium, Eibar.

Today is not Ángel Zapico's first day at his job. While Patricia Rodriguez Barrios is the newest member of the Eibar staff, Zapico is the longest-serving; his Eibar career started in 1969. He has been here working at Ipurua since before the president, manager and all of the playing staff were born and if there is one individual for whom Eibar's promotion to La Liga means the most, Zapico would have a decent claim.

Like Barrios, Zapico does find himself in a new role – kitman. There are few roles besides getting on the field and playing which Zapico hasn't held at Ipurua and his CV would tell you he has previously worked with Eibar's youth team, been the assistant manager and even been on the board of directors. The journey of life saw him leave the club in 1997, but upon finding himself out of work in 2010, the call came in: "We can offer you a job Ángel, but it would have to be as the kitman."

He jumped at the opportunity and moved back to the club where he had become as permanent a fixture as the goalposts.

It's important to point out the 'Eibar Model' is not only a financial one, but that the ethos of the club is one of community. Zapico may hail from Asturias, but he had become as much a part of the community of Eibar as anyone else at the club and his service would never be forgotten. Presented with the opportunity to help out a member of the Eibar family in 2010, the club therefore made sure Zapico was at least asked if he'd be keen to take up the role.

He has certainly been rewarded with an astonishing few years, which have brought him to this Sunday afternoon before Eibar's top-flight debut against Real Sociedad. Seated in Ipurua's *txoko*, the dining area which looks out over the pitch from the Main Stand, is Zapico and the kitmen from Real Sociedad. As has become tradition on matchdays, Zapico invites the rival team's kitmen to join him in the *txoko* – once they have prepared the kit in the away dressing room – for some chorizo and a small glass of *txakoli*, a very acidic and dry white wine from the Basque Country. Never did he expect to send the invitation out to the kitmen of La Liga.

Zapico is just one of many long-time servants of Eibar; the length of time spent here by players highlights how enjoyable the working environment is at Ipurua. While Zapico is the longest-serving member of staff at the club, the player with the longest Eibar history is also still getting up every morning for work nearby.

That man is José Ignacio Garmendia, the goalkeeper who played for Eibar so many times the club records can't even accurately recall the official number of appearances he made in the Eibar goal. No, really.

Now 55 years old, Garmendia runs a butchers store in his hometown of Villabona, about 50 kilometres to the east of Eibar, yet this is not a new venture for the Gipuzkoan; he worked there throughout his 19-year playing career as well. It was the norm during Garmendia's career from 1979 to 1998 for players to have full-time jobs and play football on a part-time basis; full-time professional football only arrived in Eibar after Garmendia had hung up his boots and gloves to focus solely on his apron. The butcher played alongside electricians such as Olano, carpenters like Rodríguez, gas men such as Gómez de Segura, bankers including Joaquín Arrieta and even a detective in Mikel Etxarri. If only the Spanish press were as fond of puns back then as they are now, they could have had a fun time reporting on Eibar.

Garmendia was not only a loyal servant of Eibar, but a heck of a player as well, having been voted Eibar's top goalkeeper of all time. Like current goalkeeper Xabi Irureta, Garmendia also won the *Segunda*'s Zamora Trophy during his time between the Ipurua sticks – on two occasions, in fact, in 1991/92 and 1995/96 – and even once grabbed a goal for himself on a wet and windy day – a '*día de perros*' recalls Garmendia, a really terrible day – in April 1988 at home to Pontevedra. The ever-humble Garmendia attributes the goal to the wind, but those like 13-year-old Álex Aranzábal who were there that day – and if you believe everyone who claims they were then the attendance figure would have been far higher than the few hundred recorded by the regional press – will tell you that the butcher meant it.

Garmendia was presented with various opportunities to move on from Eibar to join a larger club, but preferred to stay in part-time football, a situation with which he was comfortable. He oversaw generations of players coming through the Ipurua dressing room and was a much-loved figure by all, not least for the selections of meat he would bring from his butchers store to share on the dreaded long away trips by coach.

If there are two people that define the 'Eibar Model' of hard work and loyalty – both towards and from the club – then they are José Ignacio Garmendia and Ángel Zapico. Neither ever imagined seeing the club taking on the global stars of the football world. Yet here they are.

By the time Zapico completes the washing of the kits the following morning, and Garmendia opens the shutters of his store, Eibar will have picked up their first-ever La Liga win. Only time would tell if the team could earn enough wins for Zapico to invite the country's top kitmen for lunch at Ipurua for a second successive season.

3

A Fairytale Season: *Act 2*

"It's just all about hard work from everybody. That worked in the Segunda B, it worked in the Segunda and it has worked in the Primera so far."

Guillem Balague

Saturday, 29th November 2014. Balaídos, Vigo.
The final whistle has just blown here in Celta de Vigo's Balaídos ground after a, quite frankly, bizarre game of football.

One team had 29 total shots, while the other had eight. One team had nine shots on target, while the other had two. One team forced nine saves from the opposition keeper, while the other forced one. One team had 15 corners, while the other had one. One team had 73% possession, while the other had 27%. One team had over 16,000 fans, while the other had just 12 – yes, 12.

The most important stat is that the team with all the shots, corners, possession and fans scored zero goals, while the other scored one. Somehow, Eibar have won 1-0. The dozen *azulgrana* fans are having the time of their lives!

For 87 minutes of football earlier it did not look like Eibar's committed dozen would have much to cheer about. They knew they were facing a Vigo side of uncertain potency, one which regularly oscillates between awesome and disastrous. With just three minutes on the clock, it appeared they had decided to turn in a good performance tonight as Joaquín Larrivey struck Vigo's first shot. It was parried by Irureta to concede the first of those 15 corners. Shortly afterwards, Vigo carved out a further opportunity as Nolito directed a header goalwards, but Irureta was able to propel himself towards the save from one side of the goal to the other with a full-body flick as sudden and powerful as Buckaroo from that saddle-stacking children's – okay, adults too – game.

A FAIRYTALE SEASON: ACT 2

Khron-Dehli and Orellana both shot just past the post from outside the penalty area, with Eibar not affording Vigo much space closer to goal. Then, on the half-hour mark, Eibar took the lead against the run of play; a lovely floated ball from Arruabarrena dropped sweetly for Manu del Moral just inside the penalty area and the on-loan Sevilla midfielder summoned up enough boldness to shoot past Sergio Álvarez.

From then on, Eibar had something to defend – and defend they did. The key to this victory was – besides a bit of luck – Eibar's energy levels. This match was shown on the *Energy* TV channel – usually a sign of the least anticipated fixture of the weekend – and Eibar's starting XI displayed enough energy to make the producers proud as they defended their lead for the remaining hour of play. Derek Boateng, in particular, was a Duracell bunny of a central midfielder. The buccaneering Ghanaian spent the 90 minutes suffocating the Vigo midfield, stretching into tackles with muscular abandon and cutting off the supply lines to the strikers as best he could. Even up front, Eibar's indefatigable forward line worked their socks off, employing more pressing than an entire maternity ward. Dani García was able to ease the pressure time and time again, nonchalantly spreading accurate passes to all corners of the field like a snooker player working the table.

Vigo were far from lethargic themselves; they put in as much effort as Eibar, but no amount of huff and puff could blow Eibar's defensive wall down. Irureta was consistently busy in the second half, saving from Larrivey, Charles and Fernández, but the hosts lacked guile in the final third, ferreting away chance after chance. In the 89th minute, another opportunity begged to be put away, but the profligate Larrivey couldn't convert, nor could he score with a header just minutes later in the first minute of stoppage time.

Still there was more! A further three minutes of injury time had to be contested and Eibar played enough long clearances to embarrass a rugby union fly-half. With seconds left, one found its way back to the edge of the Eibar penalty area and a long-distance Khron-Dehli shot was deflected on to the crossbar by the stretching leg of Boateng, but then cleared for the final time to that beautiful sound of the referee's full-time whistle.

This has been a quite unbelievable win in the fullest sense of the adjective. Yet a win is a win even if many will, justifiably, argue that Vigo were the better team. Playing beautiful football and losing just as beautifully suits some teams in La Liga, but not Eibar. This team understands what is necessary to win and, while it may not be pretty, they are perfecting their way of playing the game.

To fully appreciate Eibar's style of play, one must first understand just how limited their resources are. Remember Eibar's playing budget is the smallest in the league by far, at under €9million, meaning the club cannot realistically purchase any players. With a 23-man squad, nearly a third of the budget would be taken up by player wages even if Eibar paid the very minimum salary permitted by the league, which by and large it does. On top comes coaching salaries, registration fees, training equipment expenditure and travelling costs. When it comes to player acquisition, Eibar really is scraping the barrel so it's little wonder the club has the least talented squad in the division. It would be no use pretending the players are future *Ballon d'Or* winners and playing open attacking football as the lack of quality would quickly show and Eibar would lose week in, week out. No, instead Eibar must use the limited quality on their roster wisely, and that is exactly what they have been doing.

I spoke to Guillem Balague about Eibar's style of play and success so far this season. Guillem explained: "The style of Eibar is very much defined by, number one, the lack of quality of the team, which means that they are all very aware that unless they work together the whole thing won't work."

He carried on, explaining how Eibar make good use of the workrate and speed of wingers Saúl Berjón and Javi Lara: "[Their success] is all based on the same kind of concept which is a lot of running without the ball. When they have the ball they don't like to be direct, as in longballs. They like to go down the wings and put crosses in.

"Remember that seven of the regulars are players that have been in the first-team line-up since they were in the *Segunda B* division and that is an extraordinary situation."

It certainly is a feel-good story to see these players starting for Eibar after having played with them in the *Segunda B* just two years' previously, but one must recognise the gulf in class between the *Segunda B* and the *Primera* is enormous and that these players, while playing well, are far from seasoned top division pros. Garitano himself is all too aware of the gulf in class, but says his team thrives on it and it is no crime to feel inferior, arguing, in fact, it helps his team remain grounded. To counter the gulf in quality, hard graft is the key says Guillem. "It's just all about hard work from everybody. It worked in the *Segunda B*, it worked in the *Segunda* and it has worked in the *Primera* so far."

Spanish football journalist Jason Pettigrove backs that up, telling me Eibar's better-than-expected results have been based on, "no prima donnas or egos in the dressing room and everyone pulling in the same direction, with the same goals and aspirations". Jason carries on: "There's little doubt in my mind Eibar would have struggled at the top level if they had a squad that didn't fully buy into what the management were trying to achieve. A real 'all for one, one for all' spirit has shone through in all of their games and, even in the ones they have lost, they've gone down fighting."

A FAIRYTALE SEASON: ACT 2

Still, even an industrial level of hard work and a high level of synergy between the players wouldn't be enough to put the ball in the opponent's net and keep it out of Irureta's. So what has Gaizka Garitano been doing tactically with this group of indisputably hardworking team players?

For most matches he is playing a 4-2-3-1 formation, which can quickly become a 4-4-1-1 if the wingers drop further back into midfield as they do against more testing opposition, or later on in matches needing to be closed out. Arruabarrena tends to be the furthest forward striker except when Piovaccari is on the pitch, in which case Arruabarrena drops back to form the tip of the midfield. It is a tactic which has worked exceptionally well and which gives Eibar two accomplished and physical target men to aim for.

The back four will vary in terms of personnel, yet has always been a four – except for the visit to the Camp Nou, when it became a five. Then again, you don't play teams like Barcelona every week. In front of the back four, Garitano likes to play a double *pivote* to protect them, usually Dani García and one other. That best 'one other' in this writer's humble opinion is Boateng, but local lad Jon Errasti is just as committed to the role and both are capable.

That just leaves the attacking trio of midfield which consists of Ander Capa on the right wing and Saúl Berjón on the left, with the centre of the midfield trio either Arruabarrena or one of Javi Lara or Manu del Moral, the other wingers.

All of this works notably well, as results such as this win against Celta de Vigo prove. As Guillem Balague explained, Plan A is to work the ball down the wings, with full-backs Bóveda and Abraham assisting where necessary. With targets such as Arruabarrena and Piovaccari, plus the winger from the opposite flank, Eibar have found success this way and been able to score just enough goals to make the few their disciplined defence concede worth something.

Besides the players on the pitch and the formations in Garitano's head, Eibar's assistants have also been key to these impressive results. Garitano has kept his two from the *Segunda*; Patxi Ferreira is his number two and Iñaki Lafuente is his goalkeeping coach. Brought in ahead of this season have been Andoni Azkargorta, Garitano's assistant in Eibar B and now opposition scout, and Mikel Calvo, who will assist Alain Gandiaga with the physical training so important for a minnow like Eibar. "In the *Primera*, everything up to and including the last detail is important, therefore in order to strengthen the technical area Eibar have made various changes and new additions," said the club in an official statement. So far these changes are working.

Thanks to this combination of hard work, team work, a sound tactical plan, proficient assistants and a little dose of luck, Eibar will travel back from Vigo looking proudly down on the rest of the bottom half of La Liga from 11th place. Over the coming weeks, they'll be looking down from higher still.

Friday, 5th December 2014. Coliseum Alfonso Pérez, Madrid.
The romantics may not agree, but realistically for Eibar the *Copa del Rey*, Spain's only knockout cup, is wholly secondary this season. While it may have provided the most memorable moments of seasons past, such as the trip to see the *Galácticos* struggle past Eibar at the Bernabéu in 2004, or the victory over Athletic Club in 2012, this season is already memorable enough that progressing far enough to draw a big name would be less exciting than it would have been in previous years.

It may sound pessimistic to suggest the *Copa del Rey* is unwinnable for Eibar, but let's look at the facts. Not since 2004 has a team hailing from a city with a population under one million lifted the trophy; and that was Real Zaragoza, hardly a minnow of Spanish football at the time. Barcelona and Real Madrid, Spain's omnipotent top dogs, have been present in five of the last six finals, each winning the trophy twice over that period. For a team like Eibar, there really is no hope.

Much of the explanation for this comes down to the fact each round is played over two legs. Cup upsets are much more common in the UK, for example, where your Manchester Uniteds and your Liverpools can have off days, as Leeds United and Oldham Athletic fans can testify. In Spain, however, the giants are afforded two lives; any upset can usually be corrected by fielding the strongest side possible in the second leg.

That each round is made up of two legs is all the more reason for smaller *Primera* teams like Eibar to prioritise the league. Four rounds must be conquered to reach the final, meaning eight extra matches. For Eibar, any extra game will take a toll on this thin squad and the thought of even four or six extra matches is enough to dismiss cup dreams for the season.

The line-up Garitano puts out for this visit to Getafe in the Last 32 round is below strength, therefore, and some of the stalwarts of the league campaign are afforded a rest; Dani García, Mikel Arruabarrena, Raúl Albentosa, Xabi Irureta, Manu del Moral, Eneko Bóveda and Saúl Berjón. It is little surprise, then, to see Eibar fall to a 3-0 defeat at the hands of Getafe; more surprising is that it takes Getafe until the final half an hour to open the scoring, though it is not for want of trying. After passing up chance after chance, two Pablo Sarabia goals and an Álvaro Vázquez back-heeled tap-in settle the first leg in Getafe's favour.

The return leg would be far more competitive, but Getafe still come out on top in front of the 2,600 fans that would make an appearance at Ipurua in the cold December rain. Two first-half Getafe goals would seal the tie – as if it hadn't been decided already – before Federico

Piovaccari's fourth goal of the season from the penalty spot in the second half.

It is a testament to the ludicrousness of Eibar's excellent December that this 5-1 aggregate cup loss would fail to dampen spirits.

Monday, 8th December 2014. Ipurua Stadium, Eibar.

It is a public holiday here in Spain today, making this 5pm Monday evening kick-off one of the few Monday fixtures of the season fans are actually excited about. All day long there has been drinking in the bars between the main square and Ipurua, not outside in the sun but tucked inside away from the swirling rain of a Basque, December Monday afternoon.

Eventually it is time to brace the cold, and luckily there is enough alcohol in the bloodstream by kick-off time to maintain a bit of warmth, so the crowds flock to Ipurua – an impressive 4,200 brave the elements. Little do they know it, but they will be rewarded with a treat of a football match.

For this visit of Almería, Garitano employs the same 4-2-3-1 formation mentioned earlier, but with a tweak. He plays two natural left wingers, Saúl Berjón and Manu del Moral, on either flank which results in 72% of Eibar's play in the Almería half going down the left wing or centre as Moral drifts inwards from the right wing in his kind of 'false seven' role. More than a happy accident, this is tactical genius from Garitano; a ruse as cunning yet simple as Bugs Bunny's drag routine.

It is that vast space vacated by the puzzled Almería left-back Mané on Manu del Moral's wing that Piovaccari is able to burst into to pick up the ball in the third minute before turning and, while expertly keeping his balance on the muddy pitch beneath him, dashing towards goal to slot into the bottom corner. Manu continues to drift towards the centre in the minutes following, forcing Mané to dance to his rhythm, and Eibar build on their opener by persistently moving the ball towards the Almería goal through the centre and left channels.

In the 20th minute, Eibar's second goal arrives; this time Saúl Berjón is able to latch on to a Dani García through ball along the left flank and fire, albeit with a deflection, into the back of the net. The protagonists of the night, our two left wingers, also set up Eibar's next two goals, though not from the wings but from the corner flags.

First, Saúl Berjón hoists the ball up for Raúl Albentosa to nod in, while Eibar's fourth – yes, a fourth goal! – comes when Manu del Moral's corner is diverted into the net by Eibar's other centre-back Raúl Navas. Navas's goal comes in the second half, by which point Almería have pulled one back, thus easing any nerves.

Saúl Berjón picks up an injury and is withdrawn to a standing ovation. This also ends Manu del Moral's role as the ghosting threat on the right wing as substitute Ander Capa, a natural right winger, fills in. The two play a major role in Eibar's fifth of the evening when, on 74 minutes, left-back Abraham's pass towards the centre is dummied by Manu and picked up in the middle of the park by Capa, who is similarly inching towards the centre from his right wing. Capa traps the ball before targeting the top corner with both force and success from outside the area. It is 5-1 and Eibar are soaring.

Two minutes later it is 5-2 when Edgar converts a cross at the back post, but there are definitely some home supporters too busy jumping up and down and singing to have even realised. The popular chant 'I will fight, until I die, because without you Eibar, I don't know how to live' – which is much catchier when it rhymes in Spanish – rings around the ground. 'One more goal, one more goal,' is the next chant from the Ipurua crowd, tongues simultaneously wedged in cheeks. Watching your team lose in the rain is never fun, but watching your team win in such conditions brings with it a special kind of joy. These fans are as happy to be singing in the rain as Gene Kelly.

The one extra goal doesn't come, but the final score here is an incredible 5-2. Eibar have laid down a marker for future visitors to Ipurua: expect an easy game at your peril.

Future visitors have also seen just how tricky Ipurua's pitch will be to play on. The rains here today have been like a monsoon; there is little that could have been done to make the pitch more playable, making the comments of one of Almería's team doctors uncalled for. Antonio Rios Luna would say after the match: "I cannot understand how the LFP [the league] allows you to play at the elite level on a pitch like Eibar's. It is third worldly and dangerous for the players."

Nobody would argue the Ipurua turf is impeccable – and in one further rainy game in January it will look anything but. However, the Ipurua pitch has appeared no worse than any other in such heavy weather. Sid Lowe agrees, telling me: "Eibar is a classic Basque cliché, but actually I think it [the pitch] hasn't been that bad. It's not a great pitch, but then the reality is that football is played outdoors. [It has been good] considering the conditions it is played on because Eibar leads to a very very very wet valley and it's really quite exposed."

To blame a 5-2 defeat on the quality of the pitch – the Almería doctor's comments didn't come before the match but, tellingly, within ten minutes of the full-time whistle – is a cheap shot, but it is not one which takes anything away from this fantastic performance of Eibar's players, managers and fans in the stands. As Almería gripe about the state of the pitch, Eibar's colourful fans are finishing the bank holiday in style with some whiskys, songs and dancing in the rain-thrashed town centre.

It's going to be a late Monday night!

A FAIRYTALE SEASON: ACT 2

Sunday, 14th December 2014. Sánchez Pizjuán Stadium, Seville.

The *cláusulas del miedo* are a particularly controversial topic in Spanish football. These are the clauses included in loan deal contracts which forbid the loaned player from lining up against their parent club unless a fee is paid. Literally translated as 'clauses of fear', many clubs employ them and Eibar is well used to the details given how many loan players are on Eibar's books each season.

Dídac Vilà and Federico Piovaccari's contracts didn't require any such clause as neither AC Milan nor Sampdoria look set to join La Liga any time soon. Barring an encounter in the cup, Abraham would also be available for all of Eibar's fixtures since Real Zaragoza were left behind by Eibar in the *Segunda* division – which just goes to show how weak Eibar's squad is when the left-back is unwanted by a *Segunda* club.

The two loanees on Eibar's books who would face their parent clubs over the course of the season are Real Sociedad's Raúl Navas and Sevilla's Manu del Moral. Whereas Real Sociedad allowed Navas to play in the season's opening match – which they lost 1-0 with Navas a standout performer – today's rivals Sevilla have been less keen to face one of their own and the good old *cláusula del miedo* means Eibar will not play the man who opened up so much space against Almería the previous Monday. It would cost them €50,000 to play him, a not insignificant fee for a club like Eibar.

Regardless, Manu del Moral would likely not have been deployed in that 'false seven' role today anyway. This is Sevilla we are talking about, a team with a mighty home record – nine wins in 11 so far this season – in the always bouncing Sánchez Pizjuán Stadium. No, today requires a much more defensive and disciplined performance against a side streets ahead of Eibar in terms of quality. For this reason, Garitano opts for a more orthodox set-up to his team. Irureta starts in goal, behind a back four of Bóveda, Navas, Albentosa and Lillo, all of whom are starting in their preferred positions. In front of the defence, the double *pivote* roles are filled by Dani García and Derek Boateng, while the midfield trio sees Arruabarrena in the centre, Capa to his right and left-back Abraham to his left – providing an extra defensive element to a wing where José Antonio Reyes and Aleix Vidal could cause damage. At the tip of Eibar's starting XI is Piovaccari as the traditional centre-forward and target man.

Once again, Garitano has got his tactics spot on. Some managers high on confidence after a 5-2 win would come out all guns blazing, but Garitano has expertly avoided any over-confidence and Eibar's defensive approach is proving difficult for Sevilla to break down. On top of frustrating Sevilla's forward line, Eibar are able to create the odd chance on the break, the first of which falls Ander Capa's way;

the winger does well to get a shot on target and win a corner with no support alongside him in the box. It's Sevilla's turn next to have a go and Irureta does well to react to a drilled Carlos Bacca shot before Derek Boateng rifles a similarly fierce low shot at the other end, which Beto palms away.

Although the resulting play is flagged – correctly – for offside, it deserves a mention as Piovaccari's overhead kick to reach the rebound from Boateng's strike is as skilled as they come, but Beto's second save in as many seconds is equal to it.

Back to pieces of the action which do count, and in the second half Grzegorz Krychowiak should have made his chance from a corner count, only for his shot to hit Bóveda in the chest one yard from goal, to keep the scores level. Minutes later Sevilla's frustration with Eibar shows as a melee breaks out in the area. As Albentosa and Sevilla's Alejandro Arribas grapple with each other while they await a Reyes cross, Albentosa trips and hits the deck where he is swiped at by Arribas's boot. He riposte with a kick of his own right foot and both players pick up yellow cards.

Again, the pressure from Sevilla grows and yet another corner – one of 11 in the match – flies into the box and Irureta rushes out to claim it, but for once doesn't quite reach it. The ball falls to forward Kévin Gameiro who immediately shoots towards Irureta's vacated goal, but the keeper leaps like a salmon to just get a hand to the shot and divert the ball out of play for yet another corner. A series of fruitless corners later and the ball is finally in the back of Irureta's net. Thankfully for him and his team-mates, it doesn't count, however, as the very brave, but correct, linesman flags as Bacca is in an offside position when he dummies Stéphane M'bia's volley.

Sevilla continue to press for a winner and look more like finding one when Denis Suárez is substituted on for Gameiro, who had suffered a torrid afternoon competing against the Eibar defensive wall. Albentosa, in particular, has been immense and he didn't just have Gameiro in his back pocket, but had him buried so deep in it that Eibar kitman Zapico will surely find Gameiro crawling out of his washing machine the next day, left in a pocket like a forgotten receipt or tissue. Still, although the arrival of Suárez's fresh legs and ideas has Eibar on the ropes, it is still all foreplay with no finish from Sevilla and Eibar defend in numbers, never embarrassed to appear overrun. Suárez shoots wide twice in the closing minutes, as does Reyes, before M'bia's header over the bar proves to be the match's final action. Eibar have held on for a memorable point.

Since their 4-0 defeat to Real Madrid, Eibar have picked up seven points from a possible nine. Impressive doesn't even cut it; this is awe-inspiring.

A FAIRYTALE SEASON: ACT 2

Saturday, 20th December 2014. Ipurua Stadium, Eibar.
"If it ain't broke, don't fix it." How far from the truth that phrase is in the case of Eibar this Saturday evening.

Eibar's spectacular run of form is put to the test with the visit of an excellent Valencia side, who have lost just three matches all season, and Garitano is already thinking one step ahead. Not wanting his side to become too predictable, Garitano changes things a little for this glamour fixture by switching to a 3-2-2-2-1 formation – the first time all season he has not played with at least four at the back.

Albentosa takes up the central position in the back three, with Navas to his right and Lillo on the left. Right-back Bóveda is deployed on the right of midfield, in front of the eternal double *pivote* of Boateng and Dani García, with Saúl Berjón taking the left midfield position. The attacking triangle consists of Piovaccari and Arruabarrena, both playing behind Manu del Moral, who is given yet another experimental role after his exploits against Almería.

It is a bold move from the manager, especially when others would have been wary of tampering with the plan behind this successful run. However, Garitano knows how quickly things move at this level and if Eibar are to have any chance of rounding off an historic, remarkable and fairytale 2014 with a win then this risk is necessary. And it works. Ish.

After a fairly safe opening 15 minutes from both sides, Eibar create the first chance of the match when Piovaccari receives the ball from Manu, swivelling to face the goal and then launching a missile towards the far corner which Diego Alves diverts for a corner kick. That sight of goal galvanises Eibar, who push on in search of further chances and Piovaccari gets his Christmas wish ten minutes later, dribbling through Javi Fuego, only to send his shot high enough to worry Santa's sleigh and earn a place on the naughty list.

Moments later, Valencia are able to turn an attacking play from Eibar into the match's opening goal. Having cleared from the box, Rodrigo De Paul picks up the ball and sends a 'Hail Mary' long ball forward which somehow finds its way to Pablo Piatti, who is able to square to Paco Alcácer to allow the Spain international his first league goal since September, and his easiest of the campaign.

Eibar don't panic and keep up their attacking threat through Arruabarrena, who has a propensity for overlapping even when playing behind a traditional number nine and who is in no way shy of overlapping today's experimental number nine Manu to provide the necessary support. Arruabarrena is the very man who has the best chance to equalise before the break when he controls a Saúl Berjón cross with his chest and shoots, only for his effort to be deflected into the hands of Diego Alves.

Now in the second half, with Abraham having replaced Saúl Berjón, Eibar go for the equaliser backed by an Ipurua so loud the sound of drums, singing and cheering will still be echoing around the four stands come Christmas morning. Spurred on by the home choir, Piovaccari earns his nomination for the 'Best Winning of an Unwinnable Ball of the Season' award. Twenty yards away from the dropping ball, and with not one but two Valencia players between him and the prize, Piovaccari has absolutely no right to win it, but the determined Italian does just that; he races across the pitch past Lucas Orbán before sliding in to *just* reach the ball before Nicolás Otamendi. Immediately bouncing back to his feet, Piovaccari makes a beeline for the box where he unleashes a deadly low ball which Arruabarrena is just a fraction away from redirecting into the net. Piovaccari's brave effort receives the loudest applause of the night, but it deserved even more than that. It deserved a goal.

Piovaccari has a kind of who-knows-what-he'll-do-next-least-of-all-himself feel to his game, but is proving capable of producing magic on a not irregular basis. Runs like that are behind his increasing support from the terraces as this rugged and volatile centre-forward is becoming *their* rugged and volatile centre-forward. Runs like that explain why Eibar fans are proud of Piovaccari and runs like that epitomise the hard work, as we've discussed, that is necessary if Eibar are to survive in this league.

Unfortunately for Piovaccari, his cross never quite found the back of the net and proves to have been Eibar's make or break moment as Valencia begin to see out this match in the way the top clubs know how, sucking the life out of the remaining minutes.

It does indeed finish 1-0, but Eibar have acquitted themselves more than admirably and Garitano's boldness in switching a winning formation was so very nearly rewarded with a deserved point. As we shall later discover, Eibar have not made it this far by resting on their laurels and their double promotion has come about because of president Álex Aranzábal's willingness to take the occasional calculated risk. That he hired a manager similarly intrepid is little surprise and today, although this risky experimental formation didn't work out entirely as planned, Eibar are still in the top half of the table.

Sunday, 28th December 2014. San Mamés, Bilbao.

It may well be Spanish football's winter break, but for Xabi Irureta, Eneko Bóveda, Ander Capa, Dani García and Mikel Arruabarrena, the football doesn't stop; all five have been called up to the Basque national team. They are the first Eibar players to receive the call since 2007 when Jon Urzelai featured, along with a certain Gaizka Garitano. Garitano may not be here on this occasion – he is enjoying his break by taking in even more football in a trip to England where he spent Boxing Day watching Chelsea versus West Ham at lunchtime before racing across London to catch Arsenal versus QPR in the evening kick-off – but thanks to Eibar's excellent first half of the season five of his players are able to enjoy the privilege of wearing the green of the Basque selection.

And while this match may well be taking place in Spanish football's winter break, this is not, of course, 'Spanish football'. In this, the first match to be played by the Basque selection at the fully-completed San Mamés, the opponents this evening are the Catalan national team – in order to celebrate the Basque side's centenary when they played the Catalans at the old San Mamés on 3rd January 1915, winning 6-1. It is both the least and most Spanish 'international' match there could be, with both the home side, the *Euskal Selekzioa*, and the away side, the *Selecció Catalana,* explicitly not Spanish yet every single player involved is eligible for the Spanish national team. Three members – Gerard Piqué, Xavi and Sergio Busquets – of the 2010 Spanish World Cup-winning team are even featuring tonight.

It is not really an international match either, as neither side is officially recognised by FIFA, but for the five Eibar players debuting they are very much representing their country, still the greatest honour in football.

A march towards a San Mamés lit up in the green and red of the Basque flag – the *ikurrina* – winds through Bilbao before the match, featuring both sets of fans, and demands FIFA recognition for these two sides. The political element of the night continues in the stands where both the president of the Basque government Íñigo Urkullu, and Catalan president Artur Mas, are in attendance. It is just under two months since Mas presided over a non-binding Catalan referendum in which 80.8% of votes supported Catalan independence, even if the turnout was estimated at just 40%. It's little surprise, therefore, tonight's match has an overtly separatist shade to it and both *Kataluniako independentziaren* and *independentisme català* are supported as much as the two teams by tonight's impressive 45,000 crowd – which includes 4,000 Catalans.

Amid shouts of *'español el que no bote'* – 'he who doesn't jump is a Spaniard' – there is actually some football being played on the pitch below. Ander Capa marks his Basque debut with an assist in the third minute for Bilbao favourite Aritz Aduriz to score his tenth goal for the *Euskal Selekzioa* in nine appearances. It is actually a shot from Capa, but his effort is blocked by Aduriz who pulls the ball from under his feet to ping it into the net himself, like a table football goal when the ball is trapped by one of the forward line. The Basques dominate proceedings until around ten minutes before the half-time break when the Catalans find a foothold in the match and a Jonathan Soriano goal is incorrectly ruled out for offside in the 41st minute. Captain Sergio García makes up for it two minutes later with a goal that does stand and serves to level the score, sending an army of *senyeras* – the Catalan flag – flying into the cold December air.

Capa is the only Eibar player to start the match, but the typical wave of half-time friendly match changes sees him substituted and Bóveda, Dani García and Arruabarrena all brought on for their Basque debuts. Just after the hour mark, Xabi Irureta makes his first appearance in a Basque shirt, replacing ex-Eibar goalkeeper Gorka Iraizoz. Irureta does well to help the Basque side hold on for a draw which the Eibar man will call "the most fair result", while at the other end Arruabarrena and Ibai Gómez of Athletic both miss chances to regain the lead. In the end, the draw is fair, as Irureta says, and it also comes as little surprise; three times in the past decade these two sides have faced each other and this is the third draw.

Tonight wasn't so much about the final score as the chance to represent the Basque Country and christen the new San Mamés with the 'national' team's appearance. For Eibar's five debutants, this is an unforgettable night and the perfect way to end what has been an unforgettable 2014. The quintet may have been outnumbered in the squad by the ten Athletic players and the six from Real Sociedad, but it is Irureta, Bóveda, Capa, García and Arruabarrena who finish the year as members of the highest-placed Basque club in Spain.

The hope now? To carry on as they left off in 2015.

Sunday, 4th January 2015. Cornellà-El Prat Stadium, Barcelona.

To hear your club has a brand new signing arriving from Atlético on the very first day of the winter transfer window would excite fans of nearly every team in the world. To then discover the player is arriving from Atlético Kolkata, and not from Atlético Madrid, might change perceptions at most clubs; not so at Eibar where any player willing to put in a shift is welcomed with open arms.

Borja Fernández is one of Spanish football's great personalities, regularly appearing on radio shows and maintaining a blog called 'Happy Life'. He is a player with technical ability as well as an abundance of talent north of his feet and can play in a variety of positions besides his preferred *pivote* role. That he was adventurous enough to sign up for the first-ever edition of the Indian Super League surprised few so off he went to Kolkata to turn out for the Atlético Madrid-owned franchise at the second largest stadium in the world, the 131,000 capacity Salt Lake Stadium. It was a more than successful spell in India for the ex-Real Madrid holding midfielder as he patrolled the centre of the park for the eventual winners, playing all 90 minutes of the final against Kerala Blasters.

Kolkata's gain was Eibar's loss as Borja turned down the chance to sign for Eibar in the summer in order to pursue his Indian adventure, but the Basque side haven't appeared to miss him. Now, however, they have their man after all. It may be a few months later than hoped, but this free transfer is a massive gain for the latter half of the season and this positional chameleon will be able to fill in where necessary in one of the double *pivote* roles or else in the back four.

"Borja Fernández is a player we know well as we tried to sign him in the summer when his contract with Getafe expired," explains Garitano. "But he decided to play in India and now we have had the chance to sign him. Our intention was to have four *pivotes* and now we have them to compete for places."

Dani García, Boateng and Errasti, the other three *pivotes*, need not worry about having to fight an extra man to keep their place ahead of today's match with Espanyol – although Boateng is replaced by Errasti amid rumours the Ghanaian has fallen out of favour since returning late from the Christmas holiday, committing the ultimate sin of not giving all for the team. Borja is not yet cleared to feature for his new club even though he has been training with them since Wednesday – on the artificial Anexo pitch since Ipurua's turf has been frozen over – but his mere arrival has already lifted spirits and energised the squad ahead of the league season's return.

This is evident on the pitch of the Cornellà-El Prat Stadium – or the Power8 Stadium, if we must – as Eibar begin their first match of their 75th year with great purpose. In their first league game without the suspended Raúl Albentosa shoring up the defence, Borja Ekiza – not to be confused with new arrival Borja Fernández – makes his first start since the 4-0 loss to Real Madrid, and only his fifth of the season. Alongside are Raúl Navas, Bóveda and Lillo, while ahead of him are García and Errasti protecting the back four, and Capa, Manu and Saúl Berjón making up the attacking midfield trio behind Piovaccari, with the also-suspended Arruabarrena the other notable absentee.

Despite the absences, Garitano has engineered an Eibar side which looks comfortable throughout this match; there is an abundance of space in the centre of midfield, which Manu drives into early on before pinging a shot just wide, almost disbelieving of how easy it was to race so far forward with the ball.

Manu finds himself in space again, this time in the 34th minute, and Saúl Berjón's cutback from the byline bobbles all the way back to Manu at the edge of the box who has enough time to sit down, stand back up, turn around and strike a shot into the net. In the end he does only the latter, putting Eibar up 1-0.

Four minutes later, Berjón is to set up another goal. He stands at the corner flag and flaps his arms like a bird, but it's quickly apparent the signal is understood by Bóveda, who peels off his marker to meet the cross and head into the net with Piovaccari possibly getting a slight touch on the way in. Either way, Eibar lead 2-0 going into the break and it has been inherently comfortable.

Espanyol boss Sergio changes things around at half-time – he really has no other choice – and right-back López is sacrificed in order to play a third striker, Morillas. It is Eibar who again appear the better side. The swashbuckling Piovaccari fights off his markers up front to win a long ball and deliver it to the back of the net, but this third goal is chopped off – correctly – as he is marginally offside.

That seems to be the wake-up call for Espanyol that the half-time team talk was not and the home side begin to press further and further forward, but it is already too late. A missile from Anaitz Arbilla is tipped over by Irureta and Felipe Caicedo heads on to the post but by the time Espanyol do pull one back – a Caicedo header – there only remains time for one more chance which falls comfortably into the hands of Irureta.

It is Eibar's second trip to Barcelona in three months and, like last time, blue and claret are the colours of the victors.

Saturday, 10th January 2015. Ipurua Stadium, Eibar.

Despite the excellent defensive performance one week previously, and admission among some sections of Ipurua that Eibar may not be as reliant on the seemingly Derby County-bound Raúl Albentosa as some think, Garitano has no doubts about reinstating his star defender in the starting XI – the only change – for this league match with Getafe.

An absence of creativity in the line-up is made up for with an excellent rehearsed training ground free-kick routine after an admittedly dull opening half hour. Dani García and Saúl Berjón hover over the ball, while three Getafe players make up a wall in which they are joined by Manu del Moral. Berjón taps the free kick and the wall suddenly loses all of its mortar in an effort to race out and block what appears to be a Dani García effort at goal. Manu has peeled away in the other direction and García feigns to shoot before tidily chipping the ball towards his team-mate. There is still plenty of work for Manu to do as he is not by any means wide open, yet despite being the meat in a sandwich of two closing Getafe players he volleys García's pass into the net with his left foot.

Ipurua goes potty while Manu remains calm, opting not to celebrate against his former club for whom he remains their top *Primera* goalscorer with 37 strikes during his five seasons with Getafe.

The goal fails to liven up the match, even if it has livened up the crowd, and half-time ticks closer and closer without much incident. The second period begins with more action and a second goal. It goes the way of Eibar's Ander Capa; the right winger nets at the second attempt after his first shot is blocked by Velázquez.

Evoking memories of the win at Espanyol the previous week, the two-goal deficit is too large for Getafe to scale and by the time Eibar's opponents do cut it in half via Diego Castro's right boot, there is not enough time remaining for an equaliser.

So, there is a victory to cheer for the home support, which has been singing one song louder than most this evening; the not particularly complex 'Raúl, Raúl, Raúl Albentosa!' The fans know this is likely to be the last time they sing his name so they are looking to make the most of it as they chant his name over the club hymn which is now blaring out of the speakers. That is no small task, by the way, given the volume the club hymn is played after matches. It is usually great fun, particularly after a win, and the track features so many synthesisers it sounds like a karaoke backing track or the music of a Sonic the Hedgehog Sega game. Tonight, though, Raúl Albentosa's name is the song these fans want to sing.

If Albentosa had a similar mindset of wanting to make the most of his last performance for Eibar then he did exactly that. From cutting out long balls, to organising the free-kick routine from which Manu scores, he has been everywhere tonight and fully deserves the ovation he receives as he walks down the tunnel one last time.

Friday, 16th January 2015. Nuevo Arcángel Stadium, Córdoba.

One. Two. Three. Four. Five. Six. Seven. Eight. Nine. Goal!

Less than ten seconds have passed here in Córdoba and Florin Andone puts the home side into the lead. The Nuevo Arcángel Stadium has a 'Supportometer' which, while as gimmicky as it gets here in Spain, is already bursting next to the scoreboard which reads 1-0 and 00:10.

It goes without saying conceding the fourth fastest goal in La Liga history is a terrible start for Eibar, but it is particularly so for Borja Ekiza who is brushed off the ball far too easily by Andone. With Albentosa in England to complete his move to Derby County, Borja Ekiza – who had been agitating to start all season – was brought back into the starting line-up, while the only other change is Javi Lara coming in for the suspended Ander Capa. Piovaccari, once again, has kept Arruabarrena on the bench.

Little else of interest takes place in the first half, with the 'Supportometer' close to running on empty as there is very little to shout about except for Piovaccari's fuming at a double penalty claim. Córdoba centre-back Crespo not only defends the incoming ball with his arm, but also drags Piovaccari to the ground as he falls over. The Italian makes clear to the referee it should have been a penalty, perhaps not very politely.

In the second half there are scores to be settled, and not just on the scoreboard. Firstly, Campabadal sees red ten minutes after the break for his second yellow of the evening, bringing down Saúl Berjón as he looks to bisect the Córdoba back line. Then just two minutes later, as tensions boil, Piovaccari and goalscorer Andone fly into each other in an attempt to win the ball in the middle of the park. Both players roll around the ground in 'agony' before the referee produces a red card for Piovaccari, his actions in the previous 58 minutes doing little to win him the benefit of the doubt.

Eibar now find themselves a goal down and down to ten players, but Garitano maintains the status quo for the time being having already made one of his three substitutions at half-time when he hooked the unfortunate Borja for the experienced Txema Añibarro. Manu del Moral, therefore, advances slightly from his central midfield position to also take on the role of centre-forward, but with no success after ten minutes Garitano makes the necessary change and switches Manu for a lethal injection of pace in the form of Arruabarrena. And what a return to action it is.

A beautiful cross from Saúl Berjón near the right wing's corner flag is met in the air by the accelerating and towering Arruabarrena, and is diverted past the goalkeeper. It is safe to say the 'Supportometer' is running even lower in the seconds after the ball ripples the net.

That's how it finishes here in the south of Spain: 1-1. There is little else of note in this match besides the debut of Borja Fernández, who replaces Javi Lara late on to give Eibar an extra defensive-minded player on the park. It is ironic, with so much space available, that few chances were created towards the end, but Irureta in the Eibar goal can take a lot of credit for snuffing out Córdoba chances, having played much higher up the pitch than usual since the two sending offs – so high that pioneer of the 'false one' position Manuel Neuer would have been proud had he chosen to spend his Friday night tuning in.

It could have been a lot worse for Eibar tonight, having gone a goal down so early and a man down just when it appeared they would have a player advantage. Nevertheless, they found a way to overcome the odds and head north with yet another La Liga point to complete the first round of fixtures, called the first *vuelta*.

Up in the Basque mountains the locals are getting giddy as the club sits in eighth place in the table and jokes of European adventures. European qualification is, of course, a far from realistic dream – of that there is no doubt – and it would still be a miracle if Eibar even avoids relegation. For the time being, though, Eibar's form is the stuff of legend.

A FAIRYTALE SEASON: ACT 2

The legend will soon flame out, I'm afraid, as it quickly becomes clear just how serious and detrimental a blow losing Albentosa is when some of the best players in the world soon break through an Albentosa-shaped hole in this defence. Eibar is about to take a running start down a slip 'n' slide into a relegation dogfight.

La Liga standings after *jornada* 19

#	Team	Matches Played	Matches Won	Matches Drawn	Matches Lost	Points
8	Eibar	19	7	6	6	27
16	Elche	19	4	5	10	17
17	Deportivo	19	4	5	10	17
18	Almería	19	4	4	11	16
19	Levante	19	3	7	9	16
20	Granada	19	2	8	9	14

4

Ipurua

"It's very old-fashioned, it feels very authentic and it's got real identity, but it is what it is: a ground that holds five and a half thousand."

Sid Lowe

Tuesday, 23rd September 2014. Ipurua Stadium, Eibar.
I'm standing in the middle of a mucky football pitch. There is nothing too unusual or exciting about that, so what's so special about this moment?

Well, in just under 24 hours there will be a La Liga match taking place right beneath my feet and, incredibly, they've just let me walk all over what precious little grass there is left.

This is Ipurua Municipal Stadium. And this is the home of the most relaxed football club in Spanish football's top flight.

Not only is this the most relaxed club, but it is also the smallest and it takes us little more than five minutes to walk the full way around this enchanting little stadium's four stands, even stopping for a photo or two. "I mean, it's properly tiny," Sid Lowe exclaims. "I really like it, by the way, because it's very old-fashioned, it feels very authentic and it's got real identity, but it is what it is: a ground that holds five and a half thousand."

There's no getting away from the fact the stadium is tiny – its current capacity of 5,250 is the smallest in the league – and each of the four stands is very basic. Although there are, in reality, a couple of exits to each stand, Bill Leckie's joke that those in charge at the club have "put all their Basques in one exit" is pure genius and not at all far from the truth.

Ipurua is different. On a matchday, as in any football ground in the world, there are fans enjoying a sneaky cigarette in the toilets. Yet only here is this a valuable public service; the embers at the end of the cigarettes provide the toilets' only lighting underneath the blown lightbulbs which sit impotently above. Even making it to the toilet again highlights Ipurua's uniqueness; there is no toilet in the East Stand so this requires fans to squeeze through a turnstile to access those in the adjacent North Stand.

Eibar did receive financial help from the league and the government to modernise this creaking relic of the 1940s and to convert the terraces to fully-seated stands when it was becoming a stable *Segunda* division club in the 1990s, reducing the total capacity from 10,000 to 5,250 in the process. The original Main Stand was demolished in 1998 and replaced with a covered 2,800-capacity stand before the East and West stands were refurbished in 1999. That same year, the North Stand was demolished and rebuilt with five rows of seats in time for the 2000/01 season. Decades before these projects there was work done on the pitch's poor drainage in 1959, while floodlights were installed in 1970 to allow for evening matches – inaugurated with a 1-1 draw on 14th October 1970 between Basque giants Athletic Club and Real Sociedad. Both projects were successful and the drainage work carried out in 1959 did not need updating until 2000, when an irrigation system and automatic sprinklers were installed, while new floodlights were not required until 1989.

More recently, work was carried out on the new Main Stand between October 2004 and January 2006, with club offices, a gym, a medical room, a restaurant, a small-but-does-what-it-says-on-the-tin press room and a Jacuzzi all installed. The changing rooms were also moved to the Main Stand, having previously been located in the West Stand which, to this day, still has a tunnel. The total cost of the project was €1,800,800, half of which was paid for by Eibar City Council and SD Eibar itself, while the other half of the bill was footed by the Provincial Council of Gipuzkoa. While the club was incredibly proud of these new installations, inaugurated in February 2006, it would be hyperbole to say that Ipurua had become a state-of-the-art stadium.

Yet although it may not be particularly glamourous, this is the way the locals like it. A shiny plastic megastadium – like the 2013-built 53,000-seater San Mamés in neighbouring Bilbao – would look more than out of place in Eibar, a former industrial town as yet unconquered by the likes of Starbucks and McDonalds. Eibar's population has fallen from its peak in the 1970s of 40,000 to today's 27,000 and on first glance it is a town trapped in the late 20th century, sandwiched between a glorious past and a developing future; in touching distance of both, but not present in either. Eibar was, in fact, voted the second least attractive town in all of Spain in a 2011 survey by free morning newspaper *20 Minutos* and, while such polls are always of questionable validity, Eibar did receive a significant 27,884 of the 560,025 votes cast on 42 different towns and cities. Regardless, the locals are intensely proud of where they come from.

Tonight I'm joined by three locals and members of the ever-helpful *Eskozia La Brava* fan club, or *peña* as fan clubs are known in Spain.

The name translates as 'Scotland The Brave' and even though they've shown me great hospitality so far, I know it's not simply because I'm Scottish – I can already tell they'd be this welcoming to any visitor to Eibar.

Fittingly, I meet the *peña* president Joseba Combarro at the wall of the East Stand, where a mural has been painted of the Lion Rampant and the Saltire, alongside the SD Eibar club badge and the *ikurrina,* the Basque Country's flag. This stand has long been called *La Inglesa* due to its English style and faces *La Bombonera* stand, named after the famous fan group which occupied the West Stand in the 1980s and 1990s, even if most – not all – of that old guard have mellowed out nowadays and allowed *Eskozia La Brava* to take charge of Ipurua's *ánimo,* its renowned atmosphere and support.

Joseba is a fascinating fellow, immediately assertive as is his zeal for the football club he has supported since boyhood. He is always organising something and tonight has with him around ten football shirts, 60 Eibar scarves and 200 stickers – the kind of man you hear about only in maths problems at school. It is obvious that when it comes to learning about Eibar, Joseba is the main man and his omniscient and encyclopaedic knowledge of the club will prove invaluable, beginning with a tour of the legendary stadium.

We make our way inside – no key required, the door is left unlocked – and Joseba leads us on a walk across the pitch.

I'm sure there are few La Liga pitches where you'd keep a vigilant eye on your every step for fear of stepping in dog dirt, yet I can't help but do exactly that as I walk towards the centre circle; it just reminds me too much of a public park in the outskirts of Glasgow where I used to play football as a kid. But, of course, this is not a public park. This is a stadium in one of the world's top football leagues and it is due to host a match tomorrow evening against a very impressive Villarreal side. Imagine being allowed to take a stroll across the immaculate carpets of the Camp Nou or the Santiago Bernabéu the night before a match. Yes exactly, keep imagining.

You could say that Ipurua is a stadium like no other. However, although it is nowadays distinct from the various concrete bowls other Spanish clubs call home, it wasn't always so unique. Built in 1947, with the Main Stand completed in 1951, Ipurua was, like many other northern Spanish grounds, similar to a lot of the British lower-league stadiums of the 20th century with its open corners, large Main Stand, two towering behind-the-goal stands and the proximity to the pitch of the North Stand on the far side. A cup of Bovril and a half-time steak pie are the only British aspects this ground lacks. Spanish stadia expert Chris Clements, the man behind the popular *Estadios De España* blog, agrees.

"I guess if we were talking about Ipurua some 25 years ago, and Eibar was earning a crust floating between the second and third tier, then it would be a fairly typical small stadium in the north of Spain," Chris tells me. "It was aging, close to the centre of town and the majority of the ground was under cover. It would be referred to locally as an English-style stadium as it featured compact stands up tight to the pitch."

Ipurua may not have been an oddity in the Spanish stadium scene 25 years ago, but it seems from another planet now in the 21st century. As Chris explains: "A few things have changed in the past 25 years which make Eibar's idiosyncratic home even more at odds with the modern game. For a start, many city centre sites have been sold for development and clubs have moved to purpose-built and visually balanced – some say boring! – stadia on the edge of town. Instead Eibar developed their home, mainly because their ground was already big enough for its fanbase and because the geography of the town did not offer an obvious out-of-town site."

Chris has raised an important point about the geography of Eibar. Sitting in a narrow valley in Debabarrena – the most north-western part of the Basque province of Gipuzkoa, itself the smallest province in all of Spain – Eibar is a town literally squashed between the Basque mountains. With residential property to the north and the AP-8 motorway to the south, there is little room for expansion and none for relocation, forcing SD Eibar to make the most of the stadium it has called home since 1947.

That could prove problematic going forward given a ridiculous rule which requires all La Liga stadia to have at least 12,000 seats; a rule which Sid Lowe describes as, "Another example of Eibar effectively being punished for being small and successful and being measured against everyone else's standards."

Chris Clements is also opposed to the rule. "The club, which has average crowds of 4,000, neither needs nor can afford a newly-developed home," he tells me. "Realistically, Eibar's stay in the top tier is unlikely to extend beyond a few years at most. After the dream is over, they could then be left with a quarter-full stadium and debt. It's the league that is forcing Eibar into an Icarus-like situation. They neither want nor can afford to fly too close to the sun."

But fly close to the sun they must; or they must at least be seen to be 'attempting to expand' their already UEFA-compliant stadium by a September 2016 deadline. With no room to expand outwards, nor the desire to relocate to a characterless identikit stadium outside of town, Eibar's only option is to build upwards; that's not a popular one with the residents who currently enjoy a view of a La Liga stadium from their balconies of the two apartment blocks which overlook the stadium's

North Stand. The residents of those apartments fear *Sostoa-Tarren Kalea,* their street, will become a building site and are worried the view from their balconies will become obstructed. That the work will move the stand to just seven metres away – three metres closer than before – from their building justifies concern. One neighbour admitted he fears it will be like living under a bridge once the work is completed and he sees a noisy stand of the stadium towering over his balcony.

Despite the opposition, the club has decided to go ahead with the *Ipurua Tailerra* – translated as 'Ipurua Workshop' – plan to expand the North Stand, a move which will add 1,000 seats to the currently just five rows deep stand. The hope is that this will be more than a pharaonic construction project and instead provide more solid foundations and a lasting legacy of the year in the *Primera* even when – not if – Eibar return to the *Segunda* division in the future as the inevitable result of economic gravity sucking them back down.

All of that is for the future, but even more interesting is a look back at Ipurua and the club's fascinating past. SD Eibar was founded in 1940, but the story of the club as we know it has its roots in a date three years before then.

To fully understand the history of both Eibar and Ipurua, we need to return to the height of the brutal Spanish Civil War.

Monday, 26th April 1937. Guernica, Basque Country.

Pablo Picasso's famous painting of the bombing of Guernica – Google it and appreciate it – conveys just a hint of the panic, destruction and fear caused by the aerial bombing of the Basque town during the Spanish Civil War.

This late April Monday is one of the darkest Spain's Basque Country will ever experience – and there will be many – due to the complete wiping out of the former Basque capital Guernica by the now-famous *Legion Condor* of the German Air Force and Italy's *Aviazione Legionaria,* its Legionary Air Force. General Francisco Franco has called upon his allies of Hitler and Mussolini to orchestrate the world's first air raids on defenceless populations; the raids are the kind that will become so common in the upcoming World War II, for which this weekend's bombings are seen as a gruesome and cruel training exercise.

If the bombing of Guernica is practice for WWII then the practice for the practice exercise took place two days previously, just 22 kilometres south-east. In Eibar.

That not enough people will ever know the story of the complete destruction of Eibar this April is tragic. Guernica will be the town more commonly referenced in post-mortems of the war, but the plight of Eibar is almost as severe. As journalist James Holburn would go on to write in *The Times* on 4th May: "There is nothing to compare with the havoc wrought in Guernica except in Eibar, 80% of which was destroyed by bombs and fire."

On the Saturday morning two days before the wipeout of Guernica, the very same German and Italian planes conducted bombing over Eibar, the town which sat just a little north of the last defensive lines of the Basque army. Like Guernica, Eibar had no Republican presence in the town, but was viewed by Franco's Nationalists as a key strategic point in the ultimate goal of capturing Republican-occupied Bilbao, a city whose occupation has been seen as vital to winning the war in the north of the country and which lies just a little to the west of both Guernica and Eibar.

Despite the lack of a Republican presence, Eibar was generally in support of the leftist Republicans and had even been the first town in the whole of Spain to proclaim the coming of the Second Republic six years previously when it flew the Republican flag – of red, yellow and dark purple – at 6.30am on the morning of 16th April 1931, preceding other cities such as Barcelona by six hours, Madrid by seven hours and both Bilbao and San Sebastián by 11 hours. It remains unclear just how Eibar was so quick to proclaim the coming of the Second Republic, but a range of explanations are presented: it was the result of a phonetic mix-up or misinterpretation of a phone call to the town mayor, that well-informed fish suppliers brought the news with them that morning or that the town was simply so ardent for a return to democracy. Whatever the reason, Eibar's mayor Juan de los Toyos ordered the Republican flag to be raised by Mateo Careaga – the youngest of 18 newly-elected councillors from the majority Republican-Socialist party in the municipal elections held two days previously – and called for a firefighter to remove the plaque from the main square which read *Plaza de Alfonso II* – Alfonso II was the reigning king at the time – and to rename the square *Plaza de la II Republica* with an improvised cardboard sign.

Eibar's act led Niceto Alcalá-Zamora – the first prime minister of the Second Republic, although he would only remain as prime minister until that October – to award Eibar the title of '*Muy Ejemplar Ciudad*', of 'Very Exemplary City'.

That title and the act of proclaiming the Second Republic before any other town or city both were, and will always be, sources of great pride for the people of Eibar. They were less pleasing to Franco, however, and would be punished during the Civil War.

Eibar had already been suffering immensely since the first September of the war, which broke out in July 1936, with regular bombings and artillery fire on to the town. On 24th April 1937, the attacks escalated and, having dealt with other Basque towns such as Durango and Elgeta in the days and weeks previously, the Germans and Italians in the skies were then instructed to turn their attentions to Eibar.

From a population of 13,000 at the beginning of the war, only 5,000 now remain in Eibar in April; the majority left to fight elsewhere or sought refuge and food in Bilbao and San Sebastián. Of those that remain, 74 were killed by the weekend's bombings, while 97 suffered serious injuries. Those numbers likely underestimate the severity of the attacks as they include only officially recorded deaths and injuries. The planes dropped 7,250 kilograms of bombs over Eibar, leaving the town in a state of complete destruction with craters lining the streets and squares and with 182 buildings destroyed, affecting 882 households. Eibar is a very narrow town – it lies at the bottom of a valley – and the fact buildings are squeezed as tightly together as possible, made the task an easy one for the planes overhead. Those buildings that escaped unscathed were soon destroyed by the fire that raged through the town and continues to burn this Monday. You can count on one hand the buildings which remain completely intact after all of the weekend's events, one of which – miraculously and perhaps symbolically – is the town's church, an institution which has supported the Nationalists.

As the bombs now fall on Guernica, within earshot Franco's Nationalist troops march over the hill at the Ipurua neighbourhood of Eibar into what is left of this devastated ruin of a town. Eibar has been a renowned steel-producing town since the turn of the 20th century, the water racing down the valleys powering the steel mills and allowing for the manufacture of bicycles, sewing machines and weaponry – explaining the nickname the football team would go on to attain of the *armeros*; the gunners. Now, however, some of those weapons produced in Eibar are in the hands of the advancing Nationalists, while those not produced here have been supplied to them by the Germans and the Italians.

Alongside Franco's troops is one of the several bands of Moroccans which have been fighting for Franco during the war – and which have become notorious for their brutality and savageness when occupying towns and cities – and so begins the occupation of this emblematic socialist and Republican town. It doesn't take long at all; with Eibar being so small there is little resistance.

The following day, Franco's own planes will fly over Bilbao, but this time it is not bombs that are dropped but Nationalist leaflets. The message? 'Durango and Eibar have both been captured.'

More than captured, the two towns – like Guernica – have been unconditionally destroyed.

Saturday, 30th November 1940. Town Centre, Eibar.

It may be 20 months since the end of the Spanish Civil War, but Eibar is still officially a *región devastada,* literally a devastated area, suffering from severe flooding, a shortage of housing and the forced closure of factories destroyed by the bombing. While war rages on across the rest of Europe, Spain has stayed out of World War II as the country begins a rebuilding process, one which has commenced in Eibar but which is proving to be a slow process as many have migrated elsewhere, while others have sadly not returned from the war.

This might, therefore, not appear to be the best time to found a brand new football club, but in the eyes of the City Council there could be no better time.

It would be false to say Eibar has always had a strong footballing tradition – the sport took much longer to reach the valley town than it did other parts of Gipuzkoa such as Irún and San Sebastián – but as soon as the sport was introduced it became immensely popular. It was imported to the town by Pedro – more commonly known as Perico – Mandiola, who was the first Eibar man to enter the footballing spotlight as one of the finalists in the 1911 *Copa del Rey* – the ninth edition of the tournament – on 15th April 1911. Mandiola turned out in central midfield for Athletic Club de Bilbao as the Basques won 3-1 against Espanyol in a final that was, fittingly for Mandiola, played just 45 kilometres away from Eibar in Getxo's Josaleta Stadium. Mandiola's appearance was somewhat controversial as he was actually registered to the Madrid version of Athletic Club, which had been founded by a group of Basque students living in Madrid using the same English spelling as the Bilbao side. Along with four other members of the Madrid branch of Athletic Club, Mandiola was drafted in to play for the Bilbao team in the final, putting Eibar's name into the Spanish footballing history books some 29 years before its most successful club would be formed.

Mandiola had also made a little bit of footballing history three months before that Copa del Rey Final when he was in the starting line-up the first time Athletic Club de Madrid turned out in the red and white stripes the club – adopting the Spanish spelling in 1941, eventually becoming Atlético Madrid – would become famous for. Having previously played in blue and white, like their Bilbao sibling club, the switch was made when Athletic Club representative Juan Elorduy returned from a trip to England without the blue and white Blackburn Rovers kits he had been instructed to purchase. Instead, Elorduy returned to Spain with the red and white kit of Southampton and the new colours stuck for both Athletic teams, even if the Madrid club opted to retain their blue shorts. Thus, Mandiola became Eibar's first great footballing hero and through him Eibar had been making footballing history well before the sport was popular down Ipurua way.

The very fact his beloved hometown wasn't a great lover of football frustrated Mandiola, who made it his mission to introduce the game he loved to Eibar. Fresh from his Copa del Rey Final win, Mandiola sought to create a *footballa,* as the game was called in Basque, club in Eibar at a time when the only organised sporting outfit in the town was Sociedad Educación Física, a general sporting club which did not practise football. After much pressuring of sports fans in the town, Mandiola got his wish in 1913 when still playing for Athletic Club de Madrid – which had just achieved financial independence from Athletic Club de Bilbao – as Eibar's first football club was born: Izarra Club.

Although Izarra Club would also compete in running and cycling, it was principally a football club and, wearing green and black, on 25th May 1913, Izarra Club visited neighbouring town Bergara to play Shooting Club and were unceremoniously ripped apart 8-0 in Eibar's first-ever football match – and first ever trouncing. Little did the locals know it at the time, but exactly 101 years later to the day the town of Eibar would come to a standstill to celebrate Jota's promotion-winning goal and Eibar's rise to La Liga. But we'll get to that later…

The story of football in Eibar is a great one, but Izarra Club would not be the protagonists for long. Their stadium Campo de Otolaerdikua – the only sports stadium in Eibar until Ipurua was built in 1947 – would outlive Izarra Club, which was forced to disband in 1918. The club was able to enjoy some highs before then, not least winning the 1916 *Campeonato del Norte,* the Northern Championship, with a 2-1 win over Racing Santander at San Mamés. Two years later, however, Izarra finished last in the newly-formed Gipuzkoa Football Federation's *Primera Categoría Serie A* and was obliged to disband.

The death of Izarra Club did not signal the end for football in Eibar. On the contrary, it coincided with a footballing boom and the birth of four new teams: Sport Ariñ and Club de Los Trece were both formed in 1916 before Deportivo Club and Rotterdam Club were both formed in 1917. Like the preceding Izarra Club, these clubs also practised other sports in addition to football, of which cycling was always popular. The popularity of cycling in Eibar should come as no surprise given the bicycle manufacturing industry which kept the town's factories going and there was one point when the three most important bicycle factories in the country sat along one 100-metre stretch of Eibar. The popularity of the sport would even see Eibar host the finishing line of stages of the *Vuelta a España* cycling competition on four occasions in 1963, 1972, 1974 and 2012, with Ipurua hosting a temporary velodrome around the perimeters of its pitch for the 1963 stage finish. Along with cycling, tree axe chopping was mightily popular in Eibar for a period and many of the town's locals have achieved world record times for chopping various circumferences of trees.

But back to football, and 1922 was the year in which Unión Deportiva Eibaressa – UDE as it would be more commonly known – was launched, formed from two smaller clubs Irrintxi and Deportivo Eibarrés. UDE had immediate success, winning the *Segunda Categoría Serie C* in its first season of existence, 1922/23. The club progressed further and won its *Primera Categoría Serie B* group in both the 1924/25 and 1926/27 seasons, failing to win promotion in the resulting play-offs in the summer of 1925 but succeeding in the 1927 campaign and thus climbing to Serie A – its greatest ever success.

UDE's success didn't last particularly long and, although it produced internationals such as Ciriaco, Roberto and Muguerza, the club consolidated in 1931 and Deportivo Gallo filled the resulting void in 1932. Gallo also produced some quality players such as Guisasola, Aguirre and Larrañaga and picked up some honours, notably winning the *Torneo de Durango*. UDE was encouraged by the triumph of Deportivo Gallo and its former board took the decision to reform in 1935, beginning what should have been a sustained period of footballing activity, rivalry and prosperity in Eibar.

The Spanish Civil War put paid to that dream and with Eibar now still in ruins 20 months after the war, the City Council has encouraged Unión Deportiva Eibaressa and Deportivo Gallo – the largest two clubs to cease activities during the war – to fuse together to form one football team for the whole town of Eibar to celebrate. That football club is founded, therefore, on this Saturday evening with Juan Artamendi named as the club's president and it shall be called Eibar Football Club. This is the team that will one day evolve into a La Liga side.

The year 1940 is not an easy time to be founding football clubs. The new state, headed by the victorious General Franco, has been scrutinising all members of society and ensuring all can prove their usefulness to Spain under the 'Law of Political Responsibilities'. Interrogations continue as the state looks to find out how each individual acted in the war, but luckily for the majority of the locals the interrogations in Eibar hit a dead end as the town mayor had bravely burned all information which could prove any resident's Republican loyalties and lead to an execution.

The sports minister in this new regime is Franco's close friend General Moscardó and in the first-ever edition of *Marca* – published just 42 kilometres away in San Sebastián on 21st December 1938 – Moscardó outlined his plans for sport. Essentially, Moscardó announced all sport would be state-controlled with the state selecting the presidents of the football clubs and in July 1939 there was even a cap set on the wages footballers could earn, meaning no player could earn more than a colonel. Players also required licences to play and, unsurprisingly, these were controlled by the state and awarded with several conditions, one of which was a declaration of loyalty to the Franco regime. Despite the various hoops requiring jumping through, Franco did realise football could be powerful and so tried and succeeded in getting the national team to return to action. That would only take until 1941, when the Spanish national team – wearing blue rather than the traditional red – drew 2-2 with Portugal in Lisbon on 12th January in their first international match before the Civil War.

By the time of the Portugal encounter, Eibar Football Club would be a month and a half old, but the Basque club would have already changed its name once. Under the new regime, all names were forced to be Castilianised as a result of an *Orden del Ministerio del Interior*, an order from Interior Minister Ramón Serrano Suñer, which would forbid all *extranjerismos*, all foreign words. Like neighbours Athletic Club, Eibar had to remove the English spelling from their name and so the club became the Sociedad Deportiva Eibar that fans would know and love 75 years later. The requirement to Castilianise all names was originally included in an official state document released before the formation of Eibar's new football team on 16th May 1940, but it wasn't until the Spanish Football Federation advised all clubs to change their names that clubs began to comply. The Federation would send a memo around all clubs with the relevant instructions on 21st December 1940 and so on 1st January 1941 – 32 days into its existence – the legend of Sociedad Deportiva Eibar begins.

Sunday, 14th September 1947. Ipurua Stadium, Eibar.

What better way to inaugurate Ipurua than with a local derby? It wasn't planned this way, but on this September afternoon the first-ever match at Ipurua Municipal Stadium will be played between SD Eibar and CD Elgoibar, the team hailing from just seven kilometres up the valley. It is fate that the neighbours meet in the first round of the *Primera Regional* in the *Costa* group, a division the club has been promoted to under the charge of former Real Sociedad and Izarra Club player Celestino Olaizola.

In just seven years of existence, SD Eibar have already built up quite a relationship with the Elgoibar team, having borrowed Elgoibar's Campo de Lerum Stadium in the club's first years when SD Eibar didn't yet have a home. Elgoibar made sense as a temporary home for the Eibar club as it was only a ten-minute train journey away. That train service, however, would only run when there was a minimum of 250 passengers and on the several occasions when that total wasn't met the Eibar players had to pay the difference to the train company so that they could attend their matches.

Obviously playing in Elgoibar was not an ideal solution and the club needed a permanent stadium closer to home. The Campo de Otolaerdikua in Eibar became a temporary solution from 1943 to 1947, but it was not a football stadium and an increasing following for SD Eibar suggested one was needed. It would be Ipurua.

In Eibar's first years the club played only sporadically given there was no division for them to enter. The first and second divisions may have returned after the Civil War, but lower tiers had yet to resume and regional leagues thus appeared and disappeared with great frequency over the years following the war. When a new *Primera Categoría Regional* division was formed for the 1942/43 season, Eibar's lack of regular matches meant the club missed out and wasn't included. A restructuring of the same division the following season finally allowed Eibar to compete consistently in a league and it was this season when the club was gifted the blue and claret kit of Barcelona, colours which would endure. Having previously worn red and white stripes with black shorts like neighbouring Athletic Club, the new kit allowed Eibar to distinguish itself from its Bilbao neighbours. That first season of league action saw Eibar finish in a respectable fifth position.

It was the following campaign of 1944/45 when the first whispers of a custom-built football stadium began, with the area up by the hill of Ipurua mentioned as a suitable location. President Artamendi would be gone by the time the building of Ipurua was completed – stepping down in 1946 and handing the reins to Bernardino Odriozola Ogara – but he was one of the main driving forces behind the project, which also received both administrative and financial help from a City Council that was once again supportive and aware of the joy a successful and sustainable football team could bring to a town still recovering from the wounds of war, and in great need of something to cheer about.

So here we are on this September 14th afternoon for a football match played at Ipurua. Yet Elgoibar aren't here to simply make up the numbers; they are here to spoil the party, as is the rain which prompts the first, but not the last, iconic sprawl of umbrellas lining the Ipurua pitch. Elgoibar play the role of spoilsports with a 2-0 win thanks to a penalty from Etxeberria and a later goal from Ayesta. Still, this will go down as an historic day in Eibar's story, as will the names of the first 11 players to walk out on to Ipurua in the *azulgrana* shirt: Trecu, Deva, Arrondo, Kaiku, Sarasqueta, Mandiola, Galarraga, Gorrocha, Iriondo, Avelino and Castro.

Despite opening the season with a defeat, Eibar would improve as the campaign progressed; the playing staff would be shaken up halfway through and the talented Basque stars brought in would help the club to a fourth-place finish. In the following season of 1948/49, Eibar would lead the league for many *jornadas,* but again find Elgoibar spoiling the party by pipping them into first place.

In 1949/50 Eibar would compete in a new 14-team league, the newly-formed *Primera Regional Preferente* regional league where the prize is promotion to the national third division; a prize for which Eibar would be favourites at the start of the season. They would duly win the league before navigating the play-off rounds and beating Basconia 2-1 in the final in Basauri, on a hot afternoon on 29th June 1950.

Just ten years after its formation, SD Eibar would enter the third division – and the national arena.

Sunday, 15th May 1988. Tabira Stadium, Durango.

Un empate basta. A draw is enough.

That's the case as Eibar – not just the team but seemingly half the town – visit Durango this wonderfully sunny Sunday afternoon with the chance to secure promotion to the *Segunda* division by mathematically tying up their *Segunda B Grupo I* with a week to spare. The team has been on a fantastic run and hasn't yet lost a match in the calendar year – an invincible team nicknamed 'the Gunners' sound familiar? – and won't lose one until November, by which point Eibar will be participating in the division above.

A draw is enough, but Eibar is a club that loves the spectacular and they, of course, earn promotion in style by winning the match 1-0 – the goal comes from Toño – in front of the thousands of Eibar fans who have made the short 15-kilometre trip to neighbouring Durango, sparking an *azulgrana* pitch invasion to celebrate promotion to the second division of Spanish football.

It has been a long road for Eibar to make this jump to the *Segunda*, but this won't be the first time the Basque club graces Spain's second tier. Eibar's first and only other promotion to the second division came in the 1952/53 season when the club finished first in their group and nine points ahead of second-place Sestao to win promotion in just their third season in the *Tercera*, the third division, helped by their first agreement with Real Sociedad – signed in 1951 – to receive loan players. Immediately, Eibar had enjoyed success in the third tier, winning *Grupo IV* by five points ahead of Basque neighbours Alavés, from Vitoria-Gasteiz, in their first season at that level. Promotion from the third division, however, was as complicated then as it is now and even as winners of the group Eibar had to navigate the play-offs, at which point they were beaten. The following year the club finished second in the group before the 1952/53 campaign saw play-off success.

Upon winning that promotion, the then-president Manolo Escodín said: "Promotion to the *Segunda* was achieved, something which would have seemed like a dream five years ago." Even back in the 1950s, Eibar were making unrealistic promotion dreams reality.

That success was largely down to manager Antonio Corral, a man so keen to remain in football after his playing days he even considered becoming a referee before the opportunity to coach presented itself with SD Michelín, with whom he enjoyed success, before taking over at Eibar. He oversaw promotion, and five seasons in the *Segunda* division, despite Eibar's massive economic inferiority in his first of two stints as boss.

The club avoided expected relegation in its first *Segunda* season and overachieved by topping the whole division until the seventh *jornada*, ultimately finishing in a very impressive seventh position out of 16 teams. It was a similar story in 1954/55 when Eibar finished eighth. Things were going so well for Corral the bubble was due to burst eventually and in 1955/56 it seemed Eibar's run had come to an end. Having started the season poorly, the club was in the relegation positions by the fifth *jornada*, but the arrival on loan from Real Sociedad of promising 18-year-old goalkeeper José Araquistáin Arrieta – who would go on to lift the European Cup with Real Madrid and feature for Spain six times – saw Eibar's form improve and the club escaped relegation by finishing 14th and one place above the drop-zone. Despite Araquistáin having returned to Real Sociedad by the start of the next campaign, Eibar improved slightly and finished tenth – this time in the expanded division of 20 teams – although the club hadn't been higher than 13th until the final day of the season.

It was in the 1957/58 campaign when the bubble finally did burst and Eibar suffered relegation back to the third level of Spanish football. Corral's team started well and were as high as seventh place after the 13th *jornada,* but the form slipped and after winning just one of their final 12 matches the club finished 17th out of 18 teams and were relegated. That poor season has been attributed by many to the Eibar board's decision to sell fan icon and local goalkeeper Félix Arrizabalaga Embeita to Valencia midway through the campaign. He left just after *jornada* 14, when Eibar were tenth, and the club wouldn't find itself higher than 12th again.

To fully convey the value of Arrizabalaga, Eibar had conceded just 17 goals in the 14 matches played before his departure and just ten had been conceded in the 12 matches he actually played in – he was injured for two matches; lost 4-0 and 3-0. The two heavy defeats in Arrizabalaga's absence failed to convince the board he was indispensable and the sale was approved, after which Eibar conceded 38 goals in their remaining 20 fixtures. Arrizabalaga, meanwhile, enjoyed a great view of the second half of Valencia's season from the bench of the Mestalla Stadium; he didn't play a single game for Valencia that season while 450 kilometres away his ex-team-mates were losing their relegation battle. Corral resigned at the end of that season, while club president

Boni Guisasola was not even given the option to remain after the Arrizabalaga fiasco and departed after just one season as head honcho of the Ipurua boardroom.

Eibar then spent 18 seasons in the overcrowded third tier of Spanish football, even winning their group three times, and coming runners-up on seven occasions, before always ultimately failing in the play-offs. The first failure came in 1958/59, their first season back in the third division, as the club almost won immediate promotion with Arrizabalaga having returned to Eibar on loan – of course, it was in many ways too late by then – before finally taking over the Valencia starting job in 1959/60. After a second-place finish in their group, Eibar won their promotion play-off first leg against Arenas SD of Zaragoza, 4-0, at Ipurua. Promotion looked certain, but a four-goal advantage is only any use if you don't lose by four goals or more in the second leg. Eibar seemed unable to grasp that simple truth, however, and a 5-0 comeback for the Aragon side in the *vuelta*, the return match, saw Eibar miss out on promotion.

With spirits crushed and Arrizabalaga having departed again, Eibar finished seventh the following season; Antonio Mayo was now at the helm of a team full of locals. A third-place finish in 1960/61 was followed by table-topping campaigns in 1961/62 and 1962/63, but both seasons ended in play-off defeats, firstly to CD Eldense and then to Onteniente CF.

The 1963/64 season brought with it the return of Antonio Corral for a second stint at the club, but again the failure came in the play-offs following a runners-up league finish when, after seeing off Talavera CF, Eibar faced Gimnàstic de Tarragona in the second phase. Corral's side won 4-1 in Ipurua, but would yet again capitulate in the return leg as they had done in 1958/59. This time it wasn't all Eibar's own fault; the Basques were losing just 1-0 in Catalonia at 90 minutes before the referee inexplicably added nine minutes of stoppage time, allowing Tarragona to score two more goals and level the tie. At the time there was no away goals rule or extra time so the two clubs played a one-off tie-breaker in Madrid, which Eibar lost 2-0. That refereeing controversy still irritates Eibar fans to this day and *Mundo Deportivo* immediately realised the second-leg match was unforgettable. Juan Narbona opened his match report with the following line: "If one day you were to talk about miracles in [the history of] football, there is no doubt that it'd be worth mentioning this match which we've just seen in Tarragona." Narbona also described how players from both teams left the pitch in tears after the miracle comeback, for obviously differing reasons.

One of those tearful players was a 19-year-old José Eulogio Gárate, who would go on to become one of Atlético Madrid's all-time greats, following in the footsteps of Perico Mandiola in leaving the town of Eibar for the capital side. Unlike Mandiola, Gárate was not born in the Basque town, but in Buenos Aires, Argentina, where his parents were visiting his grandfather – a former deputy mayor of Eibar who was behind the 6.30am proclamation of the Second Republic in 1931 and who fled to Argentina immediately after the Spanish Civil War – when Gárate was born in 1944. A few months later, Gárate's parents returned to Eibar and he played for both the local club – debuting for SD Eibar at just 18 – and Sociedad Deportiva Indauchu after being forbidden from playing for his preferred choice of Athletic Club for not meeting their Basque-only policy, which was somewhat ironic given just how proudly Basque his grandfather was and that the Spanish national team deemed him Spanish enough to turn out for them 18 times.

Gárate would go on to wear red and white stripes regardless, albeit they were those of Atlético Madrid where he played until the end of his career in 1977 – an infection in his knee forced him to hang up his boots at 33 years old. The striker would win the Pichichi Award for the nation's top goalscorer on three occasions, but never outright; he shared it with Amancio in 1968/69, with Amancio and Luis Aragones in 1969/70, and then with Charly Rexach in 1970/71.

While Gárate was scoring goal after goal for Atlético, Eibar were still struggling their way through life in the third division. After the scarring defeat to Tarragona, Eibar had lost in similar fashion the following season of 1964/65 when they took a two-goal lead to Cádiz for the second leg of the final round of the play-offs, but again their opponents levelled the tie and again Eibar lost the tie-breaker in Madrid, this time 4-1.

Three more seasons came and went for the eternal promotion hopefuls as did three more play-off defeats, firstly to CD Constancia after giving up a 2-0 advantage from Ipurua, secondly to Real Jaén CF in similarly familiar fashion with a tie-breaker defeat in Madrid and thirdly to Jerez Industrial CF, by which point Antonio Corral had given up and vacated the manager's chair – though he would remain loyal to the club and serve on the board of directors as well as remain available to help whenever needed right up until his death in 2012.

Play-off despair wouldn't return to Eibar for some time; a sixth-place finish in 1968/69 wasn't good enough for a play-off berth, nor was their subsequent second place as restructuring of the league now only permitted a play-off spot to the winners. This led to league groups of higher quality and Eibar struggled, only achieving finishes of seventh, fourth and 12th in 1970/71, 1971/72 and 1972/73, respectively, with the club only escaping relegation to the regional division by one point in 1972/73.

The play-off experience soon returned to Ipurua in 1973/74 when a second-place finish gave Eibar another shot at promotion to the *Segunda*, but they lost 3-2 on aggregate to Burgos CF. The following season the club was back in the play-offs, but this time it was the relegation play-offs after avoiding automatic relegation by just one point. Facing CD Motril, Eibar won 2-0 at Ipurua and – for once – didn't collapse in the second leg, drawing 0-0 and staying up. The next year, they wouldn't be so lucky.

In 1975/76, the club finished 19th out of 20 and was automatically relegated to the *Regional Preferente* division. Eibar spent three seasons in the regional division – the fourth tier of Spanish football – in a period the club itself refers to as, 'the dark years'.

In the first year, the club finished fifth. If not winning promotion was bad enough, Eibar had technically slipped down a further division as the *Segunda B* – between the *Segunda* and *Tercera* – was introduced before the 1977/78 season, essentially making the *Regional Preferente* the fifth tier of Spanish football by default.

Not only that, but now only the winner of the *Regional Preferente* group would enter the promotion play-offs and Eibar had to wait until the 1978/79 season to claim top spot. It was in those play-offs that Eibar won their first ever tie-breaker; an Auzmendi goal gave them a 1-0 win over Anaitasuna. So Eibar had escaped the fifth tier, leaving those fallow years behind and never to return to such depths again.

That promotion was really just a case of getting back to square one for Eibar, which was still only in the fourth tier. The *maldición*, the curse, of the play-offs, continued into the 1980s when Eibar went to the play-offs five times between 1980 and 1986, losing to Catarroja CF in 1981/82, to Real Balompédica Linense in 1982/83, to Pontevedra CF in 1983/84 and to CD Valdepeñas in 1984/85.

It was at the fifth attempt in 1985/86, that the club finally won promotion to the *Segunda B* under the stewardship of Juan José Arrieta with the support of buses and buses of travelling fans such as *La Bombonera* fan group – as we'll hear about later. Eibar defeated Coria del Río and Badajoz in what were their 14th *Tercera* division promotion play-offs.

Having been out of the second tier since the 1957/58 season, Eibar were soon back as they spent little time hanging around in their first experience of the *Segunda B*. The successful Arriesta was offered a new contract after winning promotion but left for 'professional reasons' and was replaced by Alfonso Barasoain, who kept the momentum going with a sixth-place finish in the 1986/87 season, and who would be voted the club's greatest ever manager in a 2014 poll. If the first season back in the third tier of Spanish football was transitional, the second delivered in terms of promotion, which brings us to May 1988 and this glorious summer's day in Durango where Eibar win promotion to the *Segunda* at just the second attempt.

After a 30-year absence, Eibar is back in the *Segunda*. They will remain here for a record 18 seasons, an achievement equivalent to Elgin City surviving 18 years in the Scottish top division or Stoke City qualifying for Europe 18 years in a row.

Wednesday, 28th November 1990. Ipurua Stadium, Eibar.
It is Eibar's 50th birthday party. The venue? Ipurua. The guests? Three-times European champions Ajax. This is a celebration.

A packed stadium celebrates with a friendly match against the famous Dutch side. The Basques could and should – but don't – send Ajax and their ex-Real Madrid La Liga-winning coach Leo Beenhakker home vanquished; the match instead finishes 1-1.

Ajax may take the lead in the 71st minute through Swedish international Stefan Pettersson's header, but Eibar have already missed a first-half penalty and played better than the Dutch who struggle on an admittedly poor pitch. Eibar's Francisco Javier Oliden Álvarez levels the match when he nods Luis Ignacio Ibáñez Echeverría's cross past Menzo – an Ajax legend who has starred since 1985 and would continue to do so until being replaced by a young Edwin van der Sar in 1993 – in the 77th minute. The match ends in a draw.

Holding a former European champion is a moment of great pride for the locals, even if the match is 'only' a friendly, just as it was when Bordeaux visited for the 25th birthday bash. It's been a fun match too, with ex-Eibar heroes Pizo Gómez and Chuchi Hidalgo visiting from Atlético Madrid and Valladolid, respectively, to turn out in the *azulgrana* shirt once again, while famous Ajax stars such as Bryan Roy and Aron Winter feature for the visitors.

Also starting for Eibar is Anel Karabeg, making just his fourth appearance for the club. The fact this is Karabeg's fourth appearance isn't what is interesting; the fact he is the first foreigner to ever play for Eibar is.

The 28-year-old Yugoslav – who had previously played in Spain with Real Burgos CF – arrived from FK Velež Mostar, a club based in modern-day Bosnia and Herzegovina, exactly one month before this Ajax tie. His signing had required an Extraordinary General Meeting of the Eibar board of directors, who voted in majority to approve his signing. Although Spanish clubs had been permitted two foreigners each since 1973 – when pressure from Barcelona, keen to sign a former Ajax man by the name of Johan Cruyff had brought about a lifting of the previous ban – it has taken Eibar 17 years to make the most of the rule.

Even more important for Eibar and Karabeg, however, than this glamour friendly, is the weekend's league match with Deportivo La

Coruña, a game they will play in the *Segunda* division thanks to a phenomenal relegation-escaping final day the season before.

There are some things in life that run like clockwork: in summer it's warm, in autumn the leaves fall, in winter it's cold and in spring there is always one football team which miraculously escapes seemingly-certain relegation. Always. In the spring of 1990, it was SD Eibar.

Eibar had acquitted themselves well with a 16th-place finish in the 1988/89 season, their first back in the *Segunda* after their 30-year absence, and even led the division on six different *jornadas* despite relying on a tiny shoestring budget of just 75 million pesetas and on the newly-signed agreement to receive loanees from Athletic Club. The following campaign, however, was disastrous.

From the second *jornada* onwards, Eibar spent the whole season in the relegation zone bar the final day. With five matches remaining, they stood in 18th position, five points from safety, but somehow managed to escape *por los pelos,* by the skin of their teeth. Despite having won just seven matches all season, Eibar won four of the last five and drew the other to escape the relegation zone by one point on the final day as they defeated promotion-chasing Espanyol 3-2 away from home.

The win made the 50th anniversary year of 1990 a positive one and the 1990s would become a positive decade.

More comfortable mid-table finishes follow as Eibar cement their status as a worthy *Segunda* opponent, as well as two fifth-place finishes in 1994/95 and 1996/97 when the club would finish just two and four points away from the play-offs for promotion to the *Primera*. It wouldn't be until the 1998/99 season that Eibar would again dice with relegation and pull off an even more impressive great escape. Despite being 11 points from safety with only five games remaining, Eibar would again escape on the last day of the season, this time thanks to a ridiculous run of five straight wins to finish the campaign. Such miraculous relegation-defying escapes are often met with suspicion in Spain, where it is not unheard of for matches to be bought at the end of the season.

Not in the case of Eibar, a club that couldn't afford to buy its way out of trouble even if it wanted to. This would simply be pure and natural determination-cum-brilliance.

Ipurua would be the setting for the final match of that spectacular 1999 run and after consecutive wins against Osasuna, Hércules, Barcelona B and Albacete, Eibar would need to beat Toledo and pray for Mallorca B to lose and for Barcelona B to either draw or lose.

As the teams prepared for kick-off at Ipurua that afternoon, those in the stands would be tuning their radios and hoping. Two minutes later Eibar would have their lead.

Bedlam.

Three minutes later, Mallorca B's opponents Hércules would have theirs.

Extra bedlam.

One minute later, Las Palmas would go ahead against Barcelona B. The radios would hit the roof.

After just six minutes all three of the results needing to go Eibar's way would be in their favour and those three results would stay the same; only the margins would increase as Eibar won 3-0, Mallorca B lost 3-1 and Barcelona B lost 4-1.

By the time the full-time whistles approached, the radios would be long switched off. Eibar's miraculous great escape was to be sealed in the first few minutes. Ipurua would, fittingly, party like it was 1999.

Sunday, 1st July 2012. Olympic Stadium, Kiev.

Spain has come to a standstill. Again. For the third time in four unforgettable years, the Spanish national team has won a major international tournament. With this 4-0 win over Italy in the final of Euro 2012, *La Roja* once again has its hands on a highly sought-after trophy. The now familiar sight of captain Iker Casillas hoisting the cup will grace tomorrow's front and back pages.

Watching the scenes back home in the streets around Ipurua are many thinking the exact same thing: 'This trophy is in Eibar hands.'

They're exactly right. Of that starting XI in the Ukrainian capital, two players owe an awful lot to Ipurua and now, logically, so does the whole nation. The evening's first goalscorer is David Silva, who heads Cesc Fàbregas's pull-back past Italy legend Gianluigi Buffon. The goal is Silva's second of the tournament and the man from the Canary Islands has also provided three assists while starting every single match at these finals. He has been instrumental in this last piece of Spain's international treble, as well as having contributed to the two previous successes. He was moulded in Eibar.

Moulded is a good word to use because David Silva has always been talented and it would be false to suggest solely Eibar had made him the talent he is today. The Ipurua club certainly played a part, however, when Silva was sent to Eibar to 'toughen up' in the season of 2004/05 which helped to mould the Valencia playmaker into a more streetwise kind of player. Of his season at Ipurua, Silva told *Revista Líbero* magazine: "With every transfer, with every year, you learn things. The year in Eibar helped me to learn a lot of things that have since been important. It was an historic season and it was a shame not to achieve promotion."

Some of the things Silva learned have surely helped him at this Euro 2012 tournament; others less so. For example, Silva has spoken of learning humility and sportsmanship at Eibar and there is a now famous occasion in the 2004/05 season when Eibar – chasing a promotion to La Liga which the club ultimately just missed out on – played away at Lleida and, with the scores tied at 1-1 in the 91st minute, the ball fell to Silva who had a clear chance to score. Instead, Silva kicked the ball out so that an injured opponent could receive treatment. These were the kinds of values a club like Eibar taught its loanees.

On the other hand, some things Silva learned at Ipurua won't have come in quite so useful at major international tournaments. Silva learned, for example, how to scrape snow off a car's windscreen, for which the 18-year-old, who had never seen snow before, phoned his mother for advice during his time in the Basque Country.

Alongside Silva, lifting the trophy this summer's night in Kiev is Xabi Alonso who, like Silva, played in every match, scored two goals, won the previous two trophies with Spain and learned part of his trade at Ipurua.

It was the summer of 2000 when Xabi Alonso found out he would be loaned from Real Sociedad to Eibar, but he didn't find out about the move as one would expect. Rather, one morning while on holiday in the Basque Country with a group of friends, Alonso picked up a copy of the day's *Diario Vasco* and upon flicking through the pages he found a headline that read: '[Joseba] Llorente And Xabi Alonso To Be Loaned To Eibar.' This was news to Alonso, who immediately had one thought in mind: 'This is the work of my father.'

Alonso's father was Periko Alonso, a man who had managed Eibar between 1995 and 1998, and who had good links with his former club, and his son's current club Real Sociedad, at the time. His son was in no doubt as to who was behind his move and phoned his father after reading the news. His father confirmed the loan move would be the best thing for young Xabi, just 18 at the time – an assessment with which Alonso now agrees. Alonso cites the long bus journeys, such as the 1,300 kilometre round-trip to Albacete, as character-building and also says how inspiring and sobering it was to see his team-mates head to their day jobs each Monday morning while he could relax after a long – and often bruising – weekend.

Even before officially signing, Alonso had been learning at Eibar; he would attend the training sessions as a teenager when his father was manager and help Eibar's legendary goalkeeper Garmendia warm up. It is little wonder Alonso would go on to shine given he was afforded private shooting practice with one of the *Segunda*'s all-time great goalkeepers as a kid.

While Alonso and Silva are the only members of this triumphant Spain squad to have pulled on the *azulgrana* jersey of Eibar, they aren't the only players in this team to have made important visits to Ipurua early in their careers.

As Fernando Torres collects his Golden Boot Award here in Kiev, the striker probably isn't thinking back to his third-ever professional start; if so he would remember turning out for Atlético Madrid at Ipurua in the 2001/02 season when the Madrid side had been relegated to the *Segunda*. While embarrassing for Atlético, spending time playing in the bruising and battering *Segunda* was probably the perfect apprenticeship for the 17-year-old Torres.

Likewise, Iker Casillas is surely not reflecting on his first Ipurua experience in 2004 as he lifts the European Championship trophy, but that match was massive for the Real Madrid keeper who made no fewer than seven outstanding saves to avoid a *Copa del Rey* last 16 upset and help his side escape with a 1-1 first-leg draw before the *Galácticos* – including *Ballon d'Or* winners Luis Figo, Zinedine Zidane and Ronaldo – were unleashed to dispatch with Eibar in the return fixture. Casillas received high praise following the first leg; the front page of *Marca* declared the following morning that 'Casillas Showed In Ipurua That He's Possibly The Best Goalkeeper In The World.' He had certainly been made to work harder in that match than in this Euro 2012 final.

While Ipurua was welcoming future international stars to its turf at the turn of the 20th century, the Eibar team had been starring as well. With the club's fanbase still enjoying their great 1999 escape from relegation, the turn of the century saw some more comfortable league finishes over the following five seasons: 11th, 15th, 8th, 17th and 10th before a season which so nearly ended in promotion to La Liga. That was when David Silva arrived in 2004/05 for what was nearly a David Silva versus Goliath success story alongside the familiar figure of Gaizka Garitano who captained that side. Nobody foresaw it at the time, but disappointment in 2005 would turn to jubilation for Garitano less than a decade later when he finally won promotion as manager.

Before that, Eibar went from near-promotion to complete collapse. Following their near-promotion disappointment, the club lost the spine of their team in Silva, Garitano, goalkeeper Iraizoz and their top scorer Llorente, as well as manager Mendilibar who moved on to Athletic Club. Eibar finished last in the 2005/06 campaign, going through three different managers in the process and ending their record 18-year run in the *Segunda*. Their relegation was justified, having spent *jornada* 18 to *jornada* 42 in the drop-zone and sealing relegation with four games remaining.

The following years would see Ipurua yo-yo up and down between divisions as the club rattled through managers before finally striking gold with the appointment of Garitano just two days before the kick-off of Euro 2012. The confetti may already be falling on the floor of Kiev's Olympic Stadium a month after Garitano's appointment, but it won't be much longer before such jubilant celebrations return to Ipurua as well.

Ipurua has experienced the remarkable before. It has been a home of great escapes and calamitous relegations. It has witnessed highs and lows. It has welcomed football, cycling, concerts and even once acted as a helipad for an episode of popular Basque TV show *Mi Querido Klikowsky*. Quite literally, Ipurua has seen it all before.

Well, almost all of it. As Spain celebrates the joy of an international treble, Ipurua has not yet experienced the joy of its first ever *ascenso*, promotion, to La Liga. It soon will.

5

A Fairytale Season: *Act 3*

"Nobody said life in the Primera was going to be easy."

Gaizka Garitano

Saturday, 11th April 2015. Pride Park, Derby.
It was all Bobby Zamora's fault.

Perhaps it's unfair to pin all of the blame for Eibar's terrible run of form on Bobby Zamora, but the English striker undeniably changed the club's fortunes for the worse – and he had the audacity to not even realise.

Now enough Bobby Zamora bashing; the striker was, to be fair, just doing his job when he netted the 90th-minute multi-million pound goal at Wembley the previous 24th May to earn Queens Park Rangers a 1-0 play-off final win and a return to the embarrassment of riches that the English Premier League boasts, condemning Derby County to another season in the Championship as a result. One day later Eibar would join Zamora's QPR in celebrating their own promotion success when Jota knocked the most memorable goal in Eibar's history into the Ipurua East Stand's net to seal their rise to La Liga. Little did they know it at the time, but amid their own celebrations Eibar's technical staff should have been concerned about the consequences of that Zamora goal. It would go on to derail their fairytale season.

Fast forward 11 months to today's encounter at Derby's Pride Park. Around 1,400 kilometres away in Madrid, the Eibar squad is preparing for an historic match at the Santiago Bernabéu Stadium, but two of the most influential players that made the prospect of facing Real Madrid in La Liga a reality are missing. Unfortunately for Eibar, Jota and Raúl Albentosa are both here in Derby.

The former is lining up for Brentford, a club hailing from west London which is chasing a promotion to the Premier League, their second successive rise – just like Eibar. The Galician's three goals in his last four matches for the Basque club sealed their top-flight ticket, but as Jota was only on loan from Celta de Vigo, his time in the Basque mountains was soon up. While Eibar would have loved to have kept this gossamer talent for their top-flight adventure, their last little piece of pizzazz was lost when Vigo recalled the player who had been on their books since he was 13. Jota began pre-season training with the Galicians on 3rd July, but just over one month later the 23-year-old had been sold on to Brentford for an estimated €1.5million, a bargain for most clubs but one which Eibar simply couldn't justify matching to bring the season-long hero back to Ipurua.

Initially, it appeared Eibar could cope without the previous season's top scorer – Jota had netted 11 times in total in the *Segunda* campaign, ahead of second-top scorer Arruabarrena, who contributed seven goals – but the fact the club's first nine strikes came from nine different scorers should have been an early warning sign a lethal goalscorer was missing. Arruabarrena grabbed five in the first *vuelta* – the first round of fixtures – of the league, new recruit Federico Piovaccari found the net four times and Manu del Moral added a further three. Ten appearances for Ángel came and went in the first *vuelta* without a goal and it was never clear each week where, or from whom, the goals were going to come.

The success of the first *vuelta* was largely down to a formula of great defensive play, Irureta defending the goal as if it housed his own children, winning the midfield battle, relying on a couple of strokes of luck and hoping for a goal or two to come from somewhere, or someone. Obviously this was not a sustainable formula for top-flight success and it was as if Eibar were playing Russian roulette on a weekly basis, but with an extra bullet in the chamber each week. Eventually they were going to get found out.

Sure enough, they inevitably did get found out, which brings us on to Albentosa. If the Eibar formula appeared shaky, even with an excellent defence, then how would it look if the key piece to that defensive jigsaw was removed? The answer was grim and Eibar would find out when, after some will-he-won't-he speculation, Derby County signed Raúl Albentosa on 16th January – just hours before Eibar's match with Córdoba.

Albentosa's first half of the season had been exemplary. He is one of those cerebral players who take complete control of a match, designing the game rather than decorating it, as many of his La Liga counterparts could be accused of. As well as forming part of a defence which kept five clean sheets, Albentosa contributed two goals at the other end and bossed the Eibar penalty area with centre-back play as smooth as his slicked-back hair. The 6ft 4in defender played every single minute of the first *vuelt*a, minus the match against Espanyol – for which he was suspended – and the last fixture of the *vuelta* against Córdoba, by which point he was already being presented as a Derby County player here at Pride Park.

The technical staff here at Derby certainly recognised his talent and, having fallen from first place in the Championship, and looking to add extra cover in defence to avoid another season of promotion disappointment, the bargain signing of Albentosa was made for an estimated €600,000. Unfortunate for Eibar, but the fact of the matter was he couldn't be evenly split between the two teams without sawing him in two and that would have been unfair. On Albentosa that is.

For Eibar, the complete performance of the team in the away match against Espanyol, just two weeks before Albentosa's departure, hinted perhaps the club could cope without him. Such a conclusion was very quickly proven to be ill-founded and Eibar's loss was Derby's gain. It was a big blow according to Guillem Balague, who says: "When centre-back Albentosa left in January you could see that it showed too much." They couldn't simply replace him with "somebody of his quality because they don't have it. And then they started conceding goals."

Which brings us to today's match; it is a game which has nothing to do with Eibar, but which has everything to do with Eibar.

Despite missing six matches through injury in the first couple of months of his Derby career, Albentosa is now establishing himself as one of the first names on Rams' boss Steve McClaren's teamsheet. Today he lines up against ex-team-mate Jota. With both Derby and Brentford vying for promotion this is a crucial match in the run-in and although the Bees create chance after chance, often initiated by our friend Jota on the right wing and just as often being cleared by Albentosa in central defence, the visitors simply cannot add to their early 1-0 lead and Derby manage to equalise in the final minutes with a Darren Bent strike.

Back over in Spain, Eibar have an equally crucial run-in in their fight for La Liga survival. A disastrous run of form following Albentosa's departure in the middle of January has taken so much away from the good work done in the first *vuelta*. Had Derby won that play-off final back in May and avoided another promotion battle, Albentosa would undoubtedly be lining up at the Bernabéu in *azulgrana* and the disastrous run could potentially have been avoided, or have been far less severe.

Alas, Derby didn't win that play-off final and instead set off on another campaign in the Championship, a campaign which required the signing of Albentosa in January. From that point onwards Eibar's season collapsed. Let me tell you the stories of how.

Saturday, 24th January 2015. Anoeta Stadium, San Sebastián.
All bubbles burst.

After just one defeat in seven matches, this Basque derby would dish out another for Eibar. It would be quite a different derby from the visit of Real Sociedad to Ipurua on the opening day of the season, with rain having replaced the late summer sun and the stands in Sociedad's Anoeta stadium about as far away from the pitch as those at Ipurua are close to it. There are just two things worse in a football stadium than an athletics track isolating the fans from the action, in my opinion: firstly, huge spaces of empty seats are worse; secondly, vuvuzelas. At least tonight at Anoeta we've not heard the latter.

As well as the atmosphere being considerably flatter here than it was at Ipurua back in August, the faces in the Real Sociedad dugout are different after Jagoba Arrasate was replaced in November by Scotsman David Moyes. The Glaswegian has already been to Ipurua to take in Eibar's 5-2 win over Almería – with his assistant Billy McKinlay – on a wet and windy evening, which Moyes duly compared to his hometown.

Moyes's visit seems to have prepared him and his side well for the challenge of Eibar and the derby begins with chance after chance for the home side. Carlos Vela is visibly 'up for it' and lofts a dangerous free kick into the box early on before firing over the bar from just inside the box. Eibar are certainly not uncompetitive in this match; Saúl Berjón forces a diving save from Rulli as he stings a curling shot from outside the box following a purposeful run by Manu del Moral. Not long afterwards, though, Vela is again trying his luck without hitting the target, this time from distance. Then the very best chance of the first half falls to Eibar's Arruabarrena, literally falling to him on the far side of the penalty area, but the Eibar hero can only hit the face of Rulli, rather than the back of the net.

Now into the second half, a bending free kick that appeared to be heading for the post from Real's Esteban Granero catches both the attention and a fingertip of Irureta in the Eibar goal. The resulting corner is the source of the home side's goal; Xabi Prieto flicks the ball onwards from the near post, only to look round and see it nestling in the net as neither Irureta nor Abraham can reach the arcing ball, instead getting in each other's way. Garitano will tell the press he had discussed Prieto's near-post flicks to his players 'a thousand times', yet this one lapse in concentration has permitted the home side the lead.

Eibar still have half an hour to find a way back into this derby, yet Real look more likely to score the game's next goal. Vela again shoots just over before ex-Eibar man Yuri Berchiche sees his shot scooped out of the air by the agile Irureta.

Then, Eibar get their big chance to equalise. Unfortunately, however, the chance is with just-subbed-on-and-yet-to-score-this-season striker Ángel, who fails to open his tally. After shrugging off a couple of defenders, the Canary Islander proceeds to flick the ball into the arms of Rulli with the final whistle shortly following.

For the 600 travelling Eibar fans, the marathon drive back home – the distance between the two cities is exactly the 42 kilometres of a marathon – through a drizzle of depression certainly hurts, but two defeats in eight is still not bad going. Little do they know the drizzle will quickly turn to a downpour.

Saturday, 31st January 2015. Ipurua Stadium, Eibar.

The Ipurua pitch this Saturday evening is in a state most Sunday League teams would be ashamed of, and that is not an exaggeration. Still, the 'mud bowl' – as this match would be dubbed in the media – with Atlético Madrid is highly entertaining, if not quality-laden.

It is worth outlining just how rainy this evening is. Think somewhere between a waterfall and the scene from *The Day After Tomorrow* when the tidal wave crashes over New York City. Even Noah would have been wary of taking his ark for a spin at Ipurua this Saturday evening, but 5,200 committed fans are here to see the league champions try their best to leave this big puddle of a pitch with a win.

It may rain a lot in the Basque Country, but the extent of the bad weather is sometimes exaggerated. Tonight's conditions are an anomaly, it must be said, and although Eibar will have played several home matches in the rain by the end of the season, none will be as severe as this.

It is a cruel irony, therefore, that the muddiest, windiest and rainiest home match of the season has Atlético Madrid as the visitors – the one team in La Liga built to thrive on these conditions more than Eibar themselves.

For any other side in La Liga, tonight's conditions could have proven too difficult. There is absolutely no chance that a pass of over 15 metres is going to be played along the ground tonight, but Atlético Madrid are a rugged and hard-working team content to dribble with, and cross, the ball into their target man Mario Mandžukić rather than *tiki-taka* their way to victory. Such a tactic is not overly affected by these conditions, as is evident in just the seventh minute when an aimless hoofed long ball from Atlético's Tiago bounces – or rather splashes – kindly on the edge of the Eibar penalty area for Raúl García, who is able to easily set up Antoine Griezmann for the opener.

Just 15 minutes later, Atlético repeat their tactic of keeping the ball off the waterlogged pitch and again enjoy success; this time a cross into Mandžukić from Griezmann is knocked into the net. Two minutes later and – you guessed it – the tactic comes off once more. This time the high ball into the box is met by Abraham, but the Eibar defender is put under pressure and his fluffed clearance is picked up by Mandžukić and spun into the net.

Into the second half and it's Mandžukić involved again, but fortunately for Eibar he is not extending Atlético's lead. Instead, he is trying a cheeky and unnecessary rabona cross which is blocked by the less-than-impressed Lillo. Eibar's fans love what comes next as 5ft 10in Lillo stands up to the 6ft 2in Croatian, displaying the grit and bravery that has come to define this Eibar team. For those unfamiliar with Mandžukić, I'll just point out he is not the kind of player you want to rub up the wrong way.

There is little further action to note in the second half until Mandžukić is presented with a chance to complete his hat-trick, again from a cross into the box which the big striker heads into the hands of Xabi Irureta. A quick throw out from the Eibar goalkeeper sends Saúl Berjón racing down the left wing to cross the ball into the middle for Federico Piovaccari to grab a consolation goal.

This seals the match and players and fans alike spend little time hanging around, instead dashing inside to the dressing rooms, or the pub. This 3-1 defeat to the league champions is not a massive trauma, as it always seemed likely, but Eibar would surely have hoped to make home advantage on this mucky pitch count. Atlético almost appeared more suited to playing on it than Eibar did.

Notable in this match has been the loss of Albentosa in central defence. The tall and crafty centre-back was born for encounters like these and his absence is already highlighting cracks in this Eibar squad and some new additions would certainly be welcome. If there is one club, however, which does not rush out to panic-buy unwanted players at inflated prices on this, the last day of the transfer window, it is SD Eibar – even though the club is one of only five La Liga sides, along with Athletic, Barcelona, Real Madrid and Villarreal, reported to have room in their budget to make additions.

The only addition made to the squad is the loan deal from Liverpool of young 20-year-old Spanish centre-back Rafa Páez. However, as will be revealed days later on 2nd February, there had been a minor administrative error on Eibar's part in the submission of paperwork and, despite fixing the error immediately, FIFA would block the loan deal. Eibar would go on to appeal the decision and present to FIFA's judge documentation citing the approval of both Páez's party and of the Spanish Football Federation, which backed Eibar's case. Unfortunately for Eibar, the appeal would be unsuccessful even though, in the club's own words, "All parties agreed it was a simple administrative error, which was immediately corrected, and that the documentation was submitted on time." While the rejection of the appeal would be costly for Eibar – alarmingly thin at centre-back – the real tragedy will be that Páez cannot play for either club for the remainder of the season, leaving the youngster able to train with Eibar, but unable to get any match experience under his belt.

With Eibar assuming their main need – a central defender – is already met, the club remains well away from the late transfer gossip and there are to be no 'my mate reckons he saw so-and-so at an Eibar estate agent' rumours as the clock ticks down on Deadline Day.

With the Páez deal retrospectively blocked, Eibar end up making just two signings this transfer window. One was Borja Fernández, while the other is a Portuguese from the south-coast village of Vilà Nova de Milfontes. A centre-back? A winger? Some help up front? No, the new signing is 6,760 square metres of Portuguese grass. In response to the 'mud bowl' pitch, the club takes the opportunity to relay the turf and after evaluating various suppliers from France, Portugal and within Spain itself, the club opts for the grass from Vilà Nova de Milfontes, which produced turf 'best suited to the characteristics of Ipurua'.

This Portuguese signing will make its debut a fortnight later against Elche.

Monday, 16th February 2015. Ipurua Stadium, Eibar.

It is hard to lay new turf when the ground is covered in snow. I may not be a horticulturalist, but I know that much.

Heavy snowfall paid a visit to Eibar in the first week of February, creating a beautiful postcard picture scene the Ipurua groundskeeping staff surely had little appreciation for. The delay to the laying of the Ipurua pitch was not overly concerning considering Eibar would play in A Coruña on 6th February, but the sooner this snow disappears the better.

The match at Deportivo La Coruña was seen as an excellent opportunity to return to winning ways. Deportivo had been awful in the Ipurua fixture earlier in the season and their smash-and-grab job had somehow seen them escape with a 1-0 win. It was a chance to return the favour and return from Galicia with another three league points posted on the table. Ah well, it was a nice thought.

The first half was simply an onslaught of chances for the home side, with Deportivo miraculously failing to convert. Eibar would not be so lucky in the second half; Lucas Pérez pounced on Irureta's punched clearance just seven minutes after the break – not the first goal he'll score this season to sink Eibar. While Eibar never looked like finding an equaliser, Borja Ekiza's slack back-pass ten minutes from time ensured the points stayed with Deportivo – Eibar's bogey team – when Ivan Cavaleiro was the lucky recipient of Borja's generosity.

Now, ten days on and with the snow in Eibar finally cleared and replaced by typical rain, the new Portuguese pitch is finally laid and

Elche are to be the first visitors to the new Ipurua surface and, hopefully, the first victims.

While both teams usher in the opening period by stroking the ball around, enjoying the chance to do so without any nasty surprises, few chances are created until Raúl Navas has an 'ave it!' moment and drills a loose ball from 40 yards, forcing Elche's keeper Tyton to tip the ball over the bar.

The ball striking Tyton's gloves is to become a theme of this match and, moments later, the Polish goalkeeper parries another long-range strike, this time from Borja Fernández. Before half-time there is still time for Tyton to make what would be one of the double-saves of the season were it not – incorrectly, I might add – ruled out for offside. Piovaccari firstly heads a Javi Lara cross towards the corner, which Tyton saves with one hand before racing to scoop the rebound away before it crosses the line. While this passage of play is belatedly called back for Piovaccari apparently straying offside, nobody stops and both the saves and shots are genuine. Unfortunately for Eibar, five minutes into the second half the same linesman makes another incorrect offside call; an Elche free kick is nodded into the back of the net by an offside Jonathas. The goal stands, as does Irureta who appears to stop in anticipation of an offside call which is not forthcoming.

Forty minutes remain, plenty of time for a much-needed comeback and for more miracles in the Elche goal. Tyton again stars for the visitors as Javi Lara's volley is diverted from its course towards the top corner before Ander Capa's cross-goal shot finds Tyton's stretching boot in the way.

It isn't just Elche's goalkeeper making fantastic saves as Elche defender Albácar stretches out to block a Capa cross with his fingertips, but the officiating tonight is as poor as Elche's goalkeeper is good and no penalty for handball is awarded. There is still time for one more example of each before the 90 minutes are up; Piovaccari receives a red card for raising his arm in a 50:50 challenge before Tyton again denies Capa three yards from goal.

It has been a true *partidazo*, a superb performance, not only from Tyton but from a hungry Eibar side which finishes with seven shots on target to Elche's two, yet ends the evening defeated.

Still, the half-time presentation of a plaque to nearby club Amaikak Bat de Deba puts things into perspective. Eibar played their first-ever match against Amaikak Bat de Deba in 1940. While Eibar is now in the country's top division, their guests compete in the eighth tier of Spanish football. Losing a game in the top division 1-0 is not that bad after all, is it?

Jon Errasti watches *Ballon d'Or* winner Cristiano Ronaldo control a pass in his home town of Eibar, a day he never expected to witness.

That 2014 match was not the first time Eibar hosted Real Madrid. A 23-year-old Iker Casillas made seven outstanding saves when the two clubs drew 1-1 in a first leg tie of the 2003/04 *Copa del Rey*.

The decade between both those visits of Real Madrid saw Eibar yo-yo up and down Spain's lower divisions. In 2013 the club won promotion from the *Segunda B* back to the *Segunda A* and celebrated at the Town Hall.

Promotion to the *Primera* division was achieved the following season. With the club so small, not even the full pitch was covered in the resulting pitch invasion.

With what little fans the club did have, Eibar celebrated in style. The fans hold manager Gaizka Garitano aloft after their rise to the top was confirmed.

The town of 27,000 took to the streets to celebrate that second successive promotion.

Joining the town's residents for the party was a Scottish bagpiper in honour of the *Eskozia La Brava* fan group's strong Scottish ties.

Promotion had to be achieved with work off the field too. President **Á**lex Aranzábal is seen here working on the club's share issue.

With such a small budget, Eibar's inferior squad would need a wise and motivational manager. Gaizka Garitano was to be that man.

Garitano knows better than most what it is like to be an Eibar player; he captained an Eibar side that very nearly won promotion to La Liga in 2005.

Players may come and go, but Eibar can always count on their loyal, passionate and colourful fanbase.

It may be tiny, but there are few more scenic locations than Ipurua in Spanish football.

Jon Errasti plays a pass in Eibar's 2012 *Copa del Rey* match against Athletic Club de Bilbao. Errasti's side would record a shock and historic victory in this tie.

The club's connections with Scotland are represented with this mural on the wall of Ipurua's East Stand.

A young David Silva applauds an Eibar support which remains proud of their World Cup winning former player.

Xabi Alonso also won the World Cup and was also moulded in Eibar. He stands next to late ex-president Jaime Barriuso at Ipurua.
All photographs by Félix Morquecho

A FAIRYTALE SEASON: ACT 3

Sunday, 1st March 2015. Ipurua Stadium, Eibar.

Seven hundred chorizo *pintxos* and 70 litres of soup. That is how Eibar welcomes Athletic Club de Bilbao to the town.

The Sunday afternoon feast has been organised by the *Txinbera* fan group of Athletic Club, the Eibar-based *peña* of the Bilbao side, and all who stop by their headquarters – tucked up a winding hill just seconds away from the lively main square – wearing either an Athletic or Eibar shirt will be given some free lunch. Turn up in a Barcelona, Real Madrid or, even worse, Real Sociedad, shirt and there'll be no chorizo or soup for you today!

The atmosphere is jovial all around the town, but especially here at the *Txinbera*'s lunch for all. As the secretary of *Txinbera* Verónica Díez jokes to me, "Even the weather has agreed that it is an historic day and, after several days of rain, the sun has broken out."

And it is an historic day. This *Txinbera* fan group has only ever seen Athletic Club visit Eibar once with their first team, but that visit was in the *Copa del Rey* which makes today's match the first ever league visit of Athletic Club to Ipurua.

"This season is special," states Verónica. "The two teams are on an equal footing and our *Txinbera* fan group is littered with divided hearts. To give you an idea, as a fan group we organised a trip in which we filled two coaches to go to the Athletic–Eibar match [at San Mamés] and they were mostly filled with *azulgranas*, fans wearing the blue and claret of Eibar. It makes sense, the Eibar fans have their team in the *Primera* for the first time and they're enjoying it to the maximum."

There are certainly many divided hearts here at this lunch; fans of both teams are faced with the rare scenario of having to choose just one to root for today and the shouts of "*Ni Athletic ni Real*" – "Neither Athletic nor Real" – from the die-hard fans reminds all Eibar locals who they 'should' back. Making it even more difficult for many of the *Txinbera* members is the fact they are also shareholders of Eibar, having been "so keen to witness the Athletic–Eibar derby," explains Verónica.

"The relationship between the two sets of fans has always been good," she assures me. "Previously, we used to do what we called the '*Jornada de Peñas*', the 'fan clubs' day'. We would get together with all the official football fan groups from the town, each person with their shirt and the colours of their team – Eibar, Real Sociedad, Real Madrid, Celta de Vigo and Athletic Club – and would organise popular games, football games, food and drinks and would end up at Ipurua to see an Eibar match."

That pattern sounds very familiar today as both Athletic and Eibar fans alike finish tidying up at the *Txinbera* headquarters and wander up the hill together, past the old bullring, towards the stadium for this sell-out league match, one which is important for an Eibar team now just five points above the relegation zone.

At the top of the hill those lucky enough to have tickets, such as Verónica, head inside the stadium while the rest of the *rojiblancos* – the Athletic fans kitted out in red and white – who have made the short trip for the occasion despite not having a ticket find a nearby bar to take in the match. These bars' TVs might as well be on mute given how loud the noise is from Ipurua, but the fact they do indeed have the sound blaring out allows fans to hear the shock team news before this derby: Irureta has been benched.

For the past five seasons, Irureta's name has been the only certainty on the teamsheet while the places in the line-up to be earned week-to-week were elsewhere. A howler in the previous week's match – an away trip at Villarreal – has seen the prize-winning keeper relegated to the bench under Garitano's meritocratic squad selection; he is replaced by veteran keeper Jaime. It was unfortunate for Irureta his late mistake against Villarreal – allowing Luciano Vietto's timid strike to roll right underneath his body when hit straight at him – cost Eibar the game in a match which had been fairly even until that point. Garitano has shown his ruthlessness, however, perhaps intending to send a message to the whole squad that every place in the team must be earned and retained.

His replacement between the sticks has to wait some time before being called into action as Eibar create the best of the few opening chances. A glancing Piovaccari header ends up whistling past the post before Manu del Moral drives into the Athletic box, only to shoot straight at yet another player who has once kept goal for Eibar, Gorka Iraizoz.

Finally, Jaime is forced into action and it is, admittedly, a great save. Diving to his left the veteran saves a powerful header from Athletic's lone striker Guillermo. Another header, just moments later in the 36th minute, is not saved as Carlos Gurpegui leaves Jaime with no chance, bulleting De Marcos's cross into the net. Jaime is quickly involved once again, this time forced to deny his own team-mate Dani García as his attempted clearing header spins dangerously back towards his own bottom right corner. Jaime is well aware by now he will be getting little rest in this match and, sure enough, five minutes before half-time he is called into action again; this time he blocks Iker Muniaín's effort from just a yard out.

Eibar continue to turn the ball over with alarming frequency in the second half and are so passive, in fact, it is as if they haven't turned up at all. The best chance Eibar create in this second period is a long-range strike from Manu del Moral, which Iraizoz tips over the bar and into the *Eskozia La Brava* fans who once religiously sang his name.

Instead, it is Jaime who is once again the busier keeper; he makes an outstanding one-handed point-blank save from substitute Aritz Aduriz. The only other action of note before the final whistle is when Eibar-born Athletic winger Markel Susaeta is brought on to a fantastic cheer. Susaeta plays only five minutes before the final whistle sounds around the ground to confirm Eibar's 1-0 defeat, but Jaime's 'Man of the Match' performance has any doubters of Garitano's decision to drop Irureta eating their words.

The managerial decision has since been vindicated, but it only masked what was a sluggish and uninspiring Eibar performance all round. It really has been a dour affair on the pitch, in spite of the camaraderie off it, and at most clubs a sixth defeat in a row, coupled with such a performance, would normally be met with protestation from the fans.

This is not most clubs and Garitano's name is still sung with affection from the stands at the final whistle. The La Liga spotlight is intense, like living in a goldfish bowl, but the Basque manager has not yet let the pressure get to him, nor have the fans turned on him. Whatever the reason for the recent failures of Eibar, the prognosis is clear: Garitano is not to blame. He is the alpha and omega of this current Eibar; it is because of him they are where they are, playing derbies with the likes of Athletic Club. If Eibar are to stay up, it will be because Garitano masterminded it. If they are to be relegated he'll have at least increased their chances of staying up infinityfold. "Nobody said life in the *Primera* was going to be easy," the manager repeats. Eibar are supposed to get relegated remember.

And so, not worrying too much about the result, the celebrations with the visiting Bilbao fans continue into the evening under the amber glow of a Basque sunset until they eventually depart, hopefully to return again next season.

In spite of the largely sloppy match, Verónica has had an enjoyable afternoon supporting Athletic Club at Ipurua. "It's true that the match, with respect to the football on show, was pretty poor. Neither Eibar nor Athletic played to their best and we simply had the fortune to score first," she admits. "The victory was bittersweet, though, since it came at the expense of a dear and worthy rival, but we're confident that Eibar will get back to winning ways and start picking up points again.

"We want another Eibar versus Athletic next season!" Verónica exclaims. She is not alone.

Friday, 6th March 2015. Ciudad De Valencia Stadium, Valencia.
Saúl Berjón is fast becoming an Eibar hero and one of the prime candidates for the *Ballon de Hierro*. No, not the *Ballon d'Or*, but the ball of *hierro,* of iron.

The award will be handed out to Eibar's Player of the Season in June, courtesy of Eibar's ironmonger sponsor Hierros Servando. Made from scrap iron and shaped into a sphere, there are several candidates for the eight kilogram *Ballon de Hierro*.

Arruabarrena has been a fantastic leader up front and his ability to send the ball into various bottom corners around the country has certainly put him in contention, while Dani García has provided the nous in midfield all year and Eneko Bóveda's solid performances in defence have not gone unnoticed. Albentosa would also have been a candidate were he still here, while Irureta's recent benching might just rule him out despite what had been a stellar season between the posts.

Yet it is Saúl Berjón who has shone brightest since his first start in the 2-0 victory over Elche in September, becoming a permanent fixture ever since. Whether deployed on the left flank by Garitano or further up front to partner Arruabarrena, the Real Oviedo youth product has consistently provided his defence with a *salida*, an out ball, and his *Primera*-calibre passing and control always keeps the play moving towards the opposing goal.

Tonight, Berjón proves his worth yet again. Seeing Bóveda's cross into the box dropping slightly behind him, Berjón has both the will and the means to reach back and clip it into the net with a swish of his right boot before rushing away towards the corner flag to celebrate. The official league goal of the month for March would not be scored in *El Clásico*; no, Berjón's goal wins that honour.

More important for Eibar than the beauty of the goal is the fact the ball is actually in the net. Berjón's strike is Eibar's first goal in 416 minutes of league action and it could not be better timing given the potential importance of this match in the season's relegation storyline. Despite Eibar's run of six straight defeats coming into this match, Garitano's side has lost just two of those by two goals, and the other four by 1-0 scorelines. The club's goal difference is a very respectable minus nine – only Real Sociedad with minus eight has a better goal difference in the bottom half of the table – after 25 *jornadas*. Eibar have rarely been outplayed or comprehensively beaten; they are hardly a team falling apart, more so one which has been close and unlucky time after time. As Garitano explains to radio show *El Larguero*: "We've lost most games by one goal and we're lacking that little bit of luck."

However, this blip has now been stretching a little too long, making it more and more difficult to call it a blip. This away trip to Levante, the team occupying the last relegation place and which has been flirting with relegation – or, more accurately, spiking relegation's drink with Rohypnol – since the first day of the season, is massive in the context of each club's seasons. It is for this reason Berjón's volley is so special. It isn't just because it is so aesthetically pleasing, though there is that. It's the fact Eibar now lead Levante in this relegation six-pointer.

The lead, though, doesn't last for long.

In true Eibar-esque fashion, it is wiped out ten minutes later before the scoreboard clocks up another name in a further two minutes. After a first half devoid of incident, the first 20 minutes of this second period produce much more in the way of entertainment and Levante now lead by the odd goal in three.

Their first goal need not have found the back of the net behind Jaime – still keeping Irureta out the team – given no fewer than nine Eibar players are in the box as Toño's cross miraculously ghosts through all of them for David Barral to prod into the net for the equaliser.

If the equaliser was the result of poor defending then the second was simply comical. A headed ball bounces through three Eibar defenders before the too-often-calamitous Borja Ekiza finally gets a foot on it, only to clear it to Levante's Kalu Uche, via Raúl Navas's face. Uche's goal completes a two-minute turnaround which is difficult to swallow.

With the remaining half hour, Eibar cannot avoid falling to their seventh consecutive defeat and a late second yellow card for Dani García rubs further salt into their wounds, as would the news just two days later that striker Ángel will be out for a month after requiring the removal of his appendix. Never has a football team not wearing the national shirt of Scotland's fortune and momentum collapsed so drastically. Next up? The new league leaders – Barcelona.

Saturday, 14th March 2015. Ipurua Stadium, Eibar.

In a season of firsts, this weekend in the middle of March presents yet another test for SD Eibar. This Saturday afternoon sees another debut at Ipurua which is eagerly anticipated and long-overdue.

Today… Ipurua's new scoreboard makes its debut.

Okay, so the real anticipated debut of the day is of FC Barcelona, who are here to play their first-ever match at Ipurua, but the *videomarcador,* the electronic scoreboard, is without doubt a proud new addition for the locals. Its unveiling is perfectly timed and makes Ipurua look just that little bit more professional for the visit of the Barcelona stars; it's as if the club has brought out the good china for the visit of the Queen.

If Barcelona is footballing royalty in this metaphor, then the footballing king is Leo Messi. The Argentine netted against Eibar when the pair met at the Camp Nou in October, but Messi has simply gone from strength to strength since with a ridiculous start to 2015 in which the scandalously gifted forward has already scored 18 goals, grabbed three hat-tricks and provided 11 assists in the 16 games before today's in Eibar.

It is little surprise then, and in many ways fitting, to see Messi inaugurate the Ipurua *videomarcador*. The first goal comes from 12 yards out after a penalty is awarded when Messi's own shot strikes the hand of Borja Ekiza, even though the Eibar defender has little, if any, chance of getting his arm out of the way.

The Messi headlines are written even before the goal because what the new scoreboard fails to declare is the wispy Barcelona number ten has made one of those runs we see time and time again, but which never fail to take the footballing world's collective breath away. Picking the ball up inside his own half on the right flank where has been deployed, Messi is immediately under pressure from Javi Lara, but is able to turn away from the Eibar winger with effortless elegance, double tap the ball past Lara's team-mate Dídac Vilà before sprinting away from the pair – even taking the ball past Lara for a second time – along the right-hand side of the pitch, just metres away from the awed Ipurua crowd. Next to be embarrassed is Bóveda, who nearly nicks the ball away but finds the ball's shadow is as close as his stretching leg can reach before Raúl Navas becomes the victim of a glorious nutmeg. Messi isn't finished just yet and, having already sashayed past four Eibar players, the Argentine now carves out an arcing knife-through-butter pass between four Eibar bodies to reach Neymar on the left corner of the penalty box. His Brazilian strike partner can't quite match his magic and Eibar escape unpunished, with the exception of some bruised individual pride along the way.

Shortly after that moment of magic comes the penalty to give the visitors – wearing a fluorescent orange against the team which 'borrowed' their colours in 1944 – a 1-0 lead which remains the score as the clock ticks to 45 minutes. Just ten minutes into the second half, Messi doubles the Barcelona advantage. If his dizzying defender-evading run was classic Messi, then this goal certainly isn't as he scores his first-ever direct header from a corner in a Barcelona shirt. It may not be the kind of goal the Eibar locals expected to see from the opposition's star man, but they all count and 2-0 is how this match ends. Piovaccari could have halved the deficit with a half-volley that struck the crossbar, but this afternoon belongs to Lionel Messi who proves many doubters wrong as he shows he can do it on a wet and windy night in Eibar.

The home crowd is far from distraught, though, as the final whistle peeps through the rain and wind. Today was more about the occasion than the end result for many fans. Sure, the players and manager were confident about their chances before the match and keen to reiterate it would not be a stroll in the park for Barcelona – and they were proven correct given how much hard graft the Catalans had to put into the match and how much Messi brilliance was needed to secure the points. However, while Jon Errasti was justifiably dreaming big before the match, telling the press Eibar had "earned the right to dream after three marvellous seasons," it was never likely to be the Basques' day.

Meanwhile, Garitano had built up not only the belief Eibar could take something from the match, but also the necessity they did so, telling his pre-match press conference: "We can't gift them the match as we have a great need for points. It's very important for them to win the league title, but our survival is even more important to us. For Barcelona, one league title more or less won't change their history a great deal, while for us the future of our club is at stake. We're not here to simply joke around, or to think about swapping shirts at the end of the game." Such a bold statement seemed to be an ultimatum for his players to earn at least a point, but even Garitano recognised the value the occasion holds even if his side fall to defeat, admitting: "The fact the best team in the world is coming here, and people can enjoy it, does have its worth."

That worth was also understood by the Eibar City Council. In recognition of the match's importance, they allowed the dozen streets and squares that connect Ipurua with the town centre to be renamed for the weekend in honour of Eibar's all-time best XI and manager, as voted for by fans in a 2014 poll. So Ipurua Kalea has become José Eulogio Gárate Kalea in honour of the great ex-Eibar and ex-Atlético striker, while Plaza Ungaza is renamed Plaza Garmendia for the weekend, honouring the legendary goalkeeper.

Such acts have helped create the unique and celebratory atmosphere of the weekend, with the town rejoicing in the fact global behemoths FC Barcelona are visiting Eibar, by lining the streets to greet the team coach as it rolled into town, hoping for a fleeting glimpse of a football megastar. Fans had even camped out overnight to get their hands on the priceless tickets for the match – in the end they needn't have bothered since it didn't quite sell out – and neither the end result nor the rain was ever going to dampen anyone's party spirit.

Thanks to perhaps the greatest player ever, Eibar's losing streak has now extended to eight, but as the fans empty Ipurua to fill the neighbouring bars optimism remains high that the team can get out of their current rut. Inside the stadium, at his press conference, Barcelona coach Luis Enrique shares their confidence, telling the media Eibar are better than their run of results suggests: "From what I saw on the pitch today, Eibar doesn't look like a team that had been on a run of seven consecutive defeats." He adds: "I hope that they don't have problems and that they stay in this division."

For Eibar to do so, they would have to rewrite history as no team has ever lost eight consecutive matches in La Liga and avoided relegation. Eibar's league position has plummeted as a sobering re-acquaintance with league table gravity replaces the early season high.

La Liga standings after *jornada* 27

#	Team	Matches Played	Matches Won	Matches Drawn	Matches Lost	Points
14	Eibar	27	7	6	14	27
16	Almería	27	6	7	14	25
17	Deportivo	27	6	7	14	25
18	Levante	27	6	7	14	25
19	Granada	27	4	10	13	22
20	Córdoba	27	3	9	15	18

6

Ascenso

"It is my best memory at Eibar, without a doubt."

Raúl Albentosa

Saturday, 18th June 2005. Ipurua Stadium, Eibar.
Eibar's home match against Real Sociedad in August 2014 may be their first-ever match in Spain's top division, but it wouldn't be the first time Eibar had been in La Liga. Today, on a sunny 2005 summer afternoon in the Basque Country, Eibar is in La Liga. But only for 26 minutes...

The situation at the start of the day is this: Eibar are in fourth position in the *Segunda* division and only three teams can win *ascenso*, promotion to the top flight. There are no play-offs in the *Segunda* at this point in time so the only chance of an historic rise to the *Primera* for José Luis Mendilibar's Eibar is to finish above either one of the Cádiz or Celta de Vigo sides currently occupying the last two promotion spots. With 72 points, Eibar are just one point behind both those sides while they cannot catch their Basque neighbours Alavés, who boast 76 points and lead the table as the final *jornada* begins.

There is tangible optimism around Ipurua, not least because Eibar have an easier match on paper than promotion rivals Cádiz. Ahead of this last round of fixtures, Eibar's opponents Racing Ferrol are 15th and, having just last week confirmed their place in the division for the following season, have nothing but pride to play for. Cádiz, on the other hand, travel to a Xerez side which goes into the final day of the season having lost just once in nine matches – against fellow promotion challengers Celta de Vigo.

That Vigo team is also away from home today, but faces a slightly easier task against 13th-place Lleida. Still, Vigo enter the final day after a 2-1 home defeat against none other than Eibar the week before. Anything is possible.

Ipurua has every right to feel optimistic about the *armeros'* chances given the way Eibar have played this campaign. It has been a dream season, with the club having spent 20 of the previous 41 *jornadas* in the promotion places, even spending four of them on top of the table in November.

There is no doubting the talent in this squad. Twenty-three-year-old goalkeeper Gorka Iraizoz will go on to win the *Copa del Rey* with Espanyol the following season before cementing his hold on the number one jersey at Athletic Club for years to come. He has been terrific for Eibar in this 2004/05 season, conceding just 38 goals – the fourth best record in the division – and commanding Eibar's back third since the opening day, a match they won 2-1 against promotion rivals Cádiz. The match-winner was Joseba Llorente, who has since netted 18 goals, majorly improving on his return of just four in 2003/04.

Pulling the strings behind Llorente has been the fresh-faced David Silva. Even at just 18 years old, the on-loan playmaker from Valencia has dictated the attacking play of this side, playing an impressive 39 matches – 29 of them for the full 90 minutes. Silva has also scored four goals, the first of which was a vital 85th-minute winner in Cádiz as ten-man Eibar completed the double over their rivals and earned the right to contest a place in La Liga today. It was a beautiful strike – as most of Silva's are – with the Canary Islander pouncing on a throw-in into the box and, one swivel of his hips later, volleying past Armando in the Cádiz goal.

More memorable this season is the goal Silva didn't score. In a match in the 35th *jornada,* with Eibar drawing 1-1, Silva found himself with a chance to win the game in the 91st minute. However, noticing a Lleida player lying injured, the young forward kicked the ball out of play so his opponent could receive treatment, an act which won him the Pedro Zaballa Award for fair play – an award for going beyond the call of duty named after the player who, in a 1-0, 1969 loss to Real Madrid with his side Sabadell, noticed the Real keeper was unconscious when readying to shoot and so kicked the ball out, costing his side the match.

Teaching Silva such inspiring values, as well as the intricacies of the sport, has been his midfield partner, team captain and future Eibar manager Gaizka Garitano – the man who is already studying to be a coach at just 29 years old. His coaching course is in preparation for the future, but Garitano is also the man of the moment and the man of this promotion bid. He has been the engine room of this league campaign, with only goalkeeper Iraizoz having played more matches than him.

The evening begins well for Garitano and Eibar, very well in fact. A 17th-minute goal from star striker Llorente sends Ipurua wild as blue and claret balloons flood the pitch. One dungaree-clad supporter explains to reporters from Basque TV station *Euskal Telebista* that as it stands at 6.47pm on 18th June 2005, Eibar is a La Liga team, a remarkable achievement but one which relies on the outcome of the next 73 minutes.

Eight minutes later, news filters through from the Municipal de Chapín Stadium in Andalusia and it isn't good. Cádiz have taken the lead. The Vigo match remains goalless, though, so as it stands Eibar will finish the day on 75 points, Cádiz would secure 76, while Vigo would trail with just 74 points.

That's only as it stands, however, and the situation will change again; for Eibar, it will change for the worse. At 7.13pm a goal from Jandro gives Vigo a lead before half-time, just before Garitano misses one of Eibar's best chances to kill off their match here. The events of the last few minutes, which have seen Eibar pushed out of the promotion places, give rise to one of the most anxious half-time breaks Ipurua has ever played host to.

The situation evolves again just after the break, and again not in Eibar's favour. Two penalties change the situation completely, the first coming down south as Cádiz's Paz scores a 50th-minute spot kick to double his side's lead. Back here in Ipurua, however, there is little *paz*, meaning peace, when referee Arcas Piqueres awards the visiting Racing Ferrol side a penalty in the 56th minute and sends off Eibar's Antonio Karmona for the foul – Karmona's last act in this, his last game before retirement – and the penalty is duly dispatched by Bermejo. The situation then doesn't change until 8.12pm when Vigo double their lead, a goal which acts as the death sentence to Eibar's promotion hopes.

So Eibar come close but not quite close enough – a conspiracy, according to some frustrated fans, to avoid a team like Eibar tarnishing the 'glamour' of the top division. Cádiz win the division with 76 points, Celta de Vigo are runners-up with the same number, while Alavés also finish on 76 points after losing their match but still winning promotion. Fourth place is Eibar's reward for a wonderful season, but this club wanted more, even if everyone present here at Ipurua today knew they had little right to dream of tiny Eibar making it to La Liga…

The fans are certainly not bitter. Karmona, the potential villain of the evening for leaving his team-mates a man short and conceding a penalty, is paraded around the stadium by fans keen to mark his retirement positively. Inside, captain Garitano thanks the fans: "We're all quite pissed off [with the outcome], but the fans were brilliant, which I'm sure will help Eibar for the better in the seasons to come."

Garitano is right; the fans were brilliant and they have organised an open-top bus tour to celebrate the season's success. The town now packs Ungaza Square to await its heroes. A banner in English reads "You'll never walk alone" and judging by the fact most of the 27,000 population is here right now, they have a point. Before long, the bus arrives and the battle-weary team make their way into the Town Hall and on to the balcony to belt out Queen's 'We are the Champions'.

Eibar may not have been the official champions today, nor even have finished in the promotion places, yet for 26 glorious minutes this June afternoon in 2005, Eibar was in the *Primera*.

Next time, they'll be singing Queen as true champions. The La Liga dream will one day come true.

Saturday, 17th June 2006. Ipurua Stadium, Eibar.

Almost a year to the day, Ipurua is again readying itself for the last day of the *Segunda* season and the opponents are – just like last year – Racing Ferrol, while the score is – just like last year – 1-1. Even the referee Arcas Piqueres, who awarded the penalty and sent off Karmona, has returned.

Unlike last year, however, Ipurua is not packed out and there is scarce enthusiasm or optimism around the Basque valley. Today, there are only 900 in attendance, according to *Mundo Deportivo*, compared to the 4,500 the same newspaper recorded the year before. Garitano's prediction the support last season's excitement and near-promotion brought to Ipurua would stand Eibar in good stead for the long run was misjudged. Instead, Eibar begin this final day of the season already relegated; they have been since three *jornadas* previously.

This team didn't get off to a great start, instead losing to Elche at Ipurua on the opening day and already it was obvious the optimism of the previous season had deflated, with just 1,800 heading up to Ipurua to witness the 2-1 loss. The lack of optimism was justified, to be fair, given the high profile departures had left a tribute act of a team. Between the sticks Iraizoz was gone, having returned to Espanyol. Top scorer Llorente had also departed, with his switch to fellow *Segunda* rival Valladolid a cruel blow. David Silva had again been sent out on loan by Valencia, but this time to Vigo to experience the *Primera* division.

Most damaging was the loss of captain Garitano. The leader of the team that came so close to promotion was on his way to neighbouring Real Sociedad, finally getting his well-deserved chance to play in the first division.

Not only had playing staff left, but manager Mendilibar was also out the door, having accepted the Athletic Club job up the road. Eibar was left with a bare-bones squad, one which was unsurprisingly relegated after spending just nine *jornadas* of the whole season outside the relegation zone. Today's match with Racing Ferrol – also relegated – is to be Eibar's last in the *Segunda* after 18 years in the division and 711 consecutive *Segunda* matches – a record.

There is no open-top bus parade down to Ungaza Square after today's match.

Just one year later there will be. Eibar spend only one season in the division below, the *Segunda B*. Spending the majority of the season in second place, Eibar would overtake Palencia with five matches remaining to win the group and a place in the promotion play-offs, which had been the cause of such disappointment in the past.

Eibar would succeed this time, defeating Hospitalet in the first play-off round by an aggregate score of 2-0. Next up would be Rayo Vallecano in the final, with the Madrid side edging the first leg 1-0 in the capital. Two goals in quick succession in the first half at Ipurua would seal the tie in Eibar's favour and it would be the Basques enjoying promotion in front of a sell-out Ipurua crowd, including 500 Rayo Vallecano fans packed into an away end not designed for any more than 300 people. The full-time whistle would be greeted with a pitch invasion of *azulgrana* and tartan 'See You Jimmy' hats, yet the travelling Rayo fans would not be completely forgotten about by the understandably ecstatic Basques.

Rayo Vallecano fan Paul Reidy was there that day and later recalled the humility of the Eibar fans: "What was incredible, though, was the Eibar fans' reaction at the final whistle. There was the inevitable promotion pitch invasion and then a surge of Eibar fans to the stand where we were housed and they all began to chant, 'Rayyyyyyo Rayyyyyyo'." It's little wonder the two sets of fans would go on to form one of the most amicable relationships between two clubs in all of Spain.

Tuesday, 27th January 2009. Ipurua Press Room, Eibar.
At 34 years old, Álex Aranzábal is not the oldest person in the Ipurua press room today. At 34 years old, Álex Aranzábal is not even older than all of the Eibar playing staff. Yet at 34, Álex Aranzábal is today presented as the new president of SD Eibar, the youngest president in Spanish professional football.

He replaces Jaime Barriuso, the president since 2002, who has today stepped down for 'personal reasons', months after losing an election for the Gipuzkoa Football Federation and who is suffering from health problems and would sadly pass away in October 2012. Barriuso has enjoyed a successful period in charge, having overseen the 2004/05 season when Eibar came so close to promotion to the *Primera*. He also oversaw the relegation from the *Segunda* in 2005/06, even if it was followed by immediate promotion back to the second tier thanks to the play-off final win over Rayo Vallecano. Eibar then enjoyed a comfortable first season back in the division under Barriuso in 2007/08, hovering around mid-table all season. The club even got to experience two derbies against relegated Real Sociedad and managed two draws against their neighbours – 0-0 and 1-1.

The current campaign of 2008/09 is becoming disastrous. Vice-president since June 2008, Aranzábal now takes over the presidency with the club in the relegation zone. Things will only continue to worsen under the new president.

With the team having lost five of Aranzábal's first seven matches in charge, and finding itself four points from safety, Aranzábal will take his first major decision as president and sack the coach Carlos Pouso. His replacement will be Josu Uribe, but the team will fail to improve and win just one of Uribe's 15 games in charge, finishing 21st and suffering another relegation.

Although the relegation is a major failure, Aranzábal would at least have shown his board is ready to take the tough decisions necessary. Again, he would change up the management in the summer of 2009 – his second managerial appointment in just six months in charge – with the hiring of the relatively unknown Ángel Viadero Odriozola as coach. Uribe's failure to turn the situation around by collecting just eight points from the 45 available in his 15 matches in charge would leave Aranzábal no choice but to dismiss the Asturian, arguing there is no need to mix sport with personal issues and proving success for the club comes above making friends for Aranzábal. There is an oft-repeated phrase in Spanish that would come to define Aranzábal's next few years: *'El que no arriesga no gana'.* No risk, no reward.

Following a stellar first campaign back in the *Segunda B* in Aranzábal's first full season at the helm in 2009/10, which nearly ends with yet another immediate promotion back to the *Segunda* but which would ultimately end with play-off despair against Pontferradina, a frustrated Aranzábal would seek further changes.

2010 was to be a time of economic crisis in Spain and, apart from at the Camp Nou or Santiago Bernabéu, football was not immune. With incomes stretched and football more easily – and more cheaply – available on TV, attendances would fall around the country. In December 2010, Aranzábal would address this issue with Letizia Gómez of *El Correo*: "The competition, above all through TV, is getting better and better. There used to be hardly one match each weekend and now the supporter, from the armchair in his house, can choose to watch Chelsea, Real Madrid or Barcelona instead of coming up to Ipurua. This [economic] crisis affects football in general, but keeping in mind the number of residents here and the division we're in, the numbers we are getting are acceptable. There are stadiums in the *Primera* division, like Getafe's, that have attendance figures of only 8,000 people and in our division there are important towns whose stadiums are deserted. It's a terrible epidemic which is affecting football in general."

It's all very well being aware of the problem and that third division football isn't the most attractive option on a Saturday evening, but Aranzábal would have to take decisive action to counter the fact Ipurua would be more than half empty in 2010.

His solution? *Ascenso.* Only a promotion could bring the club back to life.

Aranzábal would explain to *El Correo* he had made a *plan de tres años,* a three-year plan, to get Eibar out of its rut. He'd explain Eibar could afford to go all out to win promotion to the *Segunda* "because our finances permit it" while admitting putting so much focus into winning promotion within three years would indeed be a risk but it was a calculated one.

"In life, each time somebody does something, there is a risk attached. *El que no arriesga no gana,*" Aranzábal would say. "We understand the Eibar spirit is to be brave and to risk, but with wisdom, after having evaluated and analysed the situation."

As such, Aranzábal would increase the playing budget by 30% for the 2010/11 season as well as bringing back Javier Mandiola – his fourth manager in a year and a half – who was the coach when Eibar won promotion from the *Segunda B* in 2007. There would be reason for optimism once more, but promotion back to the *Segunda* division is never easy and despite the new manager and bigger budget, the team would still struggle to get over that final hurdle. Mandiola would win 21 matches, playing attacking football and scoring 58 goals on his way to topping the group with 73 points. Yet, with no automatic promotion for winning the group, Eibar would still have to navigate the dreaded play-offs.

That's where year one of the three-year plan ends; Mandiola's side would be eliminated by Alcoyano on the away goals rule after a 0-0 away draw and 1-1 result at Ipurua.

Back to square one.

Year two of the three would see a less prolific Eibar side, but one with a better defensive record. Only 17 wins and 66 points would be picked up, but Mandiola would still earn the club a play-off spot by finishing third in *Segunda B Grupo II*. Xabi Irureta, the Eibar keeper, would have another stellar season between the sticks, picking up 15 clean sheets in the regular season and yet another in the play-offs. But his shut-out in the 0-0 second leg against Lugo at Ipurua wouldn't be enough to cancel out a 1-0 first leg defeat. The Galician side moved on and gained promotion. With two years of the three-year plan up, so too would be Mandiola's time at the club.

Aranzábal would have one last roll of the dice. Choosing the correct manager is imperative this time, but he wouldn't go for the 'safe' option of picking one of the many off-the-shelf Spanish managers so consistently on the managerial merry-go-round they've become unable to spot when the emperor is not wearing any clothes.

No, instead Aranzábal would select a wild card. *El que no arriesga no gana.*

Wednesday, 9th July 1975. Derio, Basque Country.
Gaizka Garitano Aguirre Urkizu Asla Zubikarai Madariaga Garraminia Arteche was predestined for football.

Born with eight Basque surnames on this summer's day in 1975, little Gaizka was never going to struggle to find football in his life. His father, Ángel, was a footballer – though not a particularly successful one – and would go on to carve out a more successful career as a coach, standing nervously on the touchline as the assistant manager to Mané when Gérard Houllier's Liverpool defeated his Alavés side 5-4 in the great UEFA Cup Final of 2001.

While the final in Dortmund, Germany, was a major disappointment for the Garitano family – even though Gaizka, a self-confessed Liverpool and Jamie Carragher fan, may not have been quite as upset as his father – the 2000/01 season wouldn't be all bad for the Garitanos. Just one month later, Ángel's brother Ander would lift the *Copa del Rey* with Real Zaragoza, the team with which Gaizka's uncle would spend the last six years of his career. Ander would only play the final few minutes of the final against Celta de Vigo in Sevilla, but would have started six other matches en route – including a last-32 match played against Eibar, which Ander's Zaragoza would win 1-0.

The *Copa del Rey* win would be Ander's only major honour as a player, coming at the age of 32 in his penultimate season. By the time Ander would hang up his boots, he'd have turned out for Real Zaragoza 147 times, after appearing in the red and white stripes of Athletic Club – his first club – 275 times, scoring 42 goals. Ander would go on to manage Real Zaragoza in January 2008 for a grand total of eight days, losing one cup match and winning one La Liga game before departing, reportedly with medical issues, with a 100% La Liga record as a manager.

Before, as uncle Ander was playing his last season as a professional footballer, young Gaizka – only six years younger in actual fact – would be playing his first official season as an Eibar player, turning out in midfield like his uncle. This would not come as a surprise as Gaizka was destined for football from birth, yet the sport wouldn't be his first career choice. Gaizka would actually aspire to be a *bertsolari*, a kind of Basque improvising poet for whom there are annual competitions which attract as many as 15,000 contestants. He would always have a way with words and even study for a journalism degree from the University of the Basque Country in Lejona, explaining the ease with which he would one day deal with press conferences as a manager.

But let's get back to the 2001/02 season when Gaizka would sign with Eibar. He'd already played for them on loan from Athletic Club in the 1998/99 season, with a spell at Ourense in the *Segunda B* in between. It would then take just four weeks of the season for Gaizka to cement his place in the Eibar midfield.

There are few Basque midfields Gaizka wouldn't play in during his career; in fact, only one senior Basque side, Osasuna, would miss out on the youngest Garitano's natural leadership ability. After starting his career at Athletic Club's Lezama academy – which he could see from his house – Gaizka would spend several years playing for the Bilbao B team in the *Segunda* division before making his one eight-minute appearance for the senior side as a substitute in a UEFA Cup match away to Sampdoria in September 1997, following in the footsteps of uncle Ander, as well as those of his relations Koldo Aguirre and Juan Urquizu. Gaizka would only make one appearance for the Bilbao side, however, and at the other end of his career would represent Real Sociedad the season after coming so close to promotion with Eibar in 2004/05. He would wear the blue and white of the San Sebastián club 81 times, netting nine goals, before hanging up his boots and his shinpads – the same ones the superstitious Garitano would wear all through his career, not wanting to tempt fate or injury by ever wearing a different set – after one final season at the Basque Country's other major club Alavés, his father having long gone by then.

While Gaizka and his father would never be on the same team, their paths would cross on two occasions. One of Ángel Garitano's roles as assistant to Mané was to scout the opposition and his job would have been made a lot easier when tasked with reporting on his own son when Mané and Ángel's Lleida team played the Athletic B team in the 1994/95 season. Gaizka would start that first meeting of the season and, fortunately for his mother, a goalless draw was played out. The second meeting would see Gaizka's Bilbao side fall 2-0 to his father's Lleida.

Ángel would again be tasked with scouting his son, but not until more than a decade later when a Basque derby would once again pair father and son together. Having taken over the reins at San Mamés in December 2006, Mané would again ask his assistant Ángel to scout the opposition for a derby – this time against Gaizka's Real Sociedad. Ultimately, despite having played in 15 of the previous 19 league matches, Gaizka wouldn't feature in this derby in which Athletic Club would leave Anoeta with a 2-0 win and both the Basque and Garitano bragging rights.

Father and son wouldn't meet again in football; the Mané and Ángel double act would eventually wind up in 2009, after which Ángel Garitano would never again coach in professional football, instead going on to coach local Derio youth side El Arteaga. However, Ángel certainly wouldn't lose his competitive spirit; in 2014 he'd be given a month's ban for clashing with a 19-year-old referee during a match.

By then, Gaizka would also be carrying the Garitano surname into the spotlight of Spanish football, but for the right reasons. In 2012, at just 36 years old, Gaizka Garitano would take charge at SD Eibar. He was to be Álex Aranzábal's last roll of the dice.

Sunday, 26th August 2012. Ciudad Deportiva, Zaragoza.
It all begins in front of just 200 fans. Yes, two hundred.

Eibar's *ascenso* mission begins in the least glamorous of locations as they face a Real Zaragoza B team, which has attracted no more than 150 fans. The other 50 hail from Eibar, making the trip to Aragon to see Garitano's first match in charge and, according to the *Diario Vasco*, they make much more noise than the home 'crowd'.

Those faithful fans who have made the trip deserve to see a win for their efforts, as do Garitano's team. The match finishes 0-0, but Eibar dominate from start to finish, particularly at the finish. Garitano introduces Jito with ten minutes remaining and the decision looks certain to pay off as the forward creates three wonderful chances in the 81st, 83rd and 88th minutes without being able to find the net.

It says a lot about the performance of Garitano's new-look Eibar that the Zaragoza youth team celebrates the point as if they've won the game. It also raises concerns that Eibar haven't won a match they should have.

Garitano wasn't the obvious choice to lead this quest for *ascenso* to the *Segunda* Eibar so desperately craves and needs. During his playing career, Garitano never once won a major honour – nor promotion – coming closest with Eibar that day in 2005. He did, worryingly, suffer relegation three times: forming part of the Athletic B team who suffered the side's first relegation from the *Segunda* in seven years, part of the Real Sociedad side that suffered the club's first relegation from the *Primera* in 40 years, and part of the Alavés side that suffered the club's first relegation from the *Segunda* in 14 years – just eight seasons after making the UEFA Cup Final.

The blame for those relegations cannot, obviously, be placed solely at Garitano's feet, but many in Eibar are worried Garitano lacks the *actitud ganadora*, the winning attitude, to secure promotion. Others are concerned by the fact his managerial CV could fit on a postage stamp; his only managerial credentials stem from his two years in charge of the Eibar B team, which was disbanded after Garitano's appointment for financial reasons – various youth teams do still compete, by the way, each of which is assigned a *padrino*, a godfather, from the first team. Eibar B played in the *Tercera* division, the fourth tier of Spanish football, under Garitano, finishing 16th out of 20 in 2010/11 – the B team's joint-lowest ever finish – and then 13th in 2011/12. Garitano hasn't even brought with him to the first team a band of talented youngsters à la Pep Guardiola at Barcelona. Only Ander Capa has been promoted to the first team along with Garitano.

Besides his Eibar B experience, Garitano had been an assistant to Ángel Viadero Odriozola in the 2009/10 season with the first team, but both were dismissed – by Aranzábal – just before the end of the season. Garitano's own second-in-command, Patxi Ferreira, is also in a – in his own words – 'learning phase', also causing many to doubt Aranzábal's decision to put two amateurs in charge. Yet the president's choice of a manager with a mind still pure and uncluttered by the clichés of Spanish football would soon be proven wise. Garitano's side will go on to win ten of their next 14 league matches, soaring to second place in the *Segunda B Grupo II* table.

While impressive, it wouldn't be overly remarkable as the previous two years of the three-year plan have brought third and first place league finishes before ending in failure. Shortly, however, Garitano will demonstrate he does possess *actitud ganadora* that some think he lacks. He'll do so in a *Copa del Rey* Basque derby. The biggest day of Garitano's managerial career so far will come at San Mamés, the place where it all began.

Wednesday, 12th December 2012. San Mamés, Bilbao.

12/12/12 is a special date for everyone connected with SD Eibar. Not because it symbolises love, as many in Hong Kong and Singapore believe it does. Not because it signifies the end of the world, as many doomsdayers argue. And, not because at 1:21:02am, a time/date palindrome is created. Although, admittedly, that is pretty cool.

No, this date is special for Eibar fans because today Eibar dumps big brother Athletic Club out of the *Copa del Rey*.

This isn't the first time the two clubs have met, having been paired for the first time in the 1979/80 edition of the cup when the Bilbao side triumphed 10-3 over two legs, yet this is to be the first Eibar victory over Athletic Club. It isn't even a victory, to be fair.

Having drawn the first leg with Marcelo Bielsa's side 0-0 at Ipurua, Eibar have at least given themselves a chance in this second leg – held six weeks later as a result of the rescheduling of an Athletic Europa League match due to tensions in Israel – to be held at the old San Mamés, set to be demolished the following summer to make way for the new stadium.

Eibar's fans have travelled in numbers to the neighbouring city, many of whom work in Bilbao and who join the others drinking in Pozas once 5pm hits. Despite the rain, it is a party atmosphere and *azulgrana* is everywhere. Except on the pitch, that is, where Eibar take to the field in green and white hoops, like those of Celtic.

Mikel Arruabarrena is one of those in the starting XI and he scores the vital away goal for Eibar from the penalty spot late on in this even match with few chances. It is the 71st minute when Arruabarrena smashes his penalty into the top corner – he rarely places his spot kicks, preferring instead to hit them high and hard with an impressive success rate – after a challenge on David Mainz had encouraged the referee Velasco Carballo to point to the spot.

An onslaught then begins but Irureta is equal to anything Athletic have to throw at him until, in the 88th minute, Aritz Aduriz beats the offside trap to nod in a free kick from the left wing. The goal comes too late and a stoppage time corner is headed away to prompt the full-time whistle, chaos in the away section and an ovation from the home support.

And so, while tonight is not the end of the world, it is the end of the *Copa del Rey* for the old San Mamés – a stadium which hosted its first *Copa del Rey* fixture in 1914 and which tonight, almost 100 years later, has hosted its last. Eibar have made history and the players have been permitted a night of celebration, even if Aranzábal – who, dressed in his raincoat, watched the match in the away stand with the rest of the Eibar fans rather than in the directors' box with the suits – makes it clear afterwards that promotion is the ultimate goal, calling the cup run "a very nice bonus". The priority this season, of course, is to escape the *Segunda B*, although the president understands the historic significance of this result as much as anyone.

It is an historic success, as well as one which has earned the club a not insignificant €100,000 – 8% of its budget for the year – yet this may also be a success that helps to achieve the ultimate goal of *ascenso*. Although the club would crash out 5-2 to Málaga in the last 16, this victory over Athletic Club would not become worthless. There is no doubt this victory has given the Eibar players the belief and the discussed *actitud ganadora* necessary to finally navigate the dreaded play-offs.

This cup win in Bilbao might just be the most important result of Eibar's league campaign.

Saturday, 26th January 2013. Ipurua Stadium, Eibar.

Marcelo Bielsa's Athletic team may be languishing in 14th place in the La Liga table with the visit of high-flying second-placed Atlético Madrid the following day, but here he is along with former coach of the *Euskal Selekzioa,* the Basque Country team, José Ángel Iribar at Ipurua at 9am this Saturday morning.

His visit is a secret and, as such, Bielsa has parked his car at the back of the stadium and he and Iribar enter through a side door rather than the main entrance. Awaiting them are just three Eibar employees: Garitano, his assistant Patxi Ferreira and the kitman Ángel Zapico.

The visit comes on the back of a phone call Garitano received from an unknown number the day before. It turned out to be former Argentina and Chile manager, and current Athletic coach Bielsa, who announced he would be driving across to Eibar for this secret visit before conducting his Saturday training at Lezama. Garitano was unaware of the purpose of the visit at the time, but it quickly becomes clear; Bielsa is here to ensure Garitano knows Athletic took Eibar seriously in the cup match.

It should have been obvious the Bilbao side took the challenge their Basque neighbour posed seriously as star players such as Ander Herrera, Fernando Llorente, Aritz Aduriz and Iker Muniain all featured, but Bielsa wants to be sure the Eibar coaching staff doesn't think their Athletic counterparts underestimated Eibar. For that reason, Bielsa gives Garitano a gift: a folder full of his tactical planning for the cup matches.

Anyone who knows even a little about Marcelo Bielsa will know he is as studious and meticulous as managers come, so it is no surprise the folder is a large one, evidence for Garitano and his staff that their achievement against Athletic in the cup did not simply come about because they caught Athletic 'off-guard'. If anything, it appears Athletic were more prepared for Eibar than any other team Garitano has faced in the *Segunda B* this season has been.

The visit continues with Garitano and his staff showing Bielsa and Iribar around the Ipurua installations. Bielsa had wished to visit them before the first leg of the cup tie, but didn't have time to, so he is now shown around the dressing rooms and the medical rooms, as well as the restaurant which overlooks the pitch, where the Eibar squad eats together every day. Bielsa is also shown the pitch, which kitman and part-time groundskeeper Zapico explains is currently experiencing serious drainage problems, prompting Bielsa to reminisce about his experiences with various unloved pitches in Argentina.

Then it's time for the Argentine to leave. His stay has only lasted around 20 minutes, but he must return to Bilbao in time for training. Those 20 minutes are enough, however, for Garitano and his staff to once again realise the magnitude of their cup achievement. Not only had they completed a giant-killing in the cup, but that giant had been 100% prepared and still unable to stop them.

The rest of the *Segunda B* has been similarly unable to stop Garitano's Eibar. Now approaching the end of January, the Basques sit second in the league and they clock up a further success the following day, beating Tudelano 4-0 in their biggest win of the season. Oh, and in case you're curious, Bielsa's Athletic would beat Atlético Madrid 3-0, also their biggest win of the season.

Saturday, 9th March 2013. Ipurua Stadium, Eibar.
Could it all have fallen apart? Or is this just a hiccup?

After starting the season so well, Eibar come into this match-up with Noja without a win in five. Two draws and three defeats have seen Garitano's side drop to fourth position and to plummet any lower – to outside the play-off spots – would be a travesty.

Garitano knows his job is safe, but he only has to look across the dugout this afternoon for a reminder of how quickly it can change. Returning to Ipurua this Saturday, with his newly-promoted Noja side is Ángel Viadero Odriozola, here to face his old apprentice Garitano. The pair had worked together in the 2009/10 season, but both were dismissed with just two matches remaining and Garitano is keen to avoid a similar fate. He famously gives each of his starting XI a slap on the chest before they take to the field each match to get them pumped up – you can bet today's slap was a little bit harder than usual.

Yet with just five minutes remaining, it doesn't look like Garitano's slaps were strong enough, or that Eibar will achieve the win needed to get the season back on track. It doesn't even look like they'll get a draw.

On a frosty and very bare Ipurua pitch, a terrible match has played out so far. Although Eibar kidnapped the ball, there had been few chances for either side until a wonderful individual effort from Noja's Manu Oritz gave the visitors a 1-0 lead just after half-time. Now, the final whistle is drawing nearer and Eibar have finally begun to carve out some clear chances following the introduction of Garitano's three substitutions, the attacking trio of Arruabarrena, Diego and Arroyo. However, it's centre-back Aitor Arregi who equalises in the 87th minute after finding himself unmarked at a corner.

Six minutes of stoppage time are added on and Eibar keep the pressure up, winning a corner in the 94th minute. This time there is nobody obviously open and the defence manages to clear the ball, but only as far as Diego, who volleys it into the corner of the net from outside the area and is wrestled to the turf – or what's left of it – by his team-mates.

'Diego Jiménez Releases Eibar From Its Depression,' the headline reads in the following morning's *Mundo Deportivo*. How true it would prove as Eibar go on to win their next seven matches, even if none of those victories is to be particularly comfortable – five 1-0s, a 2-1 and a 2-0. Nevertheless, at the business end of the season all that matters is the accumulation of points and Eibar's run would lift them up to second place with just two games remaining. Despite drawing those two final matches, Eibar would remain in second place and enter the dreaded play-offs one more time.

Third time lucky? It had to be if the three-year plan was to succeed.

Sunday, 26th May 2013. El Collao Stadium, Alcoy.
Round one.

Having finished runners-up in their group, Eibar have three rounds of play-offs ahead of them if they are to win promotion to the *Segunda*, a daunting prospect given their unhappy relationship with the play-offs over decades past.

ASCENSO

First up is CD Alcoyano, the team from Alcoy – halfway between Valencia and Murcia – who ended Eibar's promotion hopes in the play-offs two years previously. It is a gloriously sunny evening as the two teams take to the pitch and it quickly becomes even more glorious for Eibar who, after just 20 minutes, find themselves exacting revenge, and 2-0, up thanks to goals from Garitano's B team protégé Ander Capa and Mikel Abaroa, set up by the in-form Capa. If there is one thing Eibar's history should have taught us by now – the club is never safe in the play-offs. Those seemingly-comfortable leads always slip and, indeed, that is the case today.

Alcoyano pull one back on 56 minutes, but fail to create many more chances until, just two minutes from time, the home side win a penalty from a clumsy challenge in the air by Raúl Navas. Up steps the spot-kick taker, a soon-to-be-familiar Javi Lara. Little does Lara know by converting his penalty he would be jeopardising his chance to become the scorer of Eibar's first-ever La Liga goal 15 months later.

Lara would still get that opportunity, thankfully, after Eibar survive the second leg. But only just.

Away goals do count in these play-offs and, thanks to the rule, Eibar appear to be going through. It all changes in the 77th minute of the Ipurua return leg as a result of Alcoyano substitute Álvaro's goal. It would be an all-too-familiar situation for Eibar, appearing to fall at the play-off stage. Once. Again.

One minute from time Diego Jiménez changes everything. As in the Noja match, he fires a thunderbolt into the goal in front of the *Eskozia La Brava* fans in the dying seconds of the match.

Round One? Tick.

Sunday, 9th June 2013. Carlos Tartiere Stadium, Oviedo.
Round Two.

The 20,000 fans inside the Carlos Tartiere Stadium are stunned; once again there's a last-minute Eibar goal. This round didn't start as well as the previous, with Eibar not ahead by two after 20 minutes but rather trailing by one. This week Garitano has been much more decisive and changed things just ten minutes after half-time when he brought on Mainz and Jito for Abaroa and Arruabarrena – adjusting a starting XI which contained no fewer than eight players who would start matches for Eibar in the *Primera* division.

At the time of the substitutions Eibar didn't even look like becoming a *Segunda* team. Three minutes afterwards, it was resolved thanks to super sub David Mainz who turned in an Ander Capa cross from a couple of yards after beating the offside trap.

It looked like Eibar would once again head to Ipurua with the tie on level terms, but Eibar's Guille Roldán had other ideas as he fired low and into the corner from the edge of the area. *Eskozia La Brava* celebrate the win as if it were an Old Firm derby triumph in *Eskozia* itself – which it certainly looks like with Eibar playing in green and white hoops while Oviedo play in blue with white shorts – while 20,000 Asturians leave disappointed.

Almost a thousand of those Asturians make the trip to Eibar for the return leg a week later, converting half of Ipurua's West Stand into a mosaic of blue. Eibar seal the tie, making sure to avoid the nervous finish they had endured against Alcoyano. Roldán is again the goalscorer, but this goal is manufactured by Arruabarrena, who skilfully jinks past his man on the left flank before making a beeline for the penalty box where he squares the ball for Roldán to beat Quintana in the Oviedo goal in the 79th minute to secure Eibar's place in the play-off final.

Round Two? Tick.

Saturday, 22nd June 2013. Ipurua Stadium, Eibar.
Round Three. The Final.

This is it. This is what the three-year plan comes down to.

For the first time in these play-offs for *ascenso* to the *Segunda*, Eibar are playing the first leg at home, and it suits them perfectly. Hospitalet are the opponents and within five minutes the Catalan visitors are two goals behind and seemingly out of the tie.

The goalscorers from the previous round are again the heroes; Roldán nudges a bouncing ball into the corner from the edge of the box and Mainz converts a one-on-one chance. Ipurua is bouncing with a burst of happiness that hints at emotions long-repressed. The buzz continues throughout the match as Eibar slow the game down to secure victory, until Diego Jiménez goes for the throat and dances past a couple of tackles before sending the ball into the bottom corner of the East Stand's net with just seven minutes remaining – an early goal for the stoppage time specialist.

The 3-0 result is massive and will even make the front page headline of the following morning's *Mundo Deportivo* – the only other football was, to be fair, the Confederations Cup. Eibar's place in the *Segunda* is '*En Sus Manos*' according to the newspaper. It is in their hands.

As for the scenes in the town centre this Saturday as the famous San Juan party arrives in this Basque valley one night early? Well, you can imagine…

Meanwhile, Garitano is certainly not getting carried away, bringing up in his press conference the fact Hospitalet came from a goal behind to win 2-0 at home in the previous round. "I'm happy, but I'm cautious because I know how these things work," he tells the press. "We need to be calm because any kind of euphoria now would lose us the next game before even playing it."

As it transpires, Garitano needn't worry. The second leg is to be a game of few chances, a cagey affair in which Hospitalet keep possession and Eibar are happy to let them. The home side create few clear chances and the game rapidly approaches 90 minutes without any hint of a goal being scored. It all changes with Capa's stoppage-time goal and the promotion party shortly begins as the players link arms to dance around the centre-circle, cheered on by the huge away following only marginally outnumbered by the home fans at the Feixa Llarga Stadium.

The three-year plan for promotion? Tick.

Sunday, 18th August 2013. La Victoria Stadium, Jaén.
Eibar is supposed to be relegated this season.

Eibar's budget is the smallest of the whole *Segunda* division, at €3.5million. No team comes from a smaller town, nor will any team have a smaller average attendance – 3,000. They are favourites for relegation back to the *Segunda B* and certainly not title challengers, priced at 50/1 to win the division. Even president Aranzábal – while delighted to have achieved his three-year plan and returned Eibar to a division that might just attract fans away from watching Chelsea versus Arsenal from the comfort of their armchairs – admits the club's 'natural place' is in the *Segunda B*.

So the only goal Eibar can realistically aspire to this season is survival and that begins with today's match in Andalusia against Real Jaén, also newly promoted from the *Segunda B* which makes this a potential relegation six-pointer on the season's opening day. "There are two clear candidates to go down, since they have only just come up, and they are Eibar and Jaén," explains *The Flagrant's* blog.

It is a very warm day in Jaén in the height of summer which leads to an understandably slow-tempo and lethargic match. Neither side look like scoring and most of the shots in a fairly even match are wide of the target until a deflected 41st-minute strike finds the back of the net from Eibar's new Celta de Vigo loanee Jota.

Eibar's lead is doubled on the hour mark as Raúl Navas's bandaged head meets a corner and the visitors are 2-0 in front. Real Jaén pull one goal back with five minutes remaining thanks to a screamer from Jozabed, but Eibar hang on to pick up their first *Segunda* division win since 2009.

Sunday, 15th December 2013. Ipurua Stadium, Eibar.
We fast forward a little to *jornada* 18 of the season and Eibar's most momentous weekend of the first *vuelta* of fixtures in the 2013/14 *Segunda* division.

Gaizka Garitano's side are excelling in their battle to avoid the drop and come into this match in sixth position, a not insurmountable but encouraging seven points above 19th place – the first of the four relegation spots in this 22-team division. The club could hardly expect to be any further up the table given they are operating with the lowest budget, yet two weeks previously that is exactly where they were: in fourth place and ten points above relegation.

Two defeats in a row have not overly dampened the mood and today's visit of league leaders Deportivo La Coruña – a team as disappointed to be in the division as Eibar are excited – is seen as a realistic chance to return to picking up points. A win would be an upset, of course, but as Eibar have already picked up points against Real Zaragoza – relegated with Deportivo from the top flight – and other *Segunda* heavyweights such as Barcelona B and Tenerife, never mind their 6-0 thrashing of Real Madrid Castilla, they have every right to feel confident.

A banner held up by *Eskozia La Brava* before the match of a bare-chested, kilt-wearing, sword-wielding and skull-and-crossbones-branded-shield-holding warrior – yes, *Eskozia La Brava*'s understanding of Scottish history might be a little shaky – slaying what appears to be a little boy wearing Deportivo pyjamas oozes confidence. While it gives us an idea of what we could expect if Metallica did shortbread tins, it also gives an idea of how much the fans are enjoying fighting at the top of the *Segunda* with the big boys. They love this.

They love the match even more when it finally kicks off. After an early spell of Deportivo possession, Eibar take full control and the league leaders are on the back foot. The visitors should also be down to ten men after 25 minutes when Argentine midfielder Culio is lucky to receive only a yellow card for a dangerous challenge. The referee lets Culio and Deportivo off the hook, as does Arruabarrena five minutes later when unable to knock Morales's fine cross past the Deportivo keeper.

Ten minutes after the chance Arruabarrena converts a far more difficult one, this time thunderblasting a dropping ball into the bottom corner from right in the middle of the *media luna* – the Spanish name for the penalty box arc, which literally translates as the half moon.

The second half passes by with little of note besides the fact that the incredibly distracting sun has set. It appears as if Eibar are going to hold on to the 1-0 lead to hand the league leaders just their fourth defeat from 18 when the margin of this victory is doubled. This time Arruabarrena can only manage a less spectacular half-volley from two yards out to begin a frenzy of pinching themselves amongst the fans.

With a minute remaining, Luis Fernández halves the lead, tumbling into the net along with the ball, but it's too late for the result to change further. The score finishes 2-1.

This result is amazing, which is a simple but accurate adjective to sum this up. Eibar now find themselves in fourth position and in the play-off spots for *ascenso* to the *Primera*, the land of Messi and Ronaldo, of stadiums larger than the whole town of Eibar and of neon-coloured cleats. Yes, that *Primera*. The three-year plan didn't account for such a possibility. The club was never supposed to enjoy this much success; it is almost as if it isn't permitted to.

Something strange is certainly happening up here in the Basque mountains. The dominos for winning a promotion play-off spot are now firmly in place and they are wobbling. Very soon, they will begin to topple.

Sunday, 9th February 2014. Nuevo Arcángel Stadium, Córdoba.

Nah, this isn't real. Jota has curled a strike into the bottom corner to give Eibar a 1-0 lead. *There is no way this is reality.* Sporting Gijón are losing at home. *Nope, this definitely isn't actually happening.* There are only ten minutes left and Eibar could go second in the table. *No way, somebody pinch me.* Deportivo are losing now too. *Okay, I'm definitely dreaming.* Morales has doubled the lead and Eibar are going top of the division! *Here we go, let's enjoy this!*

On a drenched, windy and Eibar-esque Sunday afternoon in the south of Spain, Eibar have just gone top of the *Segunda* division, jumping from third to first to overtake both Sporting Gijón, who have drawn against Ponferradina, and Deportivo La Coruña, who have lost in Murcia.

Just let that sink in. Eibar are the smallest team in the *Segunda* and currently the best in it.

How are they doing it? Luck isn't the answer; Eibar have been unlucky in fact. In the January transfer window Garitano's side was unable to strengthen while promotion rivals such as Deportivo La Coruña could draft in several improvements – this despite Eibar having no debt and their rivals having millions of euros worth. Instead, a mix of the tactically infallible Garitano – who would pick up his third Manager of the Month award of the season this February – with his squad of skilled and technically-gifted grafters, must be the explanation. While Atlético Madrid are doing equally miraculous things in the *Primera*, Eibar's miracle is gaining far less attention.

Garitano has admitted to being a fan of Diego Simeone's Atlético side, calling them *"hijos de puta"*, "sons of bitches", on occasions, but – insists Garitano – in an affectionate way for being so good. Having always believed in hard work, Garitano believes – like Simeone – that such work can pay off. When Atlético go on to win the 2013/14 La Liga title, miraculously holding off Barcelona and Real Madrid, Simeone will speak of the basic tenets of his title-winning team: *"Si se cree y se trabaja, se puede."*

"If you believe and you work hard, you can."

It is an ethos Atlético-admirer Garitano has undoubtedly installed at Ipurua, where his players often come back to the stadium in the afternoons to take extra voluntary training sessions; as a result they have more victories than players with Wikipedia pages. Such a fastidious approach from this squad is making it more and more likely Eibar could contest the play-offs at the end of the season, this time for promotion to the *Primera*. Or, whisper it, what if they could actually win automatic promotion?

The Cinderella story is promptly coming together, only it isn't pretty Cinderella but ugly sister Eibar that has a chance of going to the La Liga ball. Forget the ballrooms, from barrooms to boardrooms, Eibar will be the talk of the town tomorrow morning now the unfancied team is within touching distance of the top flight. Even if not expected to stay there for long, Eibar is top of the *Segunda*.

Sunday, 25th May 2014. Ipurua Stadium, Eibar.
Oh. My. Dios.

Did Jota just do that? Have Eibar just scored the goal to seal promotion? Yes. And probably yes.

Jota did just do that and Ipurua has gone crazy. His soon-to-be-famous goal comes about from a throw-in at the halfway line. It is aimed towards Urko Vera, who flicks it on further down the right wing towards Capa, the winger duly nodding the ball towards star man, Jota. The Galician controls the ball perfectly considering the torrential rain, not allowing it to bounce awkwardly but allowing it to roll just enough for him to take it with his left foot. And take it he does.

Sometimes in football, a player's age isn't defined by the ink on his birth certificate, but by moments like these. Jota's birth certificate would tell you today he is just 22 years old. That goal, however, has all the skill of a veteran ten years older.

Were he not set to be recalled by Celta de Vigo and ultimately move to Brentford, Jota would be able to dine out in Eibar for the rest of his life without ever lifting his wallet. There may only be 27,000 people, but they adore this long-haired handsome Galician with his model girlfriend. He may represent a lot of what Eibar is not, but for the rest of history he will be the face of this heroic Eibar side.

It is a side which began the day unlikely to win promotion, at least on this particular Sunday afternoon – exactly 101 years after the first ever football team from Eibar played their first ever match, that 8-0 defeat to Shooting Club. Eibar was in second place in the league before this match – their 1,006th ever in the *Segunda* – trailing Deportivo by two points after that man Jota had rescued a 1-1 draw in A Coruña the week before. After this *jornada* there remain just two matches and

Eibar kick off their match with four more points than both Barcelona B and Las Palmas behind them and five more than Murcia – who have already played one match more. Since Barcelona B cannot be promoted to the same division as their A team, an Eibar win today would mean only Las Palmas could snatch automatic promotion away, but to do so Las Palmas would need at least a draw in their own match against Recreativo Huelva – a game which, agonisingly for Eibar's players and fans, kicks off 45 minutes later than Eibar's.

By half-time in Gran Canaria, Las Palmas are winning 1-0, which is the same scoreline here at Ipurua as Eibar's match enters stoppage time. Since Jota's *golazo* wonder strike in the 61st minute, the last half an hour here has been dominated by visiting Alavés. Irureta has performed fantastically and after punching away yet another shot that has stung its way through the heavy Basque rain, the final whistle finally peeps around Ipurua.

There is no pitch invasion, however. Not yet.

In this unusual scenario, the club has no idea if promotion has been achieved yet. The final whistle signifies three massive points, but nothing is sealed. Only a defeat for Las Palmas would mathematically confirm Eibar's second consecutive *ascenso*, while a draw would virtually do so given Eibar's vastly superior goal difference.

It is thanks to how few they conceded rather than how many they scored that Eibar have such a great goal difference; Xabi Irureta won the *Segunda*'s Zamora Trophy for conceding just 26 goals in 39 matches to follow in the footsteps of Eibar goalkeeping heroes Manuel Almunia – yes, he was an Eibar *armero* before he was an Arsenal gunner – who won it in 2001/02, and José Ignacio Garmendia, who won it in 1991/92 and 1995/96.

So, with the Las Palmas game being played over the Ipurua speakers, and with many fans already having been following this fixture, Ipurua focuses in on a third half of football for the night.

Raúl Albentosa explains to me afterwards that the team never expected to win promotion that Sunday. "We were aware we could win promotion that weekend, but we each had to do our jobs and that job was to win and hope Las Palmas would *pinchara*, flop. We said it would be difficult [for Las Palmas to lose] because they're playing at home."

It certainly looks like Las Palmas are making the most of the home advantage, winning 2-0 with just half an hour to go. Albentosa explains the team are ready to accept that and focus on securing promotion the following week. But then…

"Then Recreativo de Huelva got a goal and we started to hope a little, but when they scored the second we started to jump around, willing them on. And, when they scored the third? Well, with practically 5,000 fans waiting around after attending the match we went back out to the field and we started to, almost prematurely, celebrate it. It is", adds Albentosa, "my best memory at Eibar, without a doubt."

That 82nd-minute Ezequiel Calvente Criado goal may not go down in history as Jota's will do, but it is just as important this Sunday. Eibar would surely still have won promotion, barring a miraculous comeback from their challengers coupled with an equally tragic collapse of Eibar's own confidence and form, but that goal allows the celebrations to begin right here, right now. As the players slide on their knees through the soaking wet Ipurua pitch following the full-time whistle in Gran Canaria, their loyal fans run on to join them. This is the kind of match you tell people you 'witnessed' rather than 'attended'. Everyone in this stadium knows this will become a 'where were you when?' moment and they are simply thrilled 'Ipurua' is their answer.

This is Ipurua's most important pitch invasion ever, yet there are still so few fans the pitch isn't even half-covered. Gaizka Garitano, who will win the 'Miguel Muñoz Manager of the Year' Award for this season, is held aloft in the middle of it all – his personal nightmare of 2005 has become an impossibly true ecstasy – and it is the picture that will grace the morning's newspapers. "The best manager I've ever had," says Albentosa. "Gaizka has very clear ideas, he knows how to play and he knows a lot about football. He's not particularly chatty, a man of few words, but the truth is that he relays everything to you very well."

While *Marca* would inevitably still be replete with coverage of Real Madrid's Saturday evening *la décima* triumph, the paper would dedicate its back page to Eibar, a fitting tribute from a newspaper often – and rightly – accused of ignoring Spain's smaller teams. Meanwhile, *Diario AS*'s headline would go: 'Yes, You Read That Right. Eibar Is In The *Primera*.'

Throughout all the celebrations, music plays through the Ipurua loudspeakers and Gloria Gaynor's 'I Will Survive' fittingly comes on as some thoughts already turn to the season in the *Primera*. Once again Eibar will begin a season with the aim of survival, never aiming for the very top. First, though, the club would have a chance to top the *Segunda*. Eibar could still go up as champions.

Saturday, 31st May 2014. Ipurua Stadium, Eibar.

One weekend on from the promotion Sunday, Eibar is hosting the most anticipated *fiesta* Ipurua has ever seen. CD Lugo are the visitors to Ipurua, as are 4,959 fans – essentially a full house – as Eibar celebrate their *ascenso* with Barcelona's confetti. With Barcelona having failed to win a single trophy this season – and with no Super Cup to compete in either – Eibar have very cheekily acquired Barcelona's 30 kilograms of confetti at a discounted rate. Since it won't be used at the Camp Nou any time soon and would go off otherwise – confetti has a use-by date, who knew? – it will be the likes of Jota, Errasti, Arruabarrena and Garitano drowning in these blue and claret bits of paper rather than Messi, Neymar, Piqué and Tata Martino.

Bringing in bargain bucket confetti from one of the world's superclubs is very Eibar-esque, as is the grinding out of results. Call it anti-football, call it 19th-century football, call it what you will, the way Eibar played in the 2013/14 season was exciting and brave, even if not always the kind of free-flowing attacking football the purists love. Matches featuring Eibar in this season have featured a division low of just 1.83 goals per game and today the full house predictably witness a 1-0 win. The goalscorer? Yes, of course it was Jota.

Following the match and the celebrations in Ipurua, the team take an open-top bus to the Town Hall, passing through the packed streets. It's typical that you spend ages waiting on a bus before two come along at once and that is exactly what has happened here in Eibar. After four years of waiting for an open-top bus ride to celebrate promotion to the *Segunda*, much to the pleasure of the whole town – and surely to the displeasure of the driver tasked with navigating the valley town's narrow streets – there is a second promotion celebration just one year later.

To see such joy on the faces barely distinguishable in the mass of *azulgrana* is perhaps the best thing about Eibar's rise to the top division. The football club cannot, of course, carry this whole town back to the good times on its shoulders alone. Three La Liga points won't stop the cuts to the council's budget. The visit of Ronaldo or Messi won't re-spark the town's steel-producing trade. Expanding the club's administration staff by eight people won't solve the 13% unemployment rate.

Yet nights like these certainly help. Eibar have achieved *ascenso* and is literally on the up. The town as a whole can, and will, feed on that.

Eibar is on the up in the *Segunda* table as well. With Deportivo having lost the week before, Eibar now leads the division, sitting one point ahead of the Galician giants with one fixture now remaining each. Winning the division is a real possibility and Eibar could do so with a win away at Numancia the following Sunday.

As it turns out, a win won't be necessary. Deportivo, playing the following Saturday, will lose at a Girona side desperate for a win to avoid relegation, crowning Eibar as *Segunda* champions. For the past few weeks, promotion had always been the unlikely goal for Eibar, but titles like these don't come along often for a club like Eibar and the club was not going to dismiss it as a small bonus. This is big news.

So what else would Eibar do to celebrate a season of hard work, inconceivable success and an impossible *ascenso* to the *Primera*? Have a lie down? A few beers? A holiday?

No, they would go out for a bike ride as a team.

7

A Fairytale Season: *Act 4*

"We can breathe a little bit more easily."

Unai Eraso

Thursday, 19th March 2015. Anexo, Eibar.
Smoke is rising from Ipurua. The grey cloud of fumes is visible from all across the town this sunny day in which no other cloud disturbs the blue skies, from the industrial estate in the east to the *Corte Inglés* department store in the west. One by one, the locals clamber up to Ipurua to check out what's going on beneath this cloud of smoke.

Upon arrival, each of the curious souls is greeted by a scene more suited to a *Lord of the Rings* movie than a midweek lunchtime in this sleepy valley town. Phil Ball, author of the excellent *Morbo: The story of Spanish football* describes the journey into the town of Eibar through the rugged, and normally drenched, mountains as like driving towards Mordor. Today, up by Ipurua, it looks even more like Sauron might be lurking around a corner than usual.

Beside Ipurua Stadium is one of the many training grounds which Eibar use, the *Anexo* or Annex as it would be in English. Built in 1973 using land from the old nunnery and half the size of the full-size pitch in the stadium next door, the Annex is used by Eibar most Thursdays or Fridays to host an 'open door' training session. I say 'open door', but there are no doors or gates needing opening and it would be impossible to keep the public out if they actually wanted to; the Annex is as accessible as a public park, but with slightly fewer dog walkers.

It is for that reason Garitano's squad train at various locations throughout the week, some of which can host closed-door sessions. A typical week begins with the group being split in two; one group, the players which didn't play the last match, head to nearby Arrasate-Mondragon for a heavier workload on the full-size grass pitch in order to keep fitness levels up, while the other group, those who did feature in the previous match, train in a lighter session on the Ipurua pitch. The following day is a rest day before the whole squad train at Arrasate-Mondragon. The latter half of the week – assuming there is no midweek match – sees the squad train in closed-door sessions at Ipurua in which set pieces and specific tactical work is the focus, as well as the one 'open door' session in the Annex.

Today is one such 'open door' session, but it is not ordinary. The fans have come to watch the team train, as they often do, but the difference is the fact there are as many as 160 of them and they have brought flares, flags and drums along.

It isn't at all long before all that is visible on the sidelines is the odd burst of orange, red or *azulgrana* smoke. After eight defeats in a row, this team needs a defibrillator and the fans have turned up hoping their support can restore a flicker of a pulse to Eibar's season. Even if most of them won't be able to make the 1,650 kilometre round trip to Granada for the next match, why not motivate the team right here in Eibar?

It really does have a matchday feel – perhaps even more so as flares are not actually permitted inside Spanish football stadiums – which, considering just two seasons ago Eibar were playing *Segunda B* football in front of crowds as small as 160, is quite some achievement for a Thursday lunchtime.

The manager is fully aware of the rut his side are in and has a major urge to scratch that losing itch, but Garitano has admirably so far refused to blame anyone else for the drop-off in form. Speaking after the defeat to Barcelona – the most recent of Eibar's eight consecutive losses – Garitano refused to pin any blame on the referee who awarded a harsh penalty to Barcelona for an accidental handball, instead saying: "I think that a team which has lost eight matches in a row needs to look at other aspects, improve in other aspects and avoid complaining about such things [refereeing mistakes]."

It is a far-from-common approach in modern football and one which has won Garitano many plaudits, if not many recent league points. Yet points are becoming a must and this match against Granada is as big as they come; if the squad needed fresh impetus then a match away to the second-bottom relegation rival should oblige. After eight defeats on the trot it is time to stop the haemorrhage. The loss to Barcelona was the nadir, or at least that is the hope of these 160 fans, and of Garitano.

Predicting the outcome of this weekend's match is tricky. Their first encounter, held next door at Ipurua in October, finished 1-1 and was a very even affair. Eibar may have been poor since the start of the second *vuelta* of fixtures, but Granada have been poor ever since October and have won just three times since departing Ipurua. Curiously enough, Eibar also tend to pick up better results away from home, a quirk Garitano puts down to the fact his team performs better on larger pitches. Although Ipurua's pitch is not quite as small as many assume, it is one of the division's smallest and on the larger pitches Garitano's team tend to control the game better and utilise the spaces. Ahead of this trip to Granada, Eibar have won 12 points at home and 15 away. As the smoke dies down here at the Annex, we come closer and closer to finding out whether or not Eibar will add to that away points total.

Saturday, 21st March 2015. Los Cármenes Stadium.

Following their smoke-filled training session on the Thursday, Eibar's team bus was seen off from Ipurua on the Friday with even more flares, flags, scarves and banners. That, of course, after the pre-away trip tradition of stopping at Ipurua's La Bolera bar for a coffee and a quick chat with the fans. As the team coach rolled away, a small group followed closely behind on their way to Granada's Los Cármenes Stadium while the majority stayed in the Basque Country ready to tune in to the big Saturday night game.

This match was predicted by the media to be a cagey affair between two nervous teams, thus increasing the likelihood that that is exactly what it would become. Jaime occupies the Eibar goal once again and is able to bat away an early Adrián Colunga effort before keeping an attentive eye on Piti's long-range shot as it drifts past the post. Eibar's early scares are accentuated by the calf injury Raúl Navas picks up on the half-hour mark, meaning for just the second time in Eibar's season – the other was in the 1-0 defeat away to Real Sociedad – Eibar have neither Raúl Navas nor Raúl Albentosa, their first-choice centre-backs at the start of the season, on the pitch. This is scary and the thought of a ninth straight defeat creeps into *azulgrana* minds both here in Andalusia, and back home in the Basque Country.

Such fear extends into the second half, especially when Granada's Jhon Córdoba is played through on goal. A stretching leg from Abraham, filling in at centre-back, just about manages to nudge the ball away from the Colombian striker and safely around the post.

Córdoba continues to get heavily involved and not just by repeatedly finding himself caught offside. Allan Nyom tries Granada's luck from distance and almost hits the jackpot as Jaime spills the shot towards Córdoba before the Granada striker fouls him. Eibar's chances of taking anything back north are hanging by the weakest of threads.

Then, all of a sudden, Eibar nearly take the lead. A free kick earned on one of the few occasions Eibar venture into Granada's half is lofted into the box by Javi Lara and helped towards goal by the head of Eneko Bóveda, drawing a superb acrobatic save from Olazábal in the Granada goal. Moments later, Bóveda – the right-back, remember – finds himself lurking in the six-yard box as Abraham launches a ball into the box from the left wing. This time Bóveda tries to place his header, but slightly overdoes his attempt to push it towards the far bottom corner and the ball instead bounces past the post.

Any hopes of Eibar pushing for a win are quickly ended when Manu del Moral pulls up with an injury by the time all three of Eibar's substitutions have already been made. As the *armeros* finish the match with ten men, the nerves return and it is Granada attacking in the closing stages but unable to properly test Jaime. In the end, the two teams settle for stasis and that man Jaime collects his first clean sheet in an Eibar jersey and his side their first point since 16th January.

It is undeniable Eibar have played this match more defensively than usual, keen to avoid defeat and content with one point. As this Granada side would concede nine the following weekend at the hands of Real Madrid, perhaps there would have been opportunities to score had the Basques really gone for it.

Nevertheless, a point has been secured and Eibar's *mala racha*, their bad spell, is over. After the upcoming international break it will become clear if this point can be the catalyst for the rediscovery of their mojo.

The season might just be back on track.

Friday, 3rd April 2015. Ipurua Stadium, Eibar.

Remember the match back in November when Eibar visited Rayo Vallecano and the Rayo fan group *Los Bukaneros* performed their *The Simpsons* protest against the fact teams like Rayo and Eibar are so often moved to the unpopular Friday night and Monday night slots? Well, here we are once again in the La Liga twilight zone of a Friday night for a match that when the ratings come out towards the end of the weekend will be shown to have attracted fewer viewers than the same slot on *TeleTienda*, one of Spanish TV's shopping channels.

That somebody flogging vacuum cleaners would draw more viewers than what turns out to be such a great game of football is quite depressing, but the real shame is these two sets of supporters are once again treated as if they don't matter. Probably – because to the league – they do not. It's bad enough having to watch football on any old Friday, never mind on Good Friday when some fans would rather be spending time with family.

Nevertheless, it starts off a very good Friday for Eibar, who have an excellent attacking front starting the match; the rugged Piovaccari and Arruabarrena are both involved, complemented by the silky Saúl Berjón and Ander Capa on the wings. The often-wasteful Javi Lara and Manu del Moral are both starting on the bench which gives hope that Eibar might actually make the most of any opportunities to score their first goal since Berjón's wonder volley provoked the collapse away to Levante a month earlier.

EIBAR THE BRAVE

Things begin well for an Eibar which is very much on the front foot; Piovaccari almost converts a fizzing spicy-looking cross from a Capa ball before clipping a Saúl Berjón centre into the hands of Rayo goalkeeper Cristian Álvarez moments later. The Italian certainly can't complain about being starved of service so far and with the next ball played towards him he wins the penalty that changes the match.

A Capa nudged header into the box finds the oncoming Piovaccari, who rounds the keeper only to be chopped down. The penalty is – correctly – awarded, but Álvarez – incorrectly – remains on the field as no more than a yellow card is shown. That an untouched Piovaccari would have had a 'goalscoring opportunity' to slot into the empty net is undeniable; with the ball still within reach of his left boot and no defender within the six-yard box the moment he is taken out, it should have been a red card according to the rule book. Regardless, a scalpel-sharp Mikel Arruabarrena penalty finds the roof of the net and Eibar have their deserved 1-0 lead.

When I say the penalty changes the match, it is 100% true. Despite Eibar having taken the lead, the pardon of Álvarez swings the match in Rayo's favour with the visitors now shocked into life. Eibar have been bamboozled into retreating into their own half as the rejuvenated 11 men of Paco Jémez rediscover the attacking flair soaked into the fabric of their shirts. Within five minutes the scores are level as Good – or *Bueno* – Friday becomes Alberto Bueno Friday.

The move that sets up the goal begins when Gaël Kakuta traps a dropping ball in the box, before the Chelsea loanee lays the ball off for Tito to loft a deep cross towards the arriving Bueno at the far post. Jaime in the Eibar goal begins to move towards the cross, but finds himself in no-man's land as Bueno's header loops into the back of the net.

There are five minutes left before half-time and there is a sense around Ipurua that if Eibar can just maintain the status quo then Garitano can regroup his players at the break and they will return to the dominating play they enjoyed for most of the first half. That doesn't happen, as Eibar pull a 'Levante'.

Now that is not to say letting a 1-0 lead become a 2-1 deficit within minutes is the kind of thing that Levante do, but it is exactly what Eibar did in the match away to Levante just three games ago. That night, a 1-0 advantage became a 2-1 disadvantage within 12 minutes of opening the scoring, while tonight it has taken barely seven minutes for the tables to turn.

This second goal comes from a corner and, with a man on each post and Jaime making himself as big as he can, the ball simply should not ripple the net. Captain Añibarro is simply outmuscled by Manucho who rises to send Eibar into the interval losing a match in which they have dominated for 35 minutes.

A FAIRYTALE SEASON: ACT 4

Eibar return for the second period appearing broken and only a few half-chances are created for either side; the best of which comes off the head of Manucho, only to this time be met by the hand of Jaime. Garitano, hoping to inject some fresh life into the contest, brings Javi Lara and Manu del Moral on for Capa and Errasti with 25 minutes to go, but if anything the result appears even more certain after the changes as this vanquished team can tell fate is not on their side tonight.

So the reboot of Eibar's season will have to come another night and although the fans here are happy to enjoy a few drinks with their Rayo Vallecano counterparts – for these are two special clubs with excellent relations – there is a growing sense of uneasiness about Eibar's chances of survival.

There is to be little time for glum reflection, however, with Ipurua back to life the coming Wednesday for the even trickier visit of a Málaga side chasing a Europa League spot. These fans will need to be behind their team for Eibar to have a chance of keeping any of those points in the Basque Country.

Then again, there are some comfy-looking slippers to be sold on *TeleTienda* that night. It'll be a tough choice as to what to watch.

Tuesday, 7th April 2015. Ipurua Stadium, Eibar.
"*¡Fuera! ¡Fuera! ¡Fuera!*"

"Away with you!" goes the chant to referee Jesús Gil Manzano and his assistants as they make their way towards the Ipurua tunnel for the half-time break, a chant barely audible over a cacophony of hissing and whistling. But audible enough.

The officials have made an absolute howler, to put it politely, and the locals are certainly not putting it quite as cordially to the men in yellow. The score is 0-0 in this vital midweek match against Málaga and Eibar should be ahead, but a Mikel Arruabarrena goal – having pounced on the rebound from Saúl Berjón's shot – was ruled out for offside when the striker was very clearly two yards behind the last defender.

The sense of injustice is palpable; you can smell it all around Ipurua. Or maybe that's just the sweat. It has been a nerve-wracking 45 minutes as Málaga looked to become the sixth team in a row to take three points away from Ipurua and the Andalusians had the majority of possession in that first half, and the best of the early chances, which Irureta – recalled by Garitano to the starting line-up to the delight of the fans – confidently dealt with. Quite simply, Eibar cannot afford to lose this match as it would extend their run without a win to 12 matches, which might as well be 13 as next up is a trip to the Santiago Bernabéu.

As the teams return for the second half, the fear returns with them. Arruabarrena is on hand once again to ease the fear and send pumped fists into the Ipurua air once again. Even better, this time the goal stands. A Javi Lara corner lands perfectly for Arruabarrena, who has peeled away from his marker like an *azulgrana* ninja to meet it with his forehead.

Now a different kind of fear sets in, not the fear of losing but of having something to lose. Many of the 4,008 in tonight's raucous crowd were also here last Friday and know all too well how quickly Eibar's opponents Rayo Vallecano turned the game in their favour. A repeat cannot be tolerated, but always looks a possibility as Málaga attack and attack and attack.

Admittedly, Eibar create some great opportunities on the counter, the best of which falls to Ander Capa – played through by Manu del Moral – but his low shot is well-saved by Carlos Kameni. The open nature of the match is a little too chaotic for us fans in Ipurua who are crying out for some more stability. Eventually it is introduced in the form of midfield pressure-soaking sponge Derek Boateng and a sigh of relief is heard in the stands.

The sigh becomes a scream not long afterwards when the final whistle is blown and Eibar claim the win, their first in 12 matches, which is celebrated by *Eskozia La Brava* member Robert with the waving of the largest Ghanaian flag you'll see north of Egypt in tribute to Boateng's few points-securing minutes. Meanwhile, Añibarro, born just 50 kilometres away from Ipurua, beats the ground with his fists in celebration and relief. These three points are like three stitches, patching up a serious wound that has been bothering Eibar for months. This meant a lot.

It has been a great win. In a throwback to the glory days of the season's first half, it was a hard-fought and nervous one. Málaga had a total of 13 attempts on goal – four on target – while Eibar had six attempts, hitting the target with five. It's little surprise it has been a low-scoring game given the quality of the goalkeepers, two of the more often-tested but capable custodians in the division. After tonight's match, Irureta and Kameni have, respectively, made the most and second-most saves in La Liga this season. Their totals now stand at 87 and 86.

The most important save of the night, though, might be Eibar's victory; it is no exaggeration to suggest this win might just have saved their still-shaky survival hopes.

Saturday, 11th April, Santiago Bernabéu, Madrid.
When Real Madrid visited Ipurua in November to play their first-ever league match in the tiny valley town, president Álex Aranzábal received a phone call from one of Spain's most powerful men: Florentino Pérez. The Real Madrid president let his counterpart at Eibar know he would

be unable to join Aranzábal in the Ipurua directors' box as a last-minute trip to Abu Dhabi had come up.

Now, five months later, the pair can take in a match together as they sit side-by-side in the directors' box of the Santiago Bernabéu, one of world football's most storied venues. It is a moment beyond comprehension for Aranzábal who, just two seasons previously, had become used to watching Eibar line up in stadiums that couldn't even boast four stands, never mind a directors' box. Now his club visits a stadium with a capacity more than three times the population of Eibar, one of 12 La Liga stadiums with more seats than Eibar has residents.

Over to Aranzábal's right, 2,000 of that 27,000 population have also made the trip to the iconic stadium of the European champions and they could not care less that they are missing out on the luxury of lunch in the directors' box. For them, a plastic seat in the Bernabéu is luxury enough and this big day out is to be enjoyed.

Unai Eraso, president of the *Peña Armera Bitter De Madrid* fan group, is certainly enjoying this special day in the city he now calls home. I ask Unai if the midweek win over Málaga has allowed him and his fellow supporters to enjoy this match more than they would have had the winless run continued. "Absolutely!" he exclaims. "The truth is that we had gone a lot of games without winning, since 10th January, so thanks to the victory against Málaga we can breathe a little bit more easily. So we can go into this one at the Bernabéu more relaxed because if we hadn't won [against Málaga] then taking away a positive result would have become more of a priority."

Picking up a point today would still, obviously, be useful for Eibar's ambitious hopes of survival, but Unai makes a good point. By taking care of business in midweek, it almost doesn't matter what the outcome is here today as a good time will be had by all regardless. From Unai's point of view, it would simply make his day if he could "at least celebrate a goal".

To win a point or even score a goal will be difficult, however. Real Madrid, with one eye on a midweek Champions League quarter-final with city rivals Atlético Madrid, will rest several players while others are missing through injury or suspension, but they still boast plenty of weapons. It is certainly not 'a B team' as it was put to Garitano; a certain Cristiano Ronaldo starts – one player who is interestingly not missing out through suspension.

Ronaldo – unfairly – received a yellow card in Real's previous outing at Rayo Vallecano to take his yellow cards tally to five for the season and earn him a one-match suspension which, considering Eibar is bringing the weakest squad in the league to the Bernabéu, might have been a blessing in disguise. It would have allowed Ronaldo to wipe his slate clean of yellow cards and avoid a suspension over the course of the season's run-in when matches against the likes of Valencia, Celta de Vigo and Sevilla would surely call for his services even more. Real Madrid appealed – successfully – to have Ronaldo's yellow card overturned, perhaps the highest accolade bestowed upon Eibar by the European champions. That the giants of Spanish football consider the challenge posed by the visit of Eibar worthy enough to risk their *Ballon d'Or* winner's services for later in the season is high praise for the efforts of Garitano's team so far this season.

Any satisfaction from the gesture is quickly wiped from the faces of the Eibar coaching staff as Ronaldo puts Real Madrid ahead in the 21st minute. It may have been inevitable that fate would have Ronaldo score, having been afforded the chance to play after all, but the manner of his goal is certainly unexpected.

It is from a theatrically delayed direct free kick that Ronaldo scores, which may sound like a familiar story to those who only see Ronaldo through highlight reels or Vine clips, but – and this may appear blasphemous – Ronaldo is actually really terrible at free kicks. It puzzles me sometimes just why Real Madrid keep allowing him to grab hold of the ball, place it down, step back like Jonny Wilkinson and then hoof the ball just as high every time they win a free kick near the opposition penalty area. Well, not every time, but for the last 56 times! Yes, Ronaldo has not converted any of his last 56 direct free kicks, but he does so now and, once again, it is not a good strike by any means. Irureta has absolutely no clue where the ball is heading as it skims the hair of those in the wall on its way towards him and, stupefied as if he were searching for the football in a house of mirrors, he falls out of the way allowing the ball to bounce through the centre of the goal frame.

If this goal is thanks to a stroke of luck, then it is a deserved stroke of luck. Just moments previously the hosts appeared to be taking the lead, only for Isco's long-range strike to hit the right upright before rolling perfectly straight along the white line like a bowling ball on course for a strike. The only strike, though, was off the left upright and back towards an offside Chicharito.

Just over ten minutes after Ronaldo's strike, Chicharito does get his goal as he hops up to head a cross into the far corner, like a snooker player slicing the ball masterfully into the corner diagonally opposite.

Only half an hour is gone and Eibar are not only being lectured in how to play football, but there is a fear they could be Hannibal Lecter-ed if Real Madrid keep up this pace of scoring. A fine low effort from Ronaldo heightens that fear, but Eibar do manage to hold on and arrive in the dressing rooms buried, but not quite dead, at the break. Up in the heavens of the Bernabéu the Eibar support show few signs of concern; half of them are content with a defeat but a good day out and half are convinced their team can mount a remarkable comeback.

Unai is among the latter group and the optimism is justified as Eibar play some clever football in the second half.

Although Real Madrid again set up camp right around that 18-by-44-yard rectangle, their banal pass-it-around-until-the-door-opens style is proving ineffective as Eibar's defence stifle the home side's attack and even manage to break on the counter a couple of times. That one glorious chance the *azulgrana* fans have been calling out for to score Eibar's first-ever Bernabéu goal falls to the feet of Piovaccari, but despite the pass begging to be sent on its way to the back of the net, Piovaccari's feet have other ideas and the Italian trips at exactly the wrong moment, at *the* moment. There is still time for one more chance, but it falls to Real Madrid's Jesé, who bursts past Eibar's captain Txema Añibarro before whipping the ball into the opposite bottom corner.

That goal wraps up proceedings here at the Bernabéu and it appears everyone is heading home happy. The home fans have enjoyed a comfortable victory, the away fans have enjoyed a great day out, and Adolfo – president of the *Peña Madridista De Eibar*, a Real Madrid fan group based in Eibar, and also a member of *Eskozia La Brava* – has certainly had a cauldron of both sets of joyous emotions swirling around his head.

"We had fun, there were no problems and the home fans showed their support to us," Unai tells me after the match. "In the second half I think we were better with the ball than Real Madrid and the second half was much more even," he adds – and he has a point. Still, as Unai had mentioned earlier, this match was able to be enjoyed because of the hard work done a few nights previously against Málaga. It is not at the Bernabéu that Eibar's season will be defined, even if the memories of this unbelievable campaign will focus on such glamour away trips. Today's match merely decorated this season in the *Primera*.

Sunday, 19th April 2015. Ipurua Stadium, Eibar.
Is he pointing for a goal kick? A free kick for Eibar? Surely not a penalty? Nightmare! He's given a penalty…

Here we are watching Celta de Vigo given a penalty for a comical dive from Joaquín Larrivey; he literally tripped over the turf before rolling around on the ground, claiming a spot kick and sticking a middle finger up at sportsmanship in the process. Most insultingly of all for Eibar, it wasn't even a 'good' dive. In fact, this was one of the worst dives you'll ever see – quite a statement considering fans of Spanish football in 2015 see plenty. But wait. Has the referee changed his mind?

Yes! After consulting with his linesman – who was not so easily duped – the referee has actually changed his mind and instead books the deceitful Larrivey. Now you don't see that every day. Nevertheless, as we all know, lighting doesn't strike twice and just 17 minutes later the referee gives another penalty to Vigo and on this occasion the decision does stand for a coming together between Santi Mina and Dídac Vilá. Despite the numerous *Eskozia La Brava* fans stretching blue and claret scarves in his face, Nolito slots the ball into the bottom right corner to make the score 1-0.

Not long afterwards, the half-time whistle arrives. With it, a stramash breaks out as Arruabarrena, today's captain in the absence of Añibarro, has some words with Gustavo Cabral and is rewarded with a headbutt. His Eibar team-mates immediately swarm the Argentine centre-back and, after some handbags, coaches from both teams rush on to eject their players and avoid any punishments. It eventually attracts the attention of referee Carlos Velasco Carballo, who initially appears more interested in his half-time snack, but the official fails to dish out any yellow or red cards and both Cabral and Arruabarrena return after the break. Cabral gestures to Arruabarrena that he's crazy, to which the Eibar striker clearly mouths, "*Sí, ya verás.*" "Yes, you'll soon find that out."

Not all 22 players return for the second half. Garitano makes two half-time substitutions, hooking Ander Capa and Javi Lara for the more attacking Manu del Moral and Federico Piovaccari, with the volcanic Italian telling Arruabarrena to let him know if he receives any more trouble from the feisty Vigo defenders.

The two changes improve Eibar's play, but the fundamental problem of this performance remains: Eibar keep losing the ball in dangerous areas. They are tapping the ball to each other so timidly, as if throwing an egg or priceless vase to one another. Vigo's players, time and time again, are able to arrive to the ball first. While Vigo would complete 551 – which is 86% – of their passes by the end of the 90 minutes, Eibar would complete just 61% of their 247 attempted passes. Although telling, what it doesn't reveal – proving stats often fail to tell the whole, or a particularly useful, story – is that so many of Eibar's misplaced passes have been in their own half. Losing the ball at the other end of the pitch is certainly disappointing yet never immediately dangerous, whereas consistently losing the ball just metres outside your own box is suicidal in La Liga – as I'm sure you hardly need to be told. Were it not for some fine Irureta saves and sheer wastefulness from Larrivey, Nolito and Orellana then Vigo would be out of sight.

They aren't and Eibar are still just one goal away from what would be a vital league point. Everything is thrown at Vigo, with Dejan Lekić reinforcing the strikeforce further. Manu del Moral and Saúl Berjón both have shots saved before Eibar's best chance of the match falls to Dídac Vilá with just four minutes to go. From just outside the box, the defender thumps a strike towards the far top corner, only for it to bruise the crossbar rather than the net. That was Eibar's chance.

Tonight is not their night. They'd better hope next Sunday goes their way, though. It's a big one.

Sunday, 26th April 2015. Mediterranean Games Stadium, Almería.

"Get the ball in the corner Eibar!" shouts one of the travelling support. This is perhaps the biggest game of Eibar's season so far, with 18th-place Almería just three points – or six if you assume they are to be deducted three points as punishment for a late transfer payment to Danish club Aalborg – behind Eibar in the table. Whether the gap is three or six, what is undeniable is that Almería are too close for comfort and this is a must-win match or, at least, a must-not-lose.

So with the scoreboard reading 2-0 as the five minutes of injury time begin, and with our Eibar fan willing their players to protect the score by nursing the ball by the opposition's corner flag, things must surely be going well for Garitano's team?

Wrong. This match has been a disaster so far and this must-not-lose match has now become a must-not-lose-our-head-to-head-advantage final five minutes.

First, a bit of context. The Spanish league rules mean should two teams finish a season level on points then it is not goal difference which is the deciding factor, but the head-to-head aggregate score – not including the away goals rule – between the two teams, as if they had competed over two legs in a cup competition. It is, quite frankly, a terrible rule. It encourages 'smaller' teams to field weakened starting XIs against the likes of Barcelona and Real Madrid because the managers expect to lose these games anyway and in the knowledge their team doesn't even gain much consolation from keeping the score down and their goal difference up, they might as well focus on the following fixture. Granada did exactly this when sending out a weakened XI against Real Madrid in order to rest players ahead of a home game with Celta de Vigo. Granada lost in the Bernabéu 9-1, but for them the result was no different to losing 2-1 since they are hardly likely to ever need a head-to-head advantage over the Madrid side. Were goal difference to take precedence, though, then it would have been in Granada's interest to keep the score down and all neutrals would have enjoyed a more competitive game – even if five-goal Cristiano Ronaldo might not have. My other grievance with this rule is that it is difficult to simulate the result of a two-legged cup tie from two individual league games, also promoting some strange incentives. As it is right now here in Andalusia.

Eibar do not, in the end, take on the advice of our friend in the stands, but they really should. Having won the first league match with Almería – or the first 'leg' – by a 5-2 scoreline, Eibar's head-to-head advantage over them looked safe at the beginning of this fixture. They did not even expect to lose. Now they find themselves 2-0 down and with Almería hungry for, and looking likely to get, further goals – though it is doubtable whether all 11 Almería players are even aware of the head-to-head significance – the best thing for Eibar's fleeting survival chances would be to take the ball down to the opposition's corner flag, waste some time and at least escape with the consolation of the head-to-head record remaining intact now that securing any league points seems unlikely.

Is this what football has come to? Where protecting a two-goal disadvantage in a vital relegation six-pointer is the incentive? Apparently so.

Despite Eibar's best efforts to keep pushing for the goal that would make the match 2-1, Garitano's team fails to find it and the final whistle eventually rings out after what has been a terrible 90 minutes for Eibar.

It didn't take long for Eibar to fall behind in this most important of matches, with an eighth-minute counter attack from an Eibar corner setting Thievy up to score. Eibar did develop some opportunities in the second half, but none found the net. Borja Fernández's long-range effort whistled past the post and on a less windy afternoon might have whistled a different tune, while Manu del Moral was the quarterback in the middle of a three versus two counter attack but, unable to decide whether to pass left or right, he kept hold of the ball for too long and was stripped of possession as his team-mates ran into the space where they should already have been receiving the pass.

The wastefulness would prove costly when Almería's on-loan Arsenal winger Wellington Silva won a penalty from Vilà. There was contact and it probably was a foul, but the dive was embarrassing for Silva who flipped over like a pancake upon feeling the slight tap on his boot. More embarrassing was the 2-0 scoreline for Eibar as the match was beginning to slip away from them.

Survival is also now beginning to slip away and, although Eibar would hold on to their head-to-head record, the position does not look good after the final whistle pierces the ears around the Mediterranean Games Stadium here in Almería. Once again Eibar fall to a direct rival and from the 14 matches in this second *vuelta*, the Basques have collected just four points and scored just four goals.

From the outside, it may appear as if Eibar is quickly drifting into mediocrity. Inside, though, nobody would question Eibar's work ethic; the team has consistently put in 100% effort over the course of this bad run even if, too often, the team has been bullied by opposition defences that little bit more street-wise to the workings of the *Primera*. Downstairs in the press room, however, the tide might be about to turn as manager Gaizka Garitano speaks after this latest defeat and what he says – or, rather, what he doesn't say – will send a powerful message to his dressing room.

Garitano, with his eight Basque surnames, is as Basque as bad weather. So having been asked the first question of his post-match press conference in the Basque language *euskara* by a Basque journalist from Basque TV channel *Euskal Telebista*, this Basque manager of this Basque football club replies in Basque. Obviously.

This does not make too much sense to one particular local journalist who interrupts Garitano to accuse him of rudeness for speaking his mother tongue, to which the po-faced Garitano gives a stare so intense you'd think his eyes were painted on as simultaneously the words 'pot', 'kettle' and 'black' undoubtedly pop into his head. Probably in *euskara*.

Our rude friend eventually finishes his narrow-minded point and sits down. It may be the case he doesn't understand how such press conferences work – ironically, unlike Garitano, who has a degree in journalism – but the press officer explains the chance to ask questions in *castellano* Spanish will follow and Garitano will have no problem in answering them. Although a staunch supporter of Basque independence and a speaker of *euskara* at home, Garitano always answers in whatever language he is questioned in with pleasure, whether *castellano*, *euskara* or even, on occasion, English.

That the protocol has now been made clear makes it even more surprising that the grumblings continue and a second journalist joins in. Garitano perseveres in *euskara* in an attempt to complete his first answer, but with the muttering in the background growing louder he stops mid-sentence. "*¿Pasa algo?*" he snipes. "*¿Pasa algo o qué?*" He has now switched to *castellano* and so the journalist is fully aware of what Garitano is saying: "Is there a problem? Is there a problem, or what?"

At this point the press officer Juanjo Moreno begins to lose the plot with his local journalists and defends Garitano's right to use one of Spain's five official languages, scolding the journalist – for which Eibar would thank his "excellent behaviour" in an official statement the following day – and reminding them of the situation when, for example, Barcelona visit. "We've been in the *Primera* six years," Moreno laments, "and when Barcelona visit they answer questions first in Catalan and then in Spanish." By the time he has finished, Garitano is gone. He is no longer going to indulge these journalists in this political sparring and without saying a word – in any language – he walks out the room.

The Eibar players, meanwhile, are getting ready for the long journey home but will soon hear about this incident, as will the rest of Spain for the next 24 hours as a maelstrom of a debate ensues. Although most will back Garitano there are still some who criticise the Eibar manager for answering in the language in which he was asked, such as the ever-diplomatic *Marca* which would claim he "lacked common sense."

Garitano may only have been able to say a few words in this short press conference, but the message is loud and clear: Eibar are no longer here to be bullied and told what to do. The 'pushovers' from the Basque mountains are ready to fight back.

La Liga standings after *jornada* 33

#	Team	Matches Played	Matches Won	Matches Drawn	Matches Lost	Points
16	Eibar	33	8	7	18	31
17	Almería	33	8	7	18	31
18	Deportivo	33	6	11	16	29
19	Granada	33	4	13	16	25
20	Córdoba	33	3	11	19	20

8

Ánimo

"Eskozia La Brava's only objective is to encourage and to protect Eibar wherever they play, without getting politics involved."

Joseba Combarro

Saturday, 14th June 1986. El Vivero Stadium, Badajoz.
It all began during the play-offs of the 1982/83 season, 'it' being Eibar's famous *ánimo*, its famous support.

The trip to the play-offs for promotion from the *Tercera* division to the *Segunda B* was one of several doomed play-off campaigns at the beginning of the 1980s. It was not one of the better periods in Eibar's history, neither for the town nor for the football club. The steel-producing industry was declining and workers were migrating elsewhere to leave behind a shell of a town; from a peak population of 40,000 in the early 1970s, to 35,000 in the mid-1980s.

So often in declining former industrial towns football provides the escape from the struggle of everyday life, but not here in Eibar, where the biggest migration in the town's history had coincided with the football team's fall to the inglorious regional division. Promotion back to the *Tercera* was secured in 1979, but by now this is the fourth tier of Spanish football following the invention of the intermediary *Segunda B* division. Three attempts at promotion to this new division followed the jump up from the regionals, but without success, before the 1982/83 season once again presented Eibar with a chance to win promotion through the play-offs.

Sensing an opportunity for a restoration of the club's glory in that season, Roberto Vergara gathered with some fellow Eibar fans in Akats bar to form *La Bombonera*, Eibar's first group dedicated to the *ánimo* of the football team.

In some respects, the play-offs began with the last match of the 1982/83 league season. In this campaign, the top two teams would contest the play-offs for promotion with the league winner rewarded with an easier route. Fate would have it that the final game of the season saw the top two teams, Eibar and neighbouring Durango, square off for first position and the upper hand. More than ever, Eibar needed support if the team was going to win the derby with Durango away from home and so Vergara and his friends obliged, making the short trip.

Eibar's support might one day become synonymous with Scotland, but it was actually the English flag of Saint George – a gift from an English visitor to Bilbao during the 1982 World Cup – that accompanied *La Bombonera* that summer's afternoon. Unfortunately, the red and white of the flag, and the chanting of the fans, could not inspire Eibar to victory and the match in Durango was lost 4-2. Still, Eibar had a place in the play-offs, even if promotion would have to be achieved the hard way.

The first round certainly did prove difficult as Eibar were paired against a very strong Pontevedra team and *La Bombonera* made their second trip, this time to Galicia. Again, the travelling support witnessed a defeat, 2-0, and returned to Eibar knowing that some extra oomph would be needed from the home support in the second leg on 5th June. *La Bombonera* and the rest of Ipurua provided it and were rewarded with Eibar's first-ever competitive penalty shootout – now used to decide ties – after the game was levelled. *La Bombonera* was finally afforded the chance to celebrate as the hosts triumphed and the numbers of the fan group increased further.

Next up in the play-offs was Real Balompédica Linense and, having seen off the impressive Pontevedra, Eibar were expected to dispatch a team that few rated. Some of the newly-formed *La Bombonera* made the lengthy trip to Cádiz to *animar* and support their team, but Eibar fell to a 3-1 defeat and there was no repeat comeback in the Ipurua leg; a 1-1 draw was the best Eibar could come up with.

It was back to square one for the team, but not for *La Bombonera* which had grown in number and reputation and was more than ready to launch the support Eibar deserved for the 1983/84 campaign. Throughout the season, *La Bombonera* attended each home match, and many away, to roar Eibar to a consecutive second-place finish and another shot at promotion through the play-offs. Again, a trip to Galicia was made to face Pontevedra, but this time Eibar left 3-0 losers and were unable to level the tie at Ipurua the following week.

La Bombonera refused to give up and in the following season began work on their biggest gesture yet: a huge flag produced with the help of local business Alfa, who would sponsor the club for several years and even donate an air raid siren which now sounds after goals at Ipurua. The *peña* unveiled the flag ahead of yet another play-off match, after yet another second-place finish. This time the opponents were Valdepeñas and, after witnessing a 2-0 defeat away in Castile-La Mancha, *La Bombonera* showed off their flag and gave everything they could to support the team from the West Stand – which it had now very much claimed. The team won, but only 1-0. Another play-off failure was sealed.

That brings us to this 1985/86 season, one of a stronger Eibar and an equally more vocal *La Bombonera*. The *peña* has grown so large they now struggle to fit into Akats, the bar where it all began just three seasons earlier, and with Eibar's success on the field matching the *ánimo* off it, this has been one of the most enjoyable and vibrant campaigns Ipurua has witnessed for many years.

It is a campaign which brings us to this afternoon's match in Badajoz; once again it is a play-off but by departing from the norm and actually winning their group rather than finishing runners-up, Eibar have given themselves a much better chance than ever before. The expectation has been hovering around Ipurua for the last month of the season and, having secured top spot, Eibar faced their first play-off match of the season at home. It ended 1-1 against an unfancied Coria del Río side before an historic return fixture in Seville on 1st June. As the Spanish national team graced TV screens across the country with their 1-0 defeat to Brazil in the World Cup, thousands of miles away in Guadalajara, Mexico, *La Bombonera* filled one of two whole coaches – funded by a lottery organised by the *peña* – heading south to Seville for a Spanish fourth-tier play-off match. With their boisterous support Eibar won 2-1, setting up this play-off tie against Badajoz with promotion to the *Segunda B* the prize.

If two buses to Seville seemed like a mighty statement of the size of Eibar's support then the eight buses filled to come to Badajoz – on the border with Portugal and almost as far south as Seville – is extraordinary. Several hundred fans have made this 700-kilometre trip and intend to have a promotion party here in Extremadura. With the first leg having finished 2-0 in a fit-to-burst Ipurua, Eibar's chances are good – through the fact Badajoz had the best record of all *Tercera* teams this season is worth keeping in mind.

With an *azulgrana* party going on in the away stand drowning out a nervous home support, Eibar achieve the necessary result and a 1-1 draw is enough to turn the dial up a notch or four amongst their support. A naïve sending off for Badajoz's Morgado for kicking the ball at the linesman in protest at a decision helps Eibar's cause massively after he had levelled the scores at 1-1 and looked to build some momentum to overturn the deficit. With the result confirmed well before the 90 minutes are up, the final whistle only serves to amplify the noise and prolong *La Bombonera*'s flag-waving, scarf-stretching and drum-beating *fiesta*.

It is a party which does not stay in Badajoz for long; the eight coaches quickly refill and head back north to a party at Ipurua. Eibar is a town which understands the value supporters add to the team and their *ánimo* is considered as impressive as the goals on the pitch. Eventually, several hours later, the buses roll into town and the bars which have stayed open around Ipurua fill even further. *La Bombonera* and Roberto Vergara have achieved something truly special: they have brought *ánimo* to Eibar.

A further promotion in just two years' time is unlikely but – as we know from previous chapters – will happen. Promotion to the *Primera* in just under 30 years' time is unthinkable, but – as we're again all too aware – it does happen. By that point it will be *Eskozia La Brava* taking responsibility for Ipurua's *ánimo* and Vergara and co will have retired from following Eibar to far-flung places such as Badajoz. Instead, Vergara will watch the matches from Ipurua and from La Terraza, the bar he'll own round the corner from the stadium and to which fans will often pop out at half-time for a quick beer and chat with the legend who gave birth to Eibar's famous support.

Vergara would never completely retire from co-ordinating Eibar's support, however. Remember the story about Eibar cheekily taking Barcelona's unused confetti? It is Vergara who would phone up the offices of the Camp Nou.

Tuesday, 12th October 2010. Hampden Park, Glasgow.

On the walk up towards Scotland's national stadium from the Mount Florida train station there is never any shortage of tartan merchandise, consisting of flags, 'See You Jimmy' hats and a rich variety of scarves. There are 'Bonnie Scotland' scarves, 'Flower of Scotland' scarves, plain and simple 'Scotland' scarves and there are always plenty of – unless England is the opponent – half-and-half friendship scarves.

Another popular scarf has the message 'Scotland the Brave', but for one group of supporters making their way to the stadium for tonight's Euro 2012 qualifier against newly-crowned world champions Spain there is no need to buy this scarf. They already have their 'Scotland the Brave' scarves, even if the message is written in Basque.

This is not *Eskozia La Brava*'s first trip to Scotland. Previous visits have taken in matches at Hibernian's Easter Road and Hearts' Tynecastle Stadium in Edinburgh, while here in Glasgow the group has seen Scottish league fixtures at Celtic Park and Rangers' Ibrox Stadium – although the glamour of my own team St Mirren has yet to attract a visit!

Eskozia La Brava may have become an official fan group of Eibar in 2001, but the link with Scotland stretches as far back as the 1980s and 1990s when Eibar's main *peña* was still *La Bombonera* and a fondness for Scottish whisky was established. The old guard would meet in the bars around Ipurua, places that quickly learned as well as stocking plenty of *Patxaran* – a popular Basque sloe-flavoured liqueur – they would need a few bottles of whisky to meet the demand for a 'wee dram' before and after matches. A tradition developed around February and March time of watching the Five Nations – as it was at the time – rugby tournament, partly influenced by the fact there was little else on the TV worth watching before the days of 24/7 football.

With no real affiliation to any of the five competing nations, the locals sided with the Scots for the very simple reason the alcohol in their glasses didn't hail from France, England, Ireland or Wales. If they were drinking Scottish whisky, then why not back the whisky-supplying Scots as a thank you?

The backing of the Blues may have started out for such a trivial reason, but *La Bombonera* immediately fell in love with the Scottish support for their rugby team. The vibrant colours, constant singing and never-say-die attitude of the supporters emanated through the TV screens and before long the locals were aspiring to bring this 'Braveheart' support to Ipurua. That Scotland's rugby fans would never turn on their team, instead supporting them all the more when they were losing, was a novel concept to this group of Eibar fans back in Spain where 'supporters' tend to turn on their team and whistle them when they fall behind rather than, you know, actually support them.

As such, Saltires and the Lion Rampant found a home in Ipurua throughout the 1990s as *La Bombonera* supported Eibar through season after season in the *Segunda*. Towards the end of the decade, the fan group was in transition as the old guard which had been there that sunny Badajoz afternoon in 1986 found themselves less and less able to attend matches as the responsibilities of life caught up with them. In this time of transition, the Scottish-themed support was strengthened further and the name of *Eskozia La Brava* was first mentioned as a potential fan group in its own right.

Current *Eskozia La Brava* president Joseba Combarro explains: "*Eskozia La Brava* picked up the baton as the principal fan club and support in Ipurua when *La Bombonera* wound down." It was in 2001, then, that *Eskozia La Brava* was given official status and became a unique fan group, breaking off peacefully with the old *La Bombonera*. Joseba is content: "The relationships with those who were members of *La Bombonera* are still really good."

It was in the same year that the fan group made its first trip to Scotland to take in some live – now Six Nations – rugby and experience Scotland's support first-hand at Edinburgh's Murrayfield Stadium. The trip was a huge success and a range of Scottish souvenirs, from kilts to 'See You Jimmy' hats, and whisky to Irn Bru, were brought back to the Basque Country, kick-starting the era of *Eskozia La Brava* which just over a decade later would celebrate an historic *ascenso* to La Liga by hiring a bagpiper for the promotion party.

Various trips to *Eskozia La Brava*'s 'fatherland' would take place throughout the noughties, bringing us to this 2010 trip to see world champions Spain play their first match in Scotland since 1984. It is an occasion that *Eskozia La Brava* wouldn't miss for the world, particularly with Eibar legends Xabi Alonso and David Silva in the starting XI. If there was one international match to define everything which *Eskozia La Brava* represents, it is probably this one.

The result could hardly be more perfect as well. Spain win the match, of course, but Craig Levein's Scotland side – the real pioneers of the 4-6-0 no-striker tactic Spain would use in later years – are far from embarrassed by the result and Scotland almost upset the world champions before losing out 3-2 in the end. A David Villa penalty gives Spain the lead just ahead of half-time before Andrés Iniesta doubles the advantage ten minutes into the second half, finishing off a move started by a typical Xabi Alonso defence-splitting pass.

The match is far from over and *Eskozia La Brava* get to experience the famous 'Hampden roar' first-hand as the Scottish support continue to back their side, with their support paying off just two minutes later. A Steven Naismith header past Iker Casillas sends Hampden wild, a noise matched by the equaliser – a fortunate Gerard Piqué own goal – less than ten minutes further into the second half. By this point Hampden Park is bouncing and the guests from Eibar are awestruck.

Ten minutes from time Hampden Park does simmer down a little when Basque striker Fernando Llorente meets a cross just yards from goal and duly dispatches the ball into the net. Again Hampden screams for an equaliser and, although it never arrives, the *Eskozia La Brava* representation is mightily impressed. The only thing that could have made this match even more memorable would have been a goal from one of their former stars. David Silva tried his hardest to oblige, twice being denied by excellent goalkeeping from Scotland's Allan McGregor.

As Hampden Park pours out into Glasgow's southside, Joseba and his *azulgrana*-clad friends make their way into the city centre festooned in flags and end up at their Glasgow 'local', The Horseshoe Bar near the main train station. This pub – with its 104 feet-long bar top is the longest bar in Europe and would struggle to fit into any building in Eibar – has become a favourite watering hole on the various *Eskozia La Brava* expeditions over the years and on this night the Scottish-named Spanish *peña* is, unsurprisingly, the talk of the bar after tonight's match.

It may be the case that *Eskozia La Brava* are only famous here in Glasgow tonight for their name and their Scottish links, but it is their famous support of SD Eibar which truly defines this *peña* back home.

ÁNIMO

Sunday, 24th August 2014. Xepe's Balcony, Eibar.
"*¡Que bote! ¡Que bote! ¡Que bote Ipurua!*"
"Get jumping! Get jumping! Get jumping Ipurua!"

That is the chant Xepe Gallastegui can hear from below his balcony because, unlike the majority of the seven billion people on this planet, Xepe's balcony overlooks a La Liga football stadium. It is "*un balcón de Primera*" he proudly announces. It is, "A first division balcony."

As Eibar plays its first-ever match in Spain's top tier just a few floors below, Xepe can enjoy the visit of Real Sociedad from the comfort of his own home – just as another 25 households, most of which have hung banners saying 'We see you in the *Primera* Eibar' from their balconies for this match, across the two towers of flats that stand tall over Ipurua Stadium. Over the course of the season goals from the likes of Cristiano Ronaldo, Lionel Messi and Mario Mandžukić would strike the back of the net in the closest thing Xepe has to a back garden. That must be amazing to see 19 La Liga games taking place just under your nose in a season, right?

Not necessarily so, says Xepe.

Besides the fact he actually thinks it would be cheaper purchasing a ticket than having to buy in all the wine, chorizo and cheeses he puts out for the friends who join him for matches on the balcony, it is the *ánimo* which makes Xepe long to be down there in the actual stadium amongst the noisy and most boisterous fan groups like *Eskozia La Brava*. Xepe still makes the odd trip downstairs when he can, as he did for many years as a player – he played in the first match *La Bombonera* attended in 1983 – before taking over as manager during the 1992/93 season and guiding the club to safety after a poor start had made relegation from the *Segunda* a real worry.

Now, just over 20 years later, Eibar is in the *Primera* and below Xepe's balcony the stadium really is jumping with anticipation for this match opposite Real Sociedad; a steady stream of fans has flocked towards Ipurua all afternoon with a childlike enthusiasm normally reserved for running downstairs on Christmas morning rather than for clicking through the turnstiles of a football ground. It's hardly surprising Ipurua is rocking given the magnitude of the occasion, combined with the reputation *Eskozia La Brava* has for *animando*, for motivating, the team through the sweet and sour travails of football – and they do so with a variety of songs set to tunes as foreign to football as 'Hakuna Matata' and 'Jingle Bells'. This is a fanbase which doesn't believe the highlight of a home match is a trip to the club megastore; the highlight is the chance to motivate their heroes. The players may have won promotion on the pitch, but the support of these fans from the stands indisputably played a role in winning promotion and making this red-letter day possible.

I spoke to Raúl Albentosa, who starts today's match in central defence as he did throughout the promotion-winning *Segunda* campaign, about just how important the encouragement from the fans at Ipurua was for the team. He told me, "This stadium breathes football and there is a great harmony between the players and those on the terraces because there the people come and they encourage you." Having asked him just how it feels to have the fans chanting his name, he replied: "The truth is that it gives you more confidence within yourself and more confidence for the match if the fans, rather than whistling the team even after going several games without winning, still go on supporting you. You don't find that at all clubs."

It is this idea of supporting the team despite the day's result, or the overall form of the team, that *Eskozia La Brava* identified in the Scottish support and imported to Ipurua. It is, therefore, worth keeping in mind that although Ipurua is jumping and singing and having a great time today, the support from the waving-their-shirts-as-if-they-were-pom-poms cheerleading *Eskozia La Brava* would have been exactly the same even in the *Segunda B*, as Xepe knows all too well from just a couple of season's previously.

This is exemplified through Blas, Eibar's superfan. He may be five-foot tall and you may need to cut him open and count the rings to find out his age, but Blas is among the liveliest of *Eskozia La Brava*'s committed membership. He is present at every game with his trusty blue and claret umbrella, decorated with various badges as well as more than a few holes from cigar embers. Vocal both in and around the stadium, Blas is an Eibar legend and will even become a national legend over the course of the season; his antics will regularly appear on the *Día Después* programme from *Canal+* which looks at the funnier moments from each *jornada*.

Even away from home Blas, *Eskozia La Brava* and their trusty banner will be present at every away game, albeit if only a few attend; the lowest ever away attendance was just three. They are "*pocos, pero locos*" according to Joseba. "Few, but crazy."

The Ipurua attendance today is certainly not low, but it is crazy. In the *Eskozia La Brava* section just behind the goal of the East Stand, though, the attendance is as high as it was throughout the rise up the divisions and, admirably, the club has rewarded that loyalty by freezing the cost of season tickets for these loyal fans who were season ticket holders before the 2012/13 campaign.

Of the 4,600 season ticket holders for the campaign in the *Primera*, a massive 2,500 fall into this category and are benefiting with season ticket prices set between €209 and €297, while the newer season ticket holders will pay between €265 and €396 – still lower than the cheapest season ticket this season of all 20 English Premier League clubs. The demand for these season tickets would surely be elastic anyway, but the club does not want to take advantage of its fans; these measures, insists Álex Aranzábal, are "intended to reward the faithfulness and loyalty of those who supported Eibar through difficult times." The club is ensuring promotion to the top flight is not a financial burden for those who have played their role in motivating the team towards this grand stage. Furthermore, discounts for the unemployed, disabled, retired and the young make watching Eibar affordable for all.

I should correct myself, of course, because there is no such thing as simply 'watching Eibar'. Rather, to attend a match at Ipurua is to participate. Even if no fan is allowed on the field – although, in actual fact, they normally are once the 90 minutes are up – the fans have a major role to play in motivating the players and making Ipurua a daunting place for opposition players to visit. There are few clubs where the fans feel as much a part of the club as the players, but Eibar is one of them.

That great relationship between fan and player might have its roots in the modest living standards of the members of Eibar's squad. Taking home the lowest – or close to it – salary permitted by the league, the Eibar players live a comfortable – but not excessively privileged – life and it is far easier for fans of Eibar to relate to their Saturday afternoon heroes than Real Madrid fans can relate to Cristiano Ronaldo.

Albentosa has noticed the relationship during his time living in Eibar and compares it to the relationship between family members. "You know practically everyone who works within the club, including the supporters who follow us and know us," the centre-back told me. "You know practically where they live, and they know where you live because it's a tiny town. You go out to buy some bread and everybody knows you and everybody greets you and asks you how you are. So Eibar is exactly that; a club *muy familiar*, like a family."

Albentosa, from Valencia, might be Eibar's adopted son, but there is a player in the team the fans have known for even longer, stretching back to school days. Jon Errasti was born in Eibar – the only member of the squad that was – and grew up here. So although the club's adopted players know most of the fans, Errasti even went to school with some of them and previously sat as one of them, having attended matches at Ipurua since his grandfather took him as a child.

Errasti and his grandfather were there in 2005 when Eibar so very nearly won promotion to the *Primera* division. Football legend Pelé tells an anecdote of the worst day in Brazil's footballing history – well, at least until a certain eight-goal semi-final in 2014 – when Uruguay pulled the upset of the century in defeating Brazil in Rio de Janeiro in the 1950 World Cup's final match. Nine-year-old Pelé and the young star's father were both in tears, the story goes, along with the rest of the nation, before Pelé dried his eyes and announced to his father, "One day, I'll win you the World Cup." The rest is history, and it makes for a beautiful story. While we do not know if the 17-year-old Errasti made a similar promise to his grandfather to avenge Eibar's failure in 2005 and one day win promotion, we do know his story had just as happy an ending as Pelé's.

That Errasti lived through the disappointment of Eibar's 2005 final-day failure as a fan makes this past success even more special, not just for Eibar's number eight but for the fans chanting his name from the terraces. To have 'one of their own' in the team means so much to the fan groups – and a quick unscientific tally of replica shirt names reveals he is a fan favourite, if not the fan favourite – such as *Eskozia La Brava*. The idea of Barcelona or Real Madrid fielding a player from amongst the 27,000 residents closest to their stadiums is sadly a rarity in this modern age.

I shouldn't really be surprised, therefore, to see Errasti chat to fans so casually and contently outside the bars around Ipurua after matches on his way home as he is really still a fan himself who, tangentially, happens to play for the team. Yet it is surprising to see a footballer break the pre-established paradigms of modern football and do exactly that, with his kitbag duly tucked underneath his arm. Even the manager Gaizka Garitano and president Álex Aranzábal know the majority of the fans by name, as well as a little about their profession or family circumstances. *Muy familiar* indeed.

Sunday, 30th November 2014. Manzanares River, Madrid.

There is a football match due to kick off at noon at the Vicente Calderón Stadium on the banks of Madrid's Manzanares River, yet there is little celebration, excitement or anticipation in the cold, wet and windy pre-match winter air. This is because the emergency services are currently fishing a body out of the capital city's river. It is because of football violence that 43-year-old father of two Francisco Javier Romero Taboada, known by friends as Jimmy, found himself in the freezing waters.

Jimmy arrived in the Spanish capital on a bus full of Deportivo La Coruña's left-wing ultras, the *Riazor Blues*, at around 8.30am before heading towards the stadium where the *Frente Atlético*, the right-wing ultra group of Atlético Madrid, awaited. According to the government delegate in Madrid, Cristina Cifuentes, this was a pre-arranged fight – organised through WhatsApp – between two *peñas* with a history of animosity that had festered in the 18 months since their respective clubs last faced each other on the pitch.

Remarkably – given the history of threats, insults and episodes of violence between these two sets of 'fans' – this match was declared as 'low risk', meaning fewer officers were deployed for the policing of the match and, as such, those that were deployed would not be present in the area until 10am, two hours before the kick-off. It's no coincidence, therefore, this fight was organised for an hour before and, sure enough, at 8.45am the first flares were set off while chairs, tables and metal bars were launched between the two groups. It was quickly clear that the *Riazor Blues* were outnumbered.

Jimmy was just one member of the *Riazor Blues* running for his life and had, inexplicably, found himself on the wrong side of the barrier by the river. There he was approached by a group of rival ultras who were certainly not looking to help him back over the barrier even if we cannot know or say for sure whether there was any actual push. No matter how it occurred, the tragedy is that Jimmy fell from the ledge and into the Manzanares River, where he would lie for more than 20 minutes.

By the time the emergency services arrive on the scene, and to the part of the river where Jimmy's 'clinically dead' body floats, it is already too late. It would not be until around 2pm that Jimmy would be officially pronounced dead at Madrid's Clínico San Carlos Hospital, but even as the emergency services pull him from the river there is little hope given the injuries to his head, the hypothermia suffered and the fact his heart had temporarily stopped.

Despite this harrowing incident, and the injuries suffered by a dozen more, the match would go ahead thanks to a shocking inability for the league's governing body to secure the Spanish Football Federation's permission to postpone it. It is a Sunday morning, remember, and despite four league fixtures being on today's schedule the Federation's phone is ringing out.

By the time Jimmy's death is confirmed, Atlético Madrid are 2-0 winners in a match nobody really cares about and which really should not have taken place. However, while the authorities acted too slowly, today, to postpone the match, their actions in the days ahead will affect all fans of football in Spain. Including those from up at Ipurua's East Stand…

To understand the actions of the authorities in response to this violent encounter between the *Frente Atlético* and the *Riazor Blues*, we must first explore the context of the rivalry between these two ultra groups. Given these two groups' ideological differences – the *Frente* borders on and often crosses the boundaries of fascism, while the *Riazor Blues* are about as left-wing as they come – these two groups were never going to have a friendly relationship, but what had been an indifferent relationship was first soured when the *Frente Atlético* held up a banner at a 2005 match telling their rivals: 'You are the shame of the [ultra] movement.'

This was in response to the *Blues*' supposed involvement in the death of Compostela fan Manuel Ríos Suárez in 2003 and the response of the Galician group was to bring their own banner to the return fixture at the Calderón later in the season which read: 'The ridiculous has a name: *Frente Atlético*.' The rivalry developed further still when, in September 2008, members of the *Frente Atlético* travelled north to Galicia to fight their counterparts, only to be stopped by the police just metres away from the bars where the *Riazor Blues* drink pre-match. Three years later, the *Blues* returned the favour and arrived at the surroundings of the Calderón in search of their enemies and were only stopped by police one street away from the stadium.

That such a – with hindsight – dangerous rivalry had been able to develop so rapidly through insults directed across the terraces would not be lost on the country's footballing authorities and within a fortnight new regulations would come into effect to punish chants which 'incite violence' or which 'contain offensive and/or intimidating messages'. While action is certainly required, punishing all offensive chants in football could be seen as both excessive and unenforceable.

As with all things related to La Liga, who better to speak to about these new regulations than Sid Lowe?

He explains: "My personal opinion with the reaction to Jimmy's death was that it was kind of inevitable, and a bit sad in a way, to see the reaction inevitably overstepping the mark. I think the first thing was that it was good it was taken seriously. It was good people said: 'Look, we cannot allow this kind of thing to happen.'"

I ask Sid for his thoughts on Javier Tebas's comment that, "We've got to eradicate all the ultras," to which he tells me: "My first response was: 'Alright, but before we do let's define "ultras" shall we?' There are ultras groups who don't do anything wrong, but consider themselves 'ultras', and are not. Before you start talking about eradicating groups you have to define what you mean. So let's decide what 'ultras' are first. Get rid of violent groups, but not necessarily 'ultra' groups."

Eskozia La Brava, as Eibar's principal fan group, would inevitably be tarred with the same brush as these violent groups to which Sid refers. The ever-helpful *Marca* would, in the aftermath of Jimmy's death, compile an infamous map of La Liga's 20 clubs and the main 'radical' group of each. Rather than simply state Eibar does not actually have a 'radical' fan group and risk disturbing the symmetry of the feature, *Marca* would list *Eskozia La Brava* as one such group, justifiably angering a great number of people at Ipurua, not least the *Eskozia La Brava* president Joseba who would tell me his exact feelings regarding the sullying of Eibar's name by the "shameless" folks at *Marca*.

"*Marca* equals terrorism," he tells me before backing it up. "As a result of these articles we have had many problems with security at away matches, with banners and scarves being banned. These articles only serve to create bad vibes and tension."

Like Joseba, the club itself would speak out against these accusations. An official statement would begin: "In response to information which has appeared today in relation to the fan club *Eskozia La Brava*, SD Eibar denies it is a so-called 'ultra' group, as they have demonstrated throughout their existence.

"The members of *Eskozia La Brava* have not been involved in any incident during the dozens of visits they have made in recent years to accompany the team, nor have they received any rival fans with hostility," the club would continue. "Atmospheric groups such as *Eskozia La Brava* ensure there is a good atmosphere around football, both in and around the stadium, with initiatives such as fraternisation and union with the fan groups of other football clubs."

Spanish football journalist Jason Pettigrove would also condemn the feature by *Marca*. "Those members had a right to be aggrieved," he would tell me. "Anyone who has followed Eibar's progress over the last 18 months knows nothing could be further from the truth. Vocal enthusiastic supporters? Absolutely. Ultras, by the understood definition of the same? Absolutely not. It's just a cheap shot by the newspaper to undermine the good work being done at the club."

Nobody who has visited Ipurua or welcomed *Eskozia La Brava* to their own city would reject Joseba, Jason or the club's defence of the un-menacing *peña* and it is a testament to the good behaviour of *Eskozia La Brava* and other fan groups that the club was even presented with the 2013/14 Liga Adelante Fair Play Award for its treatment of away fans and away players. The fan group is staunchly apolitical and, says Joseba, "*Eskozia La Brava*'s only objective is to encourage and to protect Eibar wherever they play, without getting politics involved. Politics should be left outside of football, it only creates problems between fan groups. Individually, yes [our members are political], but collectively we are not."

It is rare for a club's main fan group to be more politically impartial than the manager – Garitano explicitly supports Basque independence, for example – but, then again, we know by now Eibar is a rare club.

Despite being neither political nor violent, with the stricter stance of the authorities following the incident in Madrid and with the scaremongering of articles such as the aforementioned feature in *Marca*, even *Eskozia La Brava* would find it more difficult to follow their team. The club would even be charged €10,000 – later annulled – by the Anti-Violence Commission under the new regulations in relation to a song sung by *Eskozia La Brava* in their January match against Atlético Madrid, a song which essentially suggests that the Atlético manager's wife had cheated on him.

Such a charge against the club – as well as the incidences Joseba mentions of having banners and scarves confiscated – would prove that despite never labelling themselves as an 'ultra group', the simple fact, in some respects, *Eskozia La Brava* looks and feels like an ultra group would make supporting their team in this, their fairytale season in the *Primera*, more difficult. A true shame.

While the kind of hostility that was allowed to develop between the *Frente Atlético* and the *Riazor Blues* can never be permitted again, to remove all atmosphere from Spain's football stadiums is not the answer. If anything, Spanish football needs an injection of the kind of atmosphere *Eskozia La Brava* provide, not to suck it out completely with an intolerance of anything besides polite applause and the odd shout of 'well-played good Sir!'

Sid Lowe concludes his summary of the situation: "Groups like *Eskozia La Brava* are helping to make football worth going to. If they're going to start feeling themselves squeezed, it worries me."

Friday, 27th March 2015. Sacramento, California.

If *La Bombonera* were the pioneers of Ipurua's *ánimo*, and if *Eskozia La Brava* took the baton at the turn of the century and ran with it, then what is next for the support of SD Eibar?

Let's be clear: *Eskozia La Brava* is going nowhere and their numbers are increasing year after year, with a core group of teenagers ready to support Eibar religiously throughout the next decade until the time finally comes to leave that life behind them. Still, they could always use some help in promoting Eibar's cause, whether elsewhere in Ipurua, Spain or across the globe.

Unbeknownst to members of *Eskozia La Brava* this Friday evening, 9,000 kilometres away in Sacramento, California, an idea has just popped into John Sager's head.

John is a football fanatic, with a keen interest in the Russian and Serbian leagues as well as any underdog story. Having heard about Eibar's struggles in the summer of 2014, he immediately bought a share and now, having watched Eibar games where possible throughout the season, a tweet from the club's official Twitter account has caught his attention.

"Thinking about creating an SD Eibar official supporter group? Contact us at comunicacion@sdeibar.com and get free merchandising!" says the club's @sdeibar account. John may not have been thinking about forming a supporters' club or *peña* before tonight, but he is now considering the interest in Eibar across the USA and the 'need' for a fan group for Eibar fans across the pond.

While the juggernauts of the game will always attract the most interest in the States, there is a particular type of football fan, explains

John, which supports a team like Eibar. "In the USA, the English Premier League markets heavily and everyone supports Chelsea or Manchester United, or now even Manchester City. But there are a certain amount of football fans in the USA who believe there is more to the sport than raising revenue to sign the latest stars and market to the most fans. I believe Eibar have captured this ideal of something being greater than just hunting for trophies. Eibar have a spirit that cuts to the heart of football which makes the sport about something more than money."

Knowing he can count on the support of these like-minded 'soccer' fans – such as Henry Boguslavsky, who we encountered in the discussion of Eibar's share issue in the *Modelo* chapter – John decides to email the club and is put in contact with Eibar's communications director Arrate Fernández, whose enthusiasm for the idea surprises even John himself. The response from the club would be, according to John, "Beyond what I expected. But in retrospect the support from the club is not surprising. There is a reason why Eibar is a special club and has accomplished so much, and working with them in setting up the Eibar-USA *peña* has only reinforced that."

Within a month Eibar-USA would be more than just a thought in John's head; it would be reality and he would be sitting in the directors' box alongside Álex Aranzábal – and a certain Scottish manager of Real Sociedad whose ears perk up when he hears English being spoken – to take in Eibar's match against Celta de Vigo on 19th April.

John's experience would be unforgettable, further highlighting the hospitality of SD Eibar to all interested in the club, no matter where from. Following the 1-0 defeat, John would be presented with a signed 'PEÑA EIBAR USA' shirt on the pitch by Aranzábal himself as a new chapter in Eibar's overseas support begins with the birth of its first US fan group.

Other members of the fan group will make plans to visit in the next season following John's high praise of his experience in the Basque town, a scenario this tiny football club, even ignored by most of Spain in the past, could never have dreamed of before their La Liga adventure. It truly is a fantastic leap forward for the already-dedicated support of the club. In the meantime, the signed Eibar shirt will hang in De Vere's Irish Pub in Sacramento as John and co support Eibar through their final matches of the 2014/15 season.

While John's Eibar-USA fan group may be the first American *peña* of Eibar, it is not the only other *peña* joining *Eskozia La Brava* in backing the *armeros*. Eibar-USA is the eighth official fan group of the club and only the second overseas – the other being based in Cyprus. Returning to the question of who can help *Eskozia La Brava* back in Spain, there are five other official groups – three based in Eibar, one in San Sebastián and one in Madrid – already doing exactly that. The *Manix Mandiola* group has been roaring alongside *Eskozia La Brava* since 2007, while *Urko Taldea* – the San Sebastián group – and *Gatzato* were both founded as recently as 2015. In 2013, the *Peña Errasti* formed and has sat above the tunnel of Ipurua's Main Stand ever since.

The Madrid-based group is the increasingly famous *Peña Armera Bitter De Madrid*, which is presided by Unai Eraso, who we've already heard from over the course of the book. The *Bitter* fan group was founded with Eibar in the *Segunda B* on 13th April 2010 when six fans of Eibar met up in the capital city to form a group for exiles in the city. Present to found the *peña* that Tuesday night in 2010 was Unai, Jose Antonio Barberá, Lander Abarrategui, Jon Treviño, Aitor Arana and – the only one in a suit and not an Eibar shirt – president Álex Aranzábal.

Although based in the capital city, the members of this fan group have travelled to game after game, making plenty of pilgrimages to Ipurua, as well as away grounds closer to their Madrid headquarters. In doing so, a great relationship has been built up with *Eskozia La Brava*; there is no civil war between fans at this club, as there is at some others. Unai explains to me: "The largest *peña* is *Eskozia La Brava*, a charming set of fans with whom we have an excellent relationship. I know the president Joseba Combarro very well and whenever both *peñas* are together at a game, we meet up, we see each other, we chat to each other, we sing together and we laugh together."

One such match was the visit to Celta de Vigo in November 2014. Although this was a game in Spain's top division, only 12 fans could make the trip – nine from *Eskozia La Brava* and three from *Bitter*. "We were together singing and supporting the team and Eibar won 1-0," Unai recalls. "It was a great occasion!"

It is clear, therefore, Eibar will always have support. *Eskozia La Brava* is, undeniably, the ringleader of the *ánimo* for which the club is famous, but the energy and passion for the club is enhanced further thanks to the more-than-capable sidekicks such as *Bitter*, Eibar-USA, the other official *peñas* and the unofficial ones like *Supporters Jo Ta Ke*, *Eibarpool Taldea* and *Amigos SD Eibar*.

As well as Eibar's own fans, the club can count on support from other corners of the football family. Eibar is a kind of Disney protagonist; not even the most ill-hearted in football hope they fail. As one of football's rare breeds, a team respected by all, Eibar is publicly backed where other relegation candidates would not be. When was the last time the manager of Barcelona, for example, explicitly stated his preference for who he'd like to come out on top in the relegation battle? Exactly. Eibar is different.

I think a tweet from Levante fan Pål Ødegård summed this sentiment up perfectly during Eibar's poor run of form in the second *vuelta*:

"Eibar [are] on their way to their seventh straight loss. My team here is Levante, but you have to be a cold bastard to wish Eibar down."

That's exactly the point. Nobody hates Eibar. Not even their rivals. Eibar's *ánimo*, its support, is remarkable and has been since the 1980s, yet just as remarkable is there is nobody in football who actively opposes Eibar. '*Aupa Eibar!*' as they say.

9

A Fairytale Season: *Act 5*

"These are the most important matches in the history of Eibar."

Jon Errasti

Monday, 27th April 2015. Ipurua Stadium, Eibar.
As the nation focuses on Garitano's Almería press conference, the focus within Eibar itself is on the five cup finals which remain in the rest of the season. It is one of the most overused clichés in football management, up there with other staple lines such as 'only thinking about the next match' and everything seemingly taking place 'at the end of the day', but it is undeniable these five matches are as important as five finals for an Eibar side which has nosedived.

There is little time to rest following the massive blow of the defeat in the Mediterranean Games Stadium in Almería; just three days later is another Andalusian encounter – the visit of Sevilla to Ipurua on Wednesday evening. Matches will follow away to Valencia, at home to Espanyol and away to Getafe before finishing with a home tie against already-doomed Córdoba.

Much was made of the *'Tourmalet'* faced by Barcelona and Real Madrid, who over the season's final weekends would play the same teams just a few weeks apart.

From *El Clásico* on 22nd March, Barcelona would face Celta de Vigo, Almería, Sevilla, Valencia, Espanyol and Getafe in that very same order over their following six matches, the same run of fixtures with which Real Madrid would finish the season. The astute and eagle-eyed will have noticed, firstly, the patterns of the La Liga fixture generator and, secondly, that this *'Tourmalet'* is the same run of fixtures Eibar is currently in the middle of. If the media narrative that Barcelona and Real Madrid had 'cup final after cup final' is true, then this is just as appropriate for Eibar.

To have three home games in their last five fixtures is a gift for Eibar and the club is keen to make the most of it. This is why Javi Lara is sat here in the Ipurua press room with president Álex Aranzábal and marketing director Gema Baqué. Here they are presenting the campaign 'Ipurua 6,267'.

The campaign's objective is simple: to fill all 6,267 seats of the stadium for the final three home games. Not for the first time over the course of the season, Ipurua's capacity has risen, this time to the 6,267 total thanks to the opening of the western half of the new North Stand. The new stand, with the letters S, D and E spelt out with white seats for the TV cameras opposite has "great views and great seats", according to season ticket holder Andrés, who would sit there on Wednesday evening.

The club has worked the building of the new stand thus: after knocking down the whole of the previous North Stand – just five rows deep – a temporary stand was constructed on the eastern part of the stadium's northern end. This would allow work to begin on the western half of the permanent new North Stand, while season ticket holders would still have a place at that end of the ground. Once this permanent half of the stand had been constructed, the plan was to move fans from the temporary stand to the new permanent one and immediately take down the temporary stand to begin construction on its permanent replacement.

The plan has been amended, however, and the decision was taken to keep the temporary stand in place until the end of the season so Ipurua can enjoy the maximum capacity possible for the final three home games of the campaign; right now both the permanent western half of the North Stand and the temporary eastern half of the North Stand are in use.

In order to fill these extra seats, the club will sell tickets for the final three home matches through more vendors than ever before; bars across Eibar have been given tickets to sell as well, and ticket offices have been set up in Bilbao, San Sebastián and Vitoria-Gasteiz.

Throughout the launch of this campaign, Aranzábal expertly conveys both the gravity of the situation Eibar find themselves in, as well as a sense of optimism. While Eibar are looking very likely to go down, had you offered Eibar this position at the start of the season – or, imagine, two seasons ago – then there would have been only one answer. Yes!

"We are playing for more or less the same thing we played for at this time last year," explains Aranzábal. "Despite the downturn we are in at the moment, this time last year we would have signed up to be in this situation where we are not in the relegation zone, have a two-point margin and a reasonable fixture list."

How right he is. At the beginning of this season nobody gave Eibar a hope of avoiding relegation and although it is a very real possibility, the club has still not spent one single day in the relegation zone. All of this has been achieved, remember, with the league's most modest budget. Although it hurts to fall from being as high as eighth earlier in the season, Eibar could scarcely have demanded a better situation going into the final five matches.

Whether or not Eibar will still be outside of this tight relegation zone with three matches to go is another matter. Although Aranzábal points to Eibar's "reasonable" fixture list, the first two of these fixtures are the most difficult. First, soon-to-be Europa League winners Sevilla visit Ipurua, before Eibar travel to face Sevilla's rival for a Champions League spot, Valencia.

The trip to Valencia is essentially a write-off, but it is not impossible Eibar manage to pick up a point when Sevilla visit in two days' time. Sevilla have only won seven of 59 official matches in Gipuzkoa, even losing 1-0 the last time they visited Ipurua in January 2001 when the Andalusian giant spent a season in the purgatory of the *Segunda* division. Eibar managed a goalless draw at the Sánchez Pizjuán Stadium earlier in the season, the best possible result a team can expect there given that Sevilla haven't lost a home match for over a year.

Still, it will be a hugely challenging contest, hence this clarion call from the press room to fill Ipurua and give Gaizka Garitano's team as much backing as is possible. They are going to need it.

Wednesday, 29th April 2015. Ipurua Stadium, Eibar.

If the controversy of Gaizka Garitano's press conference hadn't died down on Monday, if anything it has escalated again now another match has arrived. Three days after *euskara*-gate, and with this blockbuster fixture at home to Sevilla, those at *Eskozia La Brava* have been busy preparing a banner in support of their manager and the right to speak the Basque language. They are not the only ones to condemn the actions of those couple of journalists in Almería; FC Barcelona sent an official letter to the club expressing their support and their hope that Eibar can stay in the division.

Almería, meanwhile, called the opposition to the speaking of *euskara* "regrettable", while seemingly the only person not wishing to dwell on the events further is Garitano himself. That said, *Eskozia La Brava* wish to show their support for him and do so by holding aloft a banner saying, '*Guk Euskaraz Gaizka Zergaitik Ez*', ahead of the match. While Sunday afternoon's journalists didn't think it possible for *euskara* to be translated, it actually – believe it or not – can be and translates to, 'We speak *euskara*, so why not Gaizka?' After folding away the banner in time for kick-off, another is hung right behind the goal in order to promote the official campaign for the right to speak Basque: *Euskaraz bizi nahi dut* – We want to live in Basque.

If *Eskozia La Brava* wanted their support for Garitano and the Basque language made public then they certainly get their wish when Sevilla's Carlos Bacca scores two goals in the first 15 minutes and encourages plenty of zooming in on both the ball nestled in the back of Xabi Irureta's net, and the banner just metres behind.

Unfortunately for the Eibar keeper, the blame can be pinned on him for both goals and the near sell-out Ipurua, which has been making an almighty buzz in the opening minutes, is stunned. The 'Ipurua 6,267' campaign has been able to achieve Ipurua's second largest crowd of the season – second only to the visit of Real Madrid, even outdoing the attendance of the visit of Barcelona – with 5,517 bums on seats, or at least jumping up and down above them. Considering this match is the least winnable of those remaining, and the fact it is being played midweek, that is a staggering number for a town of just 27,000 inhabitants. Imagine a full fifth of any other city wanting to come and support their team in a match always likely to end in defeat. Once again this town impresses.

Yet Irureta impresses nobody, as I was saying. For the first goal, he comes off his line towards a ball whipped in along the ground from midfield towards the centre of the box, but noticing Bacca arriving to meet the ball the Eibar keeper hesitates and it is all the time the Colombian needs to push the ball around Irureta and into the corner. Immediately the fans behind the goal begin to shout at their keeper, but it is not abuse they are dishing out. Rather, the *Eskozia La Brava* fans are desperately urging Irureta, their man, to pick himself up and regain his composure for the remaining 84 minutes of this match.

He doesn't.

In a scarily similar sequence of play just under ten minutes later, a ball comes into the penalty area and, although this time it is high from a free kick rather than low from open play, the outcome is the same. Irureta edges towards the ball then freezes on the spot. The ball ricochets off Irureta's knee – much to his surprise – and falls straight to Bacca, who simply does not miss these kinds of chances.

The game really should be over there and then, yet the crowd encourage Eibar to press on and it is the hosts looking more likely to net the game's third goal. Piovaccari is the centre-forward for the night and is doing an excellent job; he is winning fouls by putting his body on the line and sensibly committing them where necessary to stop Sevilla's chances of breaking on the counter. The Italian is quite clearly embracing the siege mentality and rhetoric of defiance that Garitano's press conference and the 'Ipurua 6,267' rallying cry have encouraged.

More than once Piovaccari manages to get his head on crosses into the box he has no right to reach, but his determination isn't accompanied by accuracy and he fails to hit the target with each attempt. Finally, however, his and Eibar's deserved breakthrough arrives. A corner in the fifth minute of the second half finds its way to Arruabarrena at the near post. The captain nudges the ball back towards the centre and Piovaccari is, of course, fighting to be in the right position and thus able to prod the ball over the line.

Gesturing for the crowd to get even louder, Piovaccari runs back to his own half and leads the Eibar push for an equaliser from the restart. The *azulgranas* take complete control and pin Sevilla back into their own area. Thanks to their pressure, Eibar manage to win a couple of corners around the hour mark yet despite trotting men up from the back, Manu del Moral – who plays against his parent club after Eibar paid the €50,000 *cláusula del miedo* at the last minute – overhits both of them. The second leads to a Sevilla counter attack in which Bacca turns provider with an assist for José Antonio Reyes, the former Arsenal man shooting down the Basque gunners' hopes of a comeback.

Sevilla force Irureta into a couple of comfortable saves before the match's end, but Eibar also keep pushing and cause more danger in the closing stages without finding a way through. This is hugely impressive from a team which has never looked capable of overturning a 2-0 deficit all season; while consistently competitive, any time Eibar have fallen more than one behind it has never been easy to envisage a comeback. Although no comeback was achieved tonight, it always seemed within the realms of possibility for Garitano's side to bring the score back to 2-2 or 3-3, even against such quality opposition.

Something has changed within this football team in that regard. Was it the extra home support, which Garitano post-match calls, "the best thing about this club?" Maybe. Was it the players sticking up for their manager? Perhaps. Was it a case of embracing 'squeaky bum time'? We shall soon find out.

Thursday, 30th April 2015. Los Cármenes Stadium, Granada.

How well Granada have done to come back into this match. Lose tonight and they would remain six points from safety with just four games left – two of them away and one at home to Atlético Madrid – yet Diego Mainz has just equalised against Espanyol with 15 minutes remaining.

Shortly afterwards, Granada's Insua breaks into the box from the left, but his shot is comfortably parried. Javier Marquez has a chance to strike from the rebound, but scuffs his shot miserably and is almost doubly punished when Caicedo breaks up the pitch for Espanyol, only to have his shot saved. This is a reminder of just how delicately balanced this result is for Granada, a team which needs to win but which simply cannot afford to lose.

Again, Granada have a chance to win this one, but Lass Bangoura's strike from the edge of the box bounces just wide. In a testament to how basketball game-esque this fixture is becoming, Espanyol march forward with Francisco Montañés finding space to shoot from inside the area. His shot, thankfully for Granada fans, is blocked by Cala. Unfortunately for Granada fans, the rebound falls straight back to the Espanyol striker whose volley whizzes past Roberto in the Granada goal. So Granada fall to yet another defeat and remain six points from safety. While still in with a chance of survival, the side from Andalusia will have to perform some mathematical gymnastics to escape relegation.

Behind them lie Córdoba. This is the one club with even less hope than Granada, especially after their 1-0 defeat away to relegation-escaping Levante on Tuesday night.

Wednesday also produced relegation battle storylines when, as well as Eibar's meeting with Sevilla, both Almería and Deportivo La Coruña were in action. The standings actually remained unchanged, with Almería unsurprisingly losing 3-0 when they visited the Bernabéu, and Deportivo travelling fruitlessly to the opposite corner of the country to lose 4-0 to the financially-troubled Elche.

From Córdoba's loss on Tuesday to Granada's loss this Thursday evening, all of this is good news for Eibar. One of the five rounds of cup finals has passed, but almost more important than Eibar's own result is that their relegation rivals have also lost. With each passing *jornada*, the column listing the number of games played becomes as important as the one listing the points totals. If Eibar can just hang on to their slim advantage for four more rounds of games then they'll be fine. That's easier said than done.

La Liga standings after *jornada* 34

#	Team	Matches Played	Matches Won	Matches Drawn	Matches Lost	Points
16	Eibar	34	8	7	19	31
17	Almería	34	8	7	19	31
18	Deportivo	34	6	11	17	29
19	Granada	34	4	13	17	25
20	Córdoba	34	3	11	20	20

Saturday, 2nd May 2015. Nuevo Arcángel Stadium, Córdoba.
This date may go down in sporting history as the day the world finally got to see Floyd Mayweather Jnr and Manny Pacquiao batter it out in a

boxing ring, yet in Spanish football it will go down as the day Córdoba were finally knocked out of La Liga.

It was a knockout blow indeed, with the Andalusians simply unable to put up a fight against the heavyweights of La Liga, Barcelona. It finished 8-0 at the Nuevo Arcángel Stadium, with it becoming more and more difficult to keep up with the score as Barcelona added goal after goal in the closing stages. For Luis Suárez it was a little easier to keep count of his tally; he simply had to look at the match ball he held in his hands after the game.

Córdoba had some counting to do themselves, but it was not quite as much fun for La Liga's bottom side. Now 11 points behind both Eibar and Almería with just three matches to play, Córdoba's first return to Spain's top flight since 1971/72 is to be a short one.

Saturday, 2nd May 2015. Riazor Stadium, A Coruña.

One of Eibar's other relegation rivals, Deportivo, fared slightly better in their Saturday match. They managed to pick up a league point at home to Villarreal. Although this was their 13th match without a win, defeat would have had Deportivo on the ropes with trips to San Mamés and the Camp Nou to come in the Galician side's final three matches.

Another positive for Deportivo is they deserved to win. Against a Villarreal side which has looked a shadow of its earlier season self in recent weeks, more clinical finishing would have seen Deportivo take a lead into the half-time break. Wastefulness allowed the second half to begin level and Villarreal quickly capitalised; Jaume Costa's deft chip over the keeper in the third minute of the second half gave the visitors the lead.

Deportivo were unlucky to be behind, but luck quickly repaid them; a Celso Borges shot two minutes later took a wicked deflection to fizzle into the back of the net. It finished 1-1, giving Deportivo a lifeline, if not a jump-start in the battle for survival. Eibar's match the following afternoon, and Almería's on the Monday evening, would determine just how much ground Deportivo gain or lose with this point.

Sunday, 3rd May 2015. Coliseum Alfonso Pérez, Madrid.

As mentioned last time we came across Granada, some mathematical gymnastics would be necessary for the Andalusian outfit to avoid the drop. Here in front of just 6,000 fans at Getafe's Coliseum Alfonso Pérez, Granada take one massive somersault up the league table under the stewardship of their third manager of the season, José Ramón Sandoval.

Granada's Youssef El Arabi scores his fifth and sixth goals of the season for the visitors, one from the penalty spot following a suspect handball decision and the second with a thumping header on the hour mark. Between his goals, Getafe had netted one of their own, but the 2-1 scoreline is how this one finishes. The heroics of Roberto in the Granada goal to halt Getafe's late quest for an equaliser are worthy of praise.

Still second bottom, but now within three points of Eibar and Almería, this has been a massive victory for Granada.

Sunday, 3rd May 2015. Mestalla Stadium, Valencia.

If Eibar have five cup finals to finish the season, then this 'final' at the Mestalla is comparable to one of those pre-season PR-for-sponsors tournaments like the Emirates or Audi Cup. Sure, it'd be nice if Eibar win today, or even earn a point, but anything taken away from their first-ever league visit to the Mestalla will be a bonus; Eibar are not supposed to win today's match.

Matches away to Valencia are about as difficult as they come in Spanish football, with only one Valencia defeat here all season – and that to a last-minute Barcelona winner. Since the turn of the year, Valencia have played ten matches at home and have won nine of them, drawing the other in the goalless derby with Villarreal. Should Eibar, the league's smallest team, come here and leave anything other than defeated, shockwaves would reverberate around the league.

For Eibar, the real tests are in the coming three matches. This is even more so a 'bonus' match after Deportivo again failed to pick up three points in last night's draw with Villarreal. Even if Eibar lose today as expected – Valencia are 1/5 odds-on favourites with most bookmakers – then they will still remain above the bottom three, which looked unlikely this time last week given the easier-looking fixture lists of Eibar's rivals.

Saúl Berjón and Derek Boateng come in for Lillo and Arruabarrena; the only two changes Garitano makes from the Sevilla game, after which he described Eibar's defending as "childish". Despite the unlikelihood of picking up a point, Garitano respects the sport by fielding a very strong, albeit defensive, starting XI.

Initially, Eibar appear unfazed by the 40,000 Champions League-hungry Valencians screaming down at the pitch. In fact, Eibar have the first great chance of the match when Piovaccari accelerates into the penalty area to somehow get his head to an Eneko Bóveda cross, an effort reminiscent of the Sevilla match as it just misses the target. Then, in the 25th minute, Valencia show us all how it's done. A cross into the box is met by Nicolás Otamendi, who goes one better than Piovaccari and bullets the ball past Irureta.

From that point onwards, Eibar's early audaciousness evaporates and the team offer up a visual dictionary definition of the word 'panic'. They struggle to string more than a couple of passes together whereas

Valencia keep the ball moving at all times, eventually working their way into shooting positions around the Eibar penalty area. They possess so much speed – not just physical pace, but quick thinking as well as movement – that Eibar simply cannot keep up.

Impressively, Garitano's side deny Valencia their second and head into the break just one goal down. The second half sees Valencia again dominate possession, but Eibar continue to defend well and Valencia's ownership of the ball comes to nothing.

Ten minutes into the second half, Manu del Moral nearly equalises. As he sends in a corner, he almost scores an Olympic goal, a goal that goes directly in from the corner kick. Diego Alves tips the spinning ball over the bar, not wanting to be the goalkeeper in the weekend's next viral YouTube video, and from the next corner Manu sends another dangerous ball into the area. This time Boateng reaches the ball before Alves, but his header flies over the crossbar.

Valencia quickly punish the wastefulness by doubling their lead two minutes later. A shot from Rodrigo De Paul rebounds off the crossbar and after ten seconds of pinball-like attempts to shoot, cross and clear the rebound, Dani Parejo picks up the ball at the edge of the area and sends it into the top corner, this effort missing the crossbar but still beyond the reach of Irureta. The keeper picks himself up and shares an embrace with the equally despairing Borja Fernández, an embrace which says; "Yup, this one's over."

Then 15 minutes later it really is over when a Dani Parejo free kick is curling towards the top corner. Irureta pushes it on to the post, but the rebound falls to Paco Alcácer who scores a goal as easy as the one he netted at Ipurua in December.

Not feeling hard done by, Eibar keep working hard and substitutes Arruabarrena and Ángel combine to grab a consolation goal with six minutes remaining.

Ángel, making his first start since surgery to remove his appendix, does ever so well to pluck the ball away from a poor André Gomes backpass before pushing the ball around Lucas Orban and racing around the other side of the defender to collect. He then delays his advance towards goal long enough for Arruabarrena to join him in attack and, after receiving a poked ball across the box from Ángel, Eibar's top scorer slots away his eighth of the season.

It is to be no more than a consolation goal for Eibar, but once again the team have lost just 3-1 to a Champions League-calibre club, as they had against Sevilla and Atlético Madrid before today. This match was never going to relegate Eibar, but a heavy loss could have sunk confidence levels perilously low. That never occurred and a disappointed but content Gaizka Garitano now looks forward rather than back.

A FAIRYTALE SEASON: ACT 5

Monday, 4th May 2015. Mediterranean Games Stadium, Almería.

At half-time, Almería's La Liga status is hanging by a thread. 2-0 down in this, their most winnable game before the season's end – with Málaga, Sevilla and Valencia to come – Almería realise they need to build a comeback in the second half against Celta de Vigo.

This is exactly what they do, even if they need a helping hand. Literally. A terrible parry from Sergio Álvarez falls straight to Thievy, who nets his second goal in as many games. Now just one behind, Almería can press on in search of the valuable point which would move them one position above Eibar in the league table. A disputable red card for Vigo's centre-back Cabral, who is judged to have fouled as the 'last man', even though Fontàs is as close to the fouled Thievy as Cabral is, helps their cause enormously.

Just over ten minutes after the expulsion, Almería get their equaliser. Jonathan Zongo finds himself in the right place at the right time to knock in a cross from the left flank.

Any hopes of pushing on for an unlikely comeback win are dashed when Mauro picks up a second yellow card for a needless shirt pull on Pablo Hernández and, with the teams once again equal in numbers, Vigo's quality shines through and it is the Galicians looking more likely to win the game in the closing stages, even hitting the post in the last minute.

A 2-2 draw is probably a fair result and it is one which Eibar will be content with as it keeps Almería well within reach at just one point ahead.

La Liga standings after *jornada* 35

#	Team	Matches Played	Matches Won	Matches Drawn	Matches Lost	Points
16	Almería	35	8	8	19	32
17	Eibar	35	8	7	20	31
18	Deportivo	35	6	12	17	30
19	Granada	35	5	13	17	28
20	Córdoba*	35	3	11	21	20

* Córdoba mathematically relegated.

Friday, 8th May 2015. Ipurua Stadium, Eibar.

These are the "most important matches in the history of Eibar" according to Jon Errasti, and the town seems to concur. A crowd of 5,648 have come to Ipurua tonight to back the team, even more than attended the Sevilla match two *jornadas* previously.

It is impossible to argue with Errasti's comment. These three matches against Espanyol, Getafe and Córdoba will – and it cannot be stressed enough – define the football club, which will either go down to the *Segunda* as expected or else strengthen its foundations as a La Liga team and consolidate its place among Spanish football's elite.

The way Eibar begin this match proves the players, many of whom will not even be here regardless of Eibar's fate, understand the magnitude of this relegation fight. They fly out of the traps and put the visiting Espanyol side – still harbouring hopes of Europa League qualification – under intense pressure with Piovaccari leading the line in front of Javi Lara, Saúl Berjón and Manu del Moral, who occupies the space where the suspended Mikel Arruabarrena would surely have played. Saúl Berjón has the first good chance.

Pleasantly surprised to find himself with so much space to shoot from the edge of the area he does exactly that, drawing a spectacular – perhaps exaggerated for the cameras – diving save from Casilla. Next, Javi Lara drives to the same vacated area around the box, but his shot sails into the partying crowd.

Then, disaster strikes. In this case, disaster being Espanyol captain Sergio García.

It is a very messy goal and one which puts Eibar in a messy situation. First, Christian Stuani rises to meet a Sergio García cross from the left and heads the ball towards the bottom corner where his effort is met by Xabi Irureta's stretching paw.

Next, Felipe Caicedo strikes the rebound off the post and the ball falls back to Sergio García in the same position on the left – he side-foots the ball into the far corner. It is a cheap goal for Eibar to concede, made even worse by the fact Borja Fernández injures himself in the process and must be replaced by Dejan Lekić, the Serbian striker with a grand total of zero goals from 20 appearances this season. Lekić hopes he can escape the shackles of the hopes and expectations all at the club have had for him.

Eibar continue to hustle for a goal, but find a now-galvanised Espanyol in their way and the visitors begin to dictate the pattern of play. The Barcelona-based side have a great opportunity to grab another and a surely insurmountable lead before the break when a counter attack culminates with a low Sergio García ball across the goalmouth. Stuani is only beaten to it by the acrobatic Eibar man Lillo.

The second half follows a familiar pattern; Eibar attack but find a strong Espanyol in their way ready to counter at the first hint of an error. Javi Lara comes close from a free kick won by Lekić, who is brought down by Espanyol keeper Casilla just outside the box. Five minutes later, another embarrassingly shambolic goalmouth scramble gifts Espanyol their not-unexpected second. Añibarro is unable to stretch quite enough to block yet another Sergio García incoming cross, which is allowed to reach Caicedo thanks to Dani García's slip, before the ball bobbles into the air and is gobbled up by Stuani who controls and shoots straight at Irureta. Unfortunately, it passes through the keeper's legs. To add insult to injury, as Irureta kicks the ball back towards the centre circle he skelps it off the face of his left-back Dídac Vilà.

Eibar are not dead yet and, backed by the roaring crowd which never ceases to lend its support, the team create several more opportunities in the last half hour. First, Piovaccari has the ball in the net but his rifled finish is chalked off for a dubious offside. The momentum this close call gives the team is so evident you have to wonder just how energised they might have been had the goal actually stood. Ángel is brought on straight after the Espanyol goal – another striker without a goal this season – and flourishes enough to dribble through the Espanyol defence as if it were fog on a couple of occasions, rewarded with a free kick and a corner for his endeavours.

Those set plays are not converted, though, and as the minutes tick down this exasperated Eibar side seem to know this is not going to be their night. They perhaps haven't deserved to win, but only a couple of unlucky and error-laden goalmouth scrambles have cost them which makes the 2-0 on the scoreboard as the full-time whistle blows a little harsh.

There are a few positives to take from this match; Garitano will be pleased by the fact Eibar did control the ball well, they made the opposition keeper sweat and the goals conceded were due to luck and individual errors rather than an underlying tactical flaw. It is not inconceivable everything will eventually click, but with only two matches remaining things need to start working for Eibar sooner rather than later.

Eskozia La Brava are certainly remaining positive and have stayed behind long after the rest of Ipurua has headed home and long after the synthesisers of the club hymn have ceased to vibrate over the sound system.

Half of them are bare-chested, enjoying the early summer evening, as they scream their support towards nobody in particular and announce just how proud they remain of their boys. Judging by the smiles on their faces, you would never know just how worried they are inside about the increasing prospect of relegation.

Saturday, 9th May 2015. Los Cármenes Stadium, Granada.
The business of cheering against your league rivals is a complex one. It is rarely 100% obvious which teams needs to be cheered against,

which teams are to be permitted the occasional win and which matches require to be drawn.

All season long, Córdoba has been one team which Eibar fans have rooted against. While few will admit to it, smiling whenever the team which won promotion via the *Segunda* play-offs falls to a defeat has been a guilty pleasure of Eibar fans these past few months. It's a no-brainer to assume that for Eibar to do the impossible and escape relegation, Córdoba is one team which has to take up one of the three relegation spots. But now that Córdoba have already secured a spot, what now?

Well, today Córdoba can finally count on some support from the Basque valleys, as Eibar look on in the hope the already-relegated Córdoba can stop Granada from taking three points which could put them right back on the road to safety.

In brief, Córdoba don't stop Granada. Eibar's relegation rivals do indeed take all three points and it is far too easy for them to win their second consecutive match for the first time this season. Córdoba, quite simply, look shattered after their 8-0 defeat to Barcelona confirmed their relegation one week previously and they trot around the field as if they have lead in their boots. The sending off of Iñigo López for a second bookable offence on the half-hour mark significantly increases the workload for each of Córdoba's remaining ten and, just before the chance of a rest arrives, Diego Mainz heads home from a deep free kick.

An inspired Granada return for the second half and look to make the most of the space left behind by López, eventually doing so in the winning of a penalty from which El Arabi seals the three points.

The roar from Los Cármenes can be heard 100 kilometres away in Almería, 700 kilometres away in Eibar and, loudest of all, 800 kilometres away in A Coruña where Deportivo fans are sweating ahead of their side's match in Bilbao.

Saturday, 9th May 2015. San Mamés, Bilbao.

We've already stopped off several times at San Mamés in this journey through Eibar's fairytale, yet this evening's action is perhaps the most significant of them all and there is not even one Eibar player on the pitch.

More important than the *Copa del Rey* visit en route to promotion from the *Segunda B,* more important than the draw in the league in September and more important than the Basque Country's friendly draw with Catalonia three months later; tonight, Deportivo's visit to San Mamés could be season-defining for Eibar.

Even a draw for the Galicians would be enough to move ahead of Eibar, condemning them to the relegation zone in the process due to the head-to-head rule and Deportivo's 1-0 and 2-0 victories. Deportivo have been Eibar's bogey team this campaign and it could yet come back to haunt the *armeros*.

Aritz Aduriz initially helps his fellow Basques out, scoring with a determined header in the 14th minute – a goal which means as much to Eibar as it does to Athletic Club. Controversy soon follows when a seemingly good Deportivo equaliser is ruled out for not much more than the fact referee Gil Manzano feels like it, allowing a sigh of relief for both Athletic and Eibar. With that slight hiccup successfully navigated, Athletic dominate the rest of the contest, but the theme of the match is one of the home side – and this is a technical term – ballsing up chance after chance.

It seems it won't matter – and a 1-0 win secured – when just three minutes of stoppage time are added on, yet in the 93rd minute the worst happens.

It may have taken until stoppage time for Deportivo's first shot on target, but Albert Lopo's late effort somehow ripples the net. His header is on target, but straight at the goalkeeper, Iago Herrerín. Devastatingly, the keeper somehow allows it to slip through his gloves.

They may do so in the most inelegant of manners, but Deportivo get their point here in Bilbao and the shockwaves hardly have to travel far to reach Ipurua. The only good news for the Eibar fans who witness the evening's events unfold here at San Mamés – and believe me, there are more than a few – is that Almería face a testing fixture against Málaga tomorrow which, if lost, brings them right back into this battle to avoid the drop.

Little do these fans know it, but Málaga would indeed come out on top in one of the season's many Andalusian derbies, though only just. An own goal from Casado would spare the blushes of Amrabat, whose shot at a near open goal would have missed had it not been bundled into the net by the Almería centre-back. Thomas would then level things up before the break, but a Javi Guerra goal with 20 minutes remaining would seal a Málaga win and, more importantly for those at the bottom, an Almería loss.

It is now incredibly complex at the bottom of the table, thanks to the league's head-to-head rule. To cut to the chase, here is the La Liga rule book's instructions for a scenario where more than one club is level on points: "If the tie is between more than two clubs, then the tie is broken using the games the clubs have played against each other: a) head-to-head points, b) head-to-head goal difference, c) head-to-head goals scored."

What is simpler to understand is that, with two weeks remaining, one point separates four teams. Only two can survive.

La Liga standings after *jornada* 36

#	Team	Matches Played	Matches Won	Matches Drawn	Matches Lost	Points
16	Almería	36	8	8	20	32
17	Deportivo	36	6	13	17	31
18	Granada	36	6	13	17	31
19	Eibar	36	8	7	21	31
20	Córdoba*	36	3	11	22	20

* Córdoba mathematically relegated.

Thursday, 14th May 2015. Barajas Airport, Madrid.

You'll have developed a sense by now that those charged with governing Spanish football are pretty disorganised. That's why it isn't actually surprising that as I land here in Madrid for Eibar's Sunday evening crunch match with Getafe I still have no idea whether or not the game will actually be played.

With just two weeks of the season remaining, an indefinite strike has been called to Spanish football and is due to officially begin on Saturday. In brief, the Spanish Football League and the Spanish government have drafted a new law which will enforce a collective sale of TV rights in Spanish football, one which will, in theory, level the playing field and reduce Barcelona and Real Madrid's share of the jackpot and increase the share of clubs like Eibar – the club which only made €11 million from TV this season. The status quo is in need of change as the current system is as behind the times as the VHS, so this is good news for everyone, minus those at the top two clubs and at Athletic Club – where any extra income will be of little use in the transfer market due to their Basque-only policy. With even Barcelona and Real Madrid reluctantly on board, it should have been very simple for this decree to pass through congress, but the Spanish Football Federation and the players' union have both objected.

They do not necessarily disagree with the idea of the new law; they are more upset at the drafting of the wording, the lack of consultation with their members and the fact even more power will be, in essence, transferred to the league. A preliminary hearing was held yesterday and the announcement from the High Court is expected today, either backing the proposed strike action or postponing it until later in the year.

When the strike was first announced on 6th May, it always seemed likely this dispute would be settled sooner or later, but the fact many *Segunda* matches are due to kick off in just two days' time – while *Primera* fixtures are all scheduled for Sunday – suggests the strike could actually happen. Once again the shit has hit the fans, the ones left to suffer.

Regardless, I'm here in Madrid for what will definitely be a vital game should it take place. The *Copa del Rey* tie away to Getafe may have mattered little, but this penultimate match of the league campaign screams importance. In some ways, this is more of a cup match than those actual cup matches. Lose and Eibar may well be out. Of the *Primera* division.

The club has recognised the importance and, as a follow-on from its 'Ipurua 6,267' campaign, have organised free buses for travelling fans. If you think that's a great gesture – and it is – the fact all players and coaching staff are forking out on five tickets each for Eibar fans is even more special. The €150 each is paying may be a drop in the ocean for some La Liga stars, but is far from an insignificant expense for these players and coaching personnel when you consider their modest wages. Once again, Eibar is outdoing itself.

As I ponder all of this, I exit the Madrid Metro system into the city centre and as my phone recovers signal it begins to vibrate. "So-and-so and so-and-so are tweeting about…" flashes up. After a couple of seconds of loading, my phone's pixels arrange themselves into a message of good news. The strike has been postponed. We have football this weekend!

Sunday, 17th May 2015. Coliseum Alfonso Pérez, Madrid.

We've jumped up and down so hard the seats beneath us have collapsed to the ground. The tide of celebration has caused an avalanche, but thankfully the morphine of the equaliser dulls any injuries. In front of us Borja Fernández screams with his fist pumped in the air and we catch a glimpse of the epic sight as we clamber up from the ground.

There is one full half and ten minutes of this one remaining and we'll have to watch them without any seats; the blue bits of plastic we were standing on when Borja nipped in at the far post to nod home a corner are now scattered across our row here in the sweltering heat – well, at least for a Scotsman – of the Coliseum Alfonso Pérez. Nobody is caring about that right now given the magnitude of the goal.

When Fredy Hinestroza opened the scoring three minutes earlier it appeared the familiar Eibar story of promising much but delivering little was about to be retold. Now, however, the scores are level and Eibar's confidence is much higher than at 0-0. The 700 Eibar fans – filling nine of the club's free buses, the record number to attend an Eibar away match – continue to back the visitors, although our row of fans now does so standing precariously on the metal bar that minutes previously had held our seats. Joseba, with his megaphone on one side of the stand, and Blas with his umbrella on the other lead the game of chanting tennis. A rally of battle cries is the backing track to the half-time whistle and it is now the moment to check the other scores.

With this being the season's penultimate week, all matches are being held simultaneously which means Almería, Deportivo and Granada are all in action. The kids in the Eibar support appear to have been tasked with monitoring the radio stations, but their half-time news is not good as Deportivo and Almería are winning against Levante and Sevilla respectively, while Granada's match back home in Gipuzkoa against Real Sociedad remains goalless.

Throughout the second half, we'll be more frequently updated with the scores elsewhere. This is good news considering the game here in southern Madrid is dying out, with Getafe content to defend the draw that will keep them safe and Eibar struggling to break down a stingy defence. First, a cheer comes up from the back of our stand as Sevilla equalise against Almería, followed by a second 'hip hip hooray' for the Seville side when they take the lead five minutes later.

The next piece of news is much less positive; Granada take the lead against Real Sociedad, the worst possible news for Eibar. The next murmurings of a radio update are even more devastating as at 7.34pm both Granada and Deportivo double their respective leads.

This is disastrous for Eibar, even if their next match is at home to already-relegated Córdoba at the same time as Almería host Valencia, Granada host Atlético Madrid and Deportivo visit Barcelona. There was hope their relegation rivals would slip up tonight to make for a comfortable final day of the season. As the final whistles sound around the country, and as the Eibar players come over to applaud the fans and toss a few sweaty shirts – this is the last outing for the blue away shirt – all of us here know next week will not be easy.

Perhaps, it should be said, the most important goal of the weekend in terms of Eibar's fight for survival was not scored in the Almería loss or the Deportivo and Granada wins, but right here in the capital. Leo Messi rounded off a precious one-two move with Pedro to seal the league title for Barcelona in the Vicente Calderón and the consequences of Barcelona having nothing to play for on the final day will be telling.

La Liga standings after *jornada* 37

#	Team	Matches Played	Matches Won	Matches Drawn	Matches Lost	Points
16	Granada	37	7	13	17	34
17	Deportivo	37	7	13	17	34
18	Eibar	37	8	8	21	32
19	Almería	37	8	8	21	32
20	Córdoba*	37	3	11	23	20

* Córdoba mathematically relegated.

A FAIRYTALE SEASON: ACT 5

6.30pm, Saturday, 23rd May 2015. Ipurua Stadium, Eibar.
Kick-off approaches on this, the most important day in Eibar's history. It is 363 days since Jota won promotion to the *Primera* right here at Ipurua. That was extraordinary, but now Eibar has a chance to pull off a feat even more remarkable than reaching Spain's top division: staying in it.

There are no fewer than 81 different scenarios for how today's action could pan out. All four matches with relegation significance – Eibar versus Córdoba, Almería versus Valencia, Barcelona versus Deportivo and Granada versus Atlético Madrid – will take place at the same time and for Eibar the scenario is actually fairly simple. They must win to have any chance of staying up.

Then they must hope for other results to go their way and this is where it gets complicated. As previously mentioned in the book, when teams are level on points it is not goal difference which separates teams but their head-to-head records – not including away goals. In the case of more than one team being level on points, teams are separated using a) head-to-head points, b) head-to-head goal difference, c) head-to-head goals scored. All four relegation-threatened teams could end up level on points should Eibar and Almería win and Deportivo and Granada draw – a scenario which would see Granada and Eibar fall to the *Segunda*. The problem for Eibar comes as soon as Deportivo enter the head-to-head equation as they lost 1-0 and 2-0 to the Galician side, whereas, individually, Eibar have a better head-to-head record over Almería and an equal head-to-head record with Granada but superior goal difference – by a whopping 11 whole goals – which would give Eibar the advantage.

While the abacuses may need to be dusted off and brought along here to a sell-out Ipurua of a record 6,065 fans, it will only be in the stands where the advanced mathematics of today's action need to be calculated. For the players it is simple: win no matter what and then see. As Eibar haven't lost any of their previous nine official matches against Córdoba – winning six and drawing three – a win is very possible, even if there has been talk of the Andalusians being offered a controversial win bonus for today's match.

All will soon unfold. Ready, set, go.

6.35pm, Saturday, 23rd May 2015. Camp Nou, Barcelona.
It had to be Messi.

The day may belong to departing captain Xavi, playing his last Camp Nou league match, but it is unsurprisingly Messi who opens the scoring with a header in just the fifth minute here at the Camp Nou.

It may seem obvious Barcelona should take the lead so early against a relegation struggler, but with nothing to play for and a fairly weak starting XI on the pitch by Barcelona's standards – third choice goalkeeper Masip starts, while other notable absentees are Gerard Piqué, Dani Alves, Jordi Alba and Luis Suárez – this is an encouraging surprise for Eibar fans.

6.36pm, Saturday, 23rd May 2015. Camp Nou, Barcelona.

News has filtered through of Messi's early strike and Ipurua is already climbing some notches as the fans dial up the atmosphere. With Deportivo losing, Eibar know if they take care of business then the impossible dream of avoiding relegation will be achieved. And then… *'Gooooooooooolllllllllll!!!!'*

It is Mikel Arruabarrena – who else! – who is embraced by all his team-mates by the corner flag, but Ander Capa deserves most of the credit for this goal. The Eibar youth product does expertly well to control a diagonal ball into the area and skilfully loft it back towards the six-yard box for Arruabarrena to score a daydream of a header past the keeper.

Just three minutes later the mood is only slightly soured by news of Almería taking the lead over Valencia. It is a massive goal for them, but Eibar remain out of the relegation zone on a head-to-head tie-breaker over Almería and Granada. Then things get even better.

Bóveda wins a corner and from the resulting set piece it is Raúl Navas who scores Eibar's second goal of the day, accurately arrowing a header from the edge of the box into the top corner to send the *Eskozia La Brava* fans behind the goal into a kaleidoscope-esque blur of pulsing blue, claret and limbs.

It is 2-0 here. It is 1-0 in Barcelona. But it isn't over until the fat lady sings.

6.44pm, Saturday, 23rd May 2015. Camp Nou, Barcelona

The ball is in the back of the net. The goal will not count on the Camp Nou scoreboard, but this incorrect offside decision will count on the league table come the end of the afternoon.

Neymar sends a perfect ball into the feet of the onside Messi who, in his typical mercurial fashion, controls with one touch and with the next puts the ball past Fabri in the Deportivo goal. Fabri is permitted a lifeline and allowed to pick the ball out of the net and take the resulting free kick. He will have plenty more work to do before his season is done.

6.58pm, Saturday, 23rd May 2015. Mediterranean Games Stadium, Almería.

As we've already heard, Almería are one goal up, but Valencia have so much to play for themselves if they want to guarantee Champions

League football ahead of Sevilla. They have a corner in the 28th minute.

The ball is sent in from the left corner by Rodrigo De Paul into the path of Nicolás Otamendi, who claps the ball into the net with his forehead.

1-1 here in the south.

7.04pm, Saturday, 23rd May 2015. Ipurua Stadium, Eibar.
We have Mexican waves here at Ipurua! As it stands Eibar are not only safe, but are in 16th position. As it stands they are 3-0 up.

The most recent goal has just been scored by Capa, who more than deserves it, not just for his work today, but for the whole season. It is Capa who steals the ball in the Córdoba half of the field and he receives the ball back via the chest of Saúl Berjón just seconds later, before turning and embarking on a foray towards goal which culminates in a cleaner-than-soap strike into the far corner, evoking the spirit of glorious final days of seasons past.

Capa's goal versus Hospitalet two years ago was the cherry on top of that promotion-winning day. Could his goal today be the cherry on top of a win that saves Eibar?

7.18pm, Saturday, 23rd May 2015. Los Cármenes Stadium, Granada.
It's half-time in Granada so it feels like it's also worth checking in on this game.

It's really not. This has been a bore of an event, played at an uninspiring methodical pace so far. It will continue to be so, with a draw suiting Atlético in terms of wrapping up automatic Champions League qualification and a draw suiting Granada, provided Almería and Deportivo don't win, which with it 2-2 at half-time at the Mediterranean Games Stadium, and 1-0 at the Camp Nou, is fine so far.

Granada coach José Ramón Sandoval would even admit as much post-match. "Openly trading blows with Atlético may not have worked out so well," he would tell the press.

7.44pm, Saturday, 23rd May 2015. Camp Nou, Barcelona.
Again, it had to be Messi.

This time Neymar does all the work and plays a superb ball into his striking partner to allow Messi the simplest of strikes to double Barcelona's lead. Half an hour remains and Barcelona look on course to celebrate their final league match of the season, and the collection of their trophy, with a win.

Even more importantly, this goal is saving Eibar. Either a three-goal Córdoba comeback – or a two-goal Deportivo comeback – is required to put Eibar down, and neither is likely. Anything is possible in football, however. Eibar themselves have proven as much.

7.44pm, Saturday, 23rd May 2015. *Los Cármenes Stadium, Granada.*

We've had a shot on goal in Granada! In the 59th minute of the match, Koke's long-range and easy-to-stop effort along the ground will register as the only shot on target in this whole shameful excuse of a football match.

If the Granada fans weren't so happy that other results are currently going their way then it would have been a shame for them to have paid to witness such a passive match. They are having a great time, particularly as the news from the Camp Nou comes through – and Almería are still drawing with Valencia.

Both those results are to change.

7.56pm, Saturday, 23rd May 2015. *Camp Nou, Barcelona.*

Deportivo La Coruña are now just one goal from safety, having pulled one back against Barcelona. Teams don't come back from two goals down at the Camp Nou, though, so Lucas Pérez's zinger of a shot must surely be a consolation goal.

Not so, as with just ten more minutes on the hypothetical Camp Nou clock – La Liga rules do not permit stadium clocks to run on the final day – Salomão strikes a rebound into the Camp Nou net, and a dagger into Eibar hearts. It comes from a free kick on the edge of the area which is blocked once by Rafinha in the wall, again by Rafinha who gets in front of Medunjanin's swing at the rebound, but then Salomão's effort is third time lucky and somehow Deportivo have cut a two-goal deficit at the Camp Nou, evoking a tear or two from the eyes of Deportivo president Tino Fernández in the stands.

The conspiracy theorists will say that Barcelona deliberately lay down for Deportivo, an argument fuelled by Deportivo centre-back Alberto Lopo's later admission to asking some Barcelona players to "ease off a little because a draw is good for all of us" and by images of goalscorer Pérez screaming "please Leo" towards Messi. Those same people will also claim matches involving Eibar's rivals have been pre-arranged in some secret smoke-filled room, as is a more frequent occurrence than one would think or hope in Spain; exchanges of *maletines*, the briefcases of corrupt payments, are not uncommon.

Giving the benefit of the doubt, one would hope the recent great run of form of Eibar's rivals is exactly that: great form. And, in all seriousness, rather than deliberately concede two goals, Barcelona probably tried to keep their lead but had 11 hearts less than the Deportivo players – who still have plenty to play for.

Yes, Barcelona's players were given three days' holiday this week and, yes, they are playing with a weaker starting XI, but although Eibar fans may not want to admit this, Eibar – like Deportivo – are also playing a weaker team than they would have at any other point in the season. Already-relegated Córdoba have given several youth players an opportunity today.

Still, unfortunately for Eibar, here in Barcelona the pending departure of Xavi in his last league match at the Camp Nou is of greater concern than the result and their hero marches off to a standing ovation on 86 minutes. His replacement, Andres Iniesta, is none too shabby himself – no pun intended. Four minutes remain, plus stoppage time, for Barcelona to get a goal and save Eibar or, ridiculously enough, for Deportivo to win the match and save Eibar. Were the away side to take all three points and move clear of Eibar in the table, Eibar would have the advantage over Granada in the tie-breaker. As it stands, with Deportivo also involved in the three-team head-to-head tie-breaker on 35 points, Eibar would lose out to both Deportivo and Granada.

Four minutes remain to find the cherry to top off this wonderful season.

8.18pm, Saturday, 23rd May 2015. Ipurua Stadium, Eibar.

Just as they have been in the directors' box of the Camp Nou, tears are falling here at Ipurua; although they drop to the ground weighted with far less joy. A 3-0 win is how it finished, a wonderful way to sign off a season in the *Primera* division no-one here in Eibar ever dreamed they would be able to complete. Staying up seemed as impossible at the beginning of the season as it does now, but that there is even still a chance of the league's by-far smallest team avoiding the drop with minutes to go in the other matches is as great an achievement as any other.

Unfortunately for Eibar's fans, the cherry to go on top of this season is not to be found here at Ipurua and an agonising reliance on results elsewhere ensues while the ever-cheesy, upbeat and video game-esque club anthem trumpets awkwardly around the stadium.

There isn't long to wait for the always-predictable Granada and Atlético goalless draw to be confirmed and by now we know that Almería have lost 3-2 to Valencia in a game Almería had to win to stand a chance. But several more minutes remain before the full-time whistle will sound across in Barcelona and Eibar need a goal; at the moment the league table does not read in Eibar's favour unless you really squint your eyes and tilt your head to the side.

At 8.21pm the whistle does eventually blow and, as one Spanish commentator puts it, "the Deportivo players appear happier than the champions". That fat lady, she has sung.

The Eibar fans have admirably avoided pondering relegation for so long. But now, like Wile E. Coyote, when he finally looks down after having broken over the cliff edge, the realisation sinks in that Eibar are going down. Still, however, they sing. With the club anthem still blaring out, the players return from the tunnel to a goosebump-evoking standing ovation. A couple of results from Barcelona and Granada will not change the fact these players are heroes.

Picture this: Eibar have finished third-bottom of a league everybody expected them to finish bottom in and they were even safe for 69 minutes of today's action. They have only fallen into the bottom three by a whisker. What if Barcelona had nicked a last-minute goal? What if Deportivo hadn't scored that late equaliser in Bilbao on 9th May? What if Raúl Navas hadn't got injured when Eibar played Granada? What if Eibar hadn't completely collapsed against Levante and Rayo Vallecano?

One more point would have saved Eibar and in previous years when the league used goal difference to separate ties they would not even have required further points. Eibar finish level on points with Deportivo and Granada above them, but their goal difference of minus 21 is four better than Deportivo's and 14 better than Granada's – Eibar's is the second-best goal difference in the whole of the bottom half of the table. Eibar, perhaps unfairly, will go down. Yes, everyone knew the rules at the start of the campaign and for that reason the result of this head-to-head three-way tie between Deportivo, Granada and Eibar is 'fair'. Yet…

I've always been a firm believer in the idea that at the end of 38 matches 'the league table never lies'. Not so much with this league table. To decide a three-way split with the results of just the four matches played against those two other teams – meaning anomalies such as Eibar's 15th September loss to Deportivo where the shot count read 14 to four in favour of Eibar are worth a quarter, instead of a 38th of the weighting – rather than with goal difference derived from the full 38 matches, makes it impossible to gain a true reflection of a team's performance over the whole season. Goal difference, in this writer's humble opinion, does reflect how consistently good or bad a team has been over the full season and I feel there should be at least some reward for losing matches by just one goal rather than five, six, seven or even eight as both Deportivo and Granada have done on occasion this season.

Granada, for example, played a weakened starting XI, with as much substance as a Pot Noodle, away to Real Madrid and duly lost 9-1 in a game which almost insulted the sport, while they saved players for the following match against Celta de Vigo where they picked up a now-even-more-important draw. Eibar also played those two sides one after the other, playing their strongest XI to lose 3-0 versus Real Madrid and then falling to a 1-0 defeat against Vigo. Of course, Granada earned a point while Eibar didn't, but should there not be a reward for trying and losing with dignity instead of not bothering? With these head-to-head rules making goal difference almost irrelevant, the integrity of the game is compromised when teams are incentivised to rest their starters in these unwinnable games away to Real Madrid.

Eibar did not, which does not mean they should be allowed to remain in the division on some sort of moral exception. Of course not. Eibar also knew the rules and it might be in their interests to rest players at the Bernabéu, but Eibar showed just why the footballing family love their story. They always compete to their maximum. Even when the perverse incentives of modern football may encourage them to do otherwise, this team retains fair play and competitive spirit which made us all fall in love with the game as kids in a public park many moons ago.

If keeping that footballing spirit intact – not to mention doing so within their budget rather than by ripping off the tax man – requires relegation, then I know Eibar will always choose that route.

And their fans will choose it with them. Here they are showering praise on Eibar's reluctant superstars. 'You made our dreams possible no matter the result' reads one of the many banners here today. What a remarkable, impossible, unforgettable and privileged season this has been. It goes without saying the fans wanted to stay up, but all here know it would have been an achievement even greater than last year's promotion. This tiny club had no right to expect a *Primera* place then, and had no right to expect one today. Sometimes in football, the underdog stories must come to an end, at which point you simply must show your gratitude for the remarkable story so far.

As Barcelona's *azulgrana* confetti this year falls over a result which has just relegated Eibar 400 kilometres away, rather than through the air of this Basque valley, Ipurua is as noisy and supportive as always.

"Eibar! Eibar! Eibar!" sings the record crowd.

8.35pm, Saturday, 23rd May. Ipurua Press Room, Eibar.

He really doesn't need to resign, yet that is exactly what an energy-sapped Gaizka Garitano does here in a subdued press room at Ipurua.

"I was very determined to stay with Eibar in the *Primera*, but I didn't accomplish the goal and I have to go," he says. "A manager who gets relegated does not have the authority to continue."

That may often be true, but Garitano is a different breed of hero in Eibar and to even have achieved one promotion was amazing. Instead, Garitano achieved the impossible and then led his team above both Córdoba and Almería and to equal points as Deportivo and Granada. There has not been even a whisper all season of Garitano being sacked; even when Eibar went on an 11-game winless run he was able to get on with his work without the Sword of Damocles hanging over him.

Contrastingly, Eibar's rivals have been ruthless with varying degrees of success. Córdoba went through three managers, as did Almería and Granada, while Deportivo have had two. Again, things work differently up here in Eibar, even if it would be fictitious to say the club has never been one to sack managers midway through a season.

"The team has worked as hard as it could all year, overcoming all the difficulties we've had in playing in this division. It's a shame because I think the lads deserved to stay in this division. It's been a bit hard and unfair, but that's football," laments a downbeat Garitano. "Life goes on and Eibar will go on," he concludes, painting a picture of optimism for "a new project".

Such honesty is refreshing given most post-match press conferences contain more lies than a typical dating website profile. Mikel Mandinabeita of the *Diario Vasco* is one of the journalists present and I speak to him afterwards about Garitano's overtly honest press conference.

"The truth is that it [his resignation] was a surprise," Mikel tells me. "We knew the manager had an automatic renovation clause should they remain in the division, but we were unsure of his future in the case of relegation. What was most surprising was he announced it right there in the heat of the moment, with his tears still wet, which caused incredulousness among those present. But all the while he displayed a dignity which is uncommon in modern football. He said his principles prevented him from continuing since he hadn't achieved the initial objective."

Garitano is painting the season as a failure; for a realist he is paradoxically idealistic. A season in which only Rayo Vallecano and Celta de Vigo finished higher relative to their budget than Eibar did need not be looked back on this way.

To almost triple Gijón's record-worst points haul of 13 surpassed expectations. To reach a high of eighth place surpassed expectations. To finish ahead of two clubs with larger budgets surpassed expectations. To record the best goal difference of the bottom eight surpassed expectations. To even be in the *Primera* in the first place surpassed expectations. This is not a failure – rather it is a muted triumph.

Regardless, Garitano feels the need to depart and it makes his final press conference a special moment, particularly for the way it concludes. Mikel describes the scenes: "Garitano then got up and there was applause, which drew him to hug each journalist present. It was a goodbye as unusual as it was emotional and it confirmed that Gaizka is a gentleman of the sport."

Eibar may have lost out today, but that sport of which Garitano is a gentleman is to shortly repay Eibar's fantastic economic model. This story is not quite finished yet.

A FAIRYTALE SEASON: ACT 5

La Liga final standings

#	Team	Matches Played	Matches Won	Matches Drawn	Matches Lost	Points
16	Deportivo	38	7	14	17	35
17	Granada	38	7	14	17	35
18	Eibar*	38	9	8	21	35
19	Almería*	38	8	8	22	32**
20	Córdoba*	38	3	11	24	20

* Eibar, Almería and Córdoba relegated.
** Almería to be deducted three further points after the season, finishing with 29 points.

10

Justicia

"The prestige of the competition is at stake."

Álex Aranzábal

Monday, 1st June 2015. Ipurua Press Room, Eibar.
We're back in the Ipurua press room where Garitano resigned just over a week ago at the end of the season. Or was it the end of the season? Not according to Álex Aranzábal.

For the second consecutive year, Eibar's season is over on the pitch, but, "not in the offices", announces Aranzábal. For the second consecutive year, it appears Eibar are to be denied a rightful place in the *Primera* because of financial rules. Here's why.

Elche is in a financial mess. The 'Elche Model' is as reckless as the 'Eibar Model' is sensible and the Valencian Community club owes €15million in debts; €9million is owed to the *Hacienda*, the Spanish tax man, while €6million is owed to its players who have gone unpaid. This, remember, is one of Raúl Albentosa's former clubs and we touched upon this subject in the *Modelo* chapter. To quickly refresh your memory, he told me: "I had been playing in Spain at various clubs and the only club which has paid me the full wage without delays has been Eibar."

Elche's financial woes do not end there.

The club has also yet to pay the full loan fee to Sevilla for the loan of our familiar friend Manu del Moral for the 2013/14 season; the forward – just like Raúl Albentosa – ironically moved from a financial mess to the country's model club which has, unsurprisingly, already squared Sevilla up for his services this season past. Furthermore, former president José Sepulcre was banned from football for 18 months in February for accounting irregularities, which included an unallocated €1,531,000 which some have alleged was used to buy football matches. It is currently being investigated by the Valencian money-laundering authorities. If Eibar is the textbook example of how to run a football club well, then Elche is the antithesis. Fate would have it, therefore, these two models of football management would come directly up against each other this June.

JUSTICIA

Because of Elche's financial debts and irregularities, the club – which finished the season 13th – is in breach of Article 76 of the *Ley Deporte, 10/1990*, the country's sports law. For that reason, the Spanish Football League's social disciplinary judge Manuel Rivero González should rule to demote Elche should their debts remain unsettled after 29th May. It surely won't come as a surprise to learn the deadline passed without the full debt repaid.

Rather than settle the €15million debt, Elche instead announced a timeline on Friday of their intentions to settle their debts. New president Juan Anguix had reached an agreement with the tax man to repay the debt in instalments and, in Elche's eyes, this should suffice to appease the judge. Not so in the Basque Country, and elsewhere in Spain, where one argument, above all others, is being raised. If Eibar had to raise the required capital to the very last cent, why should Elche be treated more favourably?

That argument is coming loudest and clearest right now from the press room of Ipurua, where president Álex Aranzábal, sporting director Fran Garagarza and finance manager Patricia Rodriguez Barrios are calling for equal treatment. It may seem a little suspect that Eibar – the team which would benefit most from Elche's administrative relegation by taking their *Primera* division place given they finished third-bottom – is the club calling for *justicia,* for justice, but as the country's model club, which recently was forced to comply with the existing laws, it has every right to speak out.

"This is not only a cause which affects Eibar, but a general cause for all of football," states Aranzábal. "It is not Eibar's position which is at stake, but the credibility of football. The prestige of the competition is at stake. We are confident the law will be enforced."

The prestige of the competition is indeed at stake. Elche owes almost as much money to its players as Eibar's entire 2014/15 sporting budget – which is unfair. Yes, Eibar was always going to be the smallest club, but if Elche did not have the money to pay its playing staff then it should have similarly downscaled; instead it had a sporting budget for the 2014/15 season larger than four other clubs and €5million larger than Eibar's, according to Spanish football finance blogger Roberto Bayon.

Perhaps even more concerning is that the Spanish tax man is yet to be fully repaid. I spoke to Sid Lowe about a similar case in 1995 when Celta de Vigo and Sevilla were both demoted for their financial sins, only to be reinstated after much toing and froing into an increased and 'shambolic' league of 22 teams. Sid explained there has been a "social change" in the two decades since. "Fans are much less inclined to support their club's ability to screw over the tax man, or the rest of us, than they once were," he suggests, before looking to the example of Sevilla. "Even the Sevilla fan, if he sees his club hasn't paid the tax man, he thinks: 'But I pay the tax man, they're chasing me if I owe them money, so why should the club get away with it?'"

In these tough economic times, football fans are much less likely to turn a blind eye to excessive spending, particularly if their own public purse is lighter as a result. Jose Enrique sums this up, saying: "Elche's problem is not just for Eibar. It is for all citizens who pay their taxes day after day. We are all *Hacienda*, the tax man."

Eskozia La Brava certainly feel this way as well. The *peña* stated: "If you're a defaulting club and you use the money of everyone to sign players rather than pay the tax man then you should be demoted."

It's easy to sympathise with these fans. Last year Eibar was debtless and strictly forced to raise over €1.7million to secure its place in the *Primera* and avoid demotion to the *Segunda B*. This year Elche is to repay debts of €15million if it is to keep its place in the *Primera* and avoid demotion to the *Segunda B*.

All now rests on the decision of Manuel Rivero González. In typical Spanish fashion, the decision was expected today but has been postponed to later in the week.

Tuesday, 2nd June 2015. FIFA Headquarters, Zurich.

The winds of change are torpedoing through the world of football at exactly the wrong time for Elche, and the right time for Eibar and all those who want fairness in the sport.

After 17 years at the helm, Sepp Blatter is to resign as president of FIFA, just days after winning re-election, which was held after a week of arrests, investigations and a general stink of corruption allegations around football's governing body. What is not surprising is that Blatter is to step down; what is surprising is he does so now after the election win.

It had appeared as if all would be swept under the carpet yet again after Blatter won the support of 133 of the 209 voting members on Friday. Surely if Blatter was going to go it would have been before the election?

Of course, there was an outcry of opposition to Blatter's re-election on social media, in newspaper column inches and from a small number of football associations. Yet everybody knows these tend to go unacknowledged. Well, they used to.

Now, the man at the top seems to have been checking the latest trends on Twitter and reading the weekend's broadsheets. Announcing his resignation, Blatter says: "While I have a mandate from the membership of FIFA, I do not feel I have a mandate from the entire world of football – the fans, the players, the clubs, the people who live, breathe and love football as much as we all do at FIFA."

This is the surprise. Sepp Blatter has sensed the opposition to his appointment from the ground level and he has listened.

Now what does this have to do with Eibar and Elche? Quite a lot actually. With the Spanish Football League's social disciplinary judge Manuel Rivero González to rule on Elche's fate later in the week, this new era of football governance – one where those at the top take notice of fans' concerns – could force Rivero González to stick to the letter of the law and demote Elche. If the head of FIFA has been influenced by fans' protests, surely Rivero González must take heed of the fans – not just Eibar's – calling for Elche to be demoted.

Whether he does or not will soon become clear.

Friday, 5th June 2015. Spanish Football League Headquarters, Madrid.

The announcement from judge Manuel Rivero González may come several days later than anticipated, but those in Eibar will be glad he took his time to properly consider what action to take. The Spanish Football League's social disciplinary judge today announces, as a result of their "very serious infractions", Elche are to be demoted one division. Eibar, consequently, is a *Primera* division team once again!

For the second consecutive season, Eibar's top-flight place is secured off the pitch. While there is rejoicing in Eibar, one cannot help but feel sorry for the fans of Elche. They are also being punished, yet it was not them in the boardroom poorly managing the club's finances. Nevertheless, this is unsurprisingly well-received in Eibar. It is poetic justice the country's model club – the one which was almost unfairly screwed over by backwards financial rules last year despite being debt-free – is the one which benefits from Elche's torturous fall.

Many will say Eibar do not deserve to play in the 2015/16 *Primera* campaign. There is some sense to that; Eibar, although agonisingly close, were simply not good enough on the pitch to earn a place. In modern football the action on the pitch is so often secondary, which is why managing budgets and paying debts on time is now as important as success on the turf.

Of this week's off-the-field battle, Aranzábal reflects: "We went down in a cruel manner, but we're now living a new chapter, one which is taking place in the offices." He adds: "We're a little bit like Lazarus; we are back to life after having been dead." The club president is also very careful this Friday to avoid premature celebration. "The events of the day are very important, but not definitive," he says. What he is referring to is the fact Elche will, unsurprisingly, appeal the ruling to demote them one division, with a fine of €180,000.

"It's a difficult situation because nothing is for sure, but we're in a better position than we were yesterday," continues Aranzábal.

"With the law in hand, we have taken a giant step towards everything becoming clear. We must continue to work because what we know right now is Eibar is a team of the *Primera*."

A long summer of legal jostling could be ahead, but Aranzábal makes the very important point that Eibar is once again a first division team and must plan for next season on that basis.

This is fantastic news for Eibar, remaining in the *Primera*, because it would have been hard to envisage a return any time soon, but they have – in some ways – been handed a poisoned chalice. Whether it was to be Elche or Eibar occupying this last *Primera* place, either side would definitely be the least competitive in the division, and have the worst squad. Elche, had they been reprieved, would have had a transfer ban and little money – as we know – to sign players. Eibar, on the other hand, will not have the means to buy players – as we know – or offer large wages.

The task of putting together a competitive team is as challenging as it was last year – for that reason. Worse still is there will be an exodus of players, of that there is no doubt; the *Primera* is simply too good a shop window. Star players such as Eneko Bóveda are set to leave, while Raúl Navas, Manu del Moral and Federico Piovaccari will end their loan spells. Only eight players are currently on Eibar's books for the 2015/16 campaign and Fran Garagarza will have an unenviable task on his hands.

Tonight, however, that is not an issue. Today's momentous verdict means Eibar's extraordinary rise to the top does not end here.

It has been a marvellous way to spend their 75th anniversary; a year of celebration has been marked by first division football, an exposition held in the city centre, the winning of promotion to the *Segunda* by the female team and a friendly match to be played against Scottish champions Celtic at Ipurua in July. The second half of this 75th year can also be enjoyed with the backdrop of top-flight football, which is a birthday present this club deserves.

Whether or not Eibar has a good or bad season in next year's top division is beside the point. This club was never supposed to be anywhere near the *Primera*, but it will complete a second year at the top table. That is unbelievable and even if Eibar do eventually suffer relegation next season, it will return to the *Segunda* as a much stronger club and, even more importantly, a much stronger town and community.

Eibar now, incredibly, has fans across the world. It has a *peña* in the US! It has had visitors from China! Fans from all corners of the globe descended on Ipurua for that final day match with Córdoba! Now when you hear someone say "an Englishman, a Scotsman and an Irishman walk into Eibar" it may not be a joke; it may simply be an account from the weekend's match at Ipurua.

The stadium capacity has been increased, the website has been redesigned, new sponsorship deals have been struck, an online store has been introduced, which will act as a great source of revenue for the future, communication with fans and shareholders has vastly improved, tickets can now be bought online – a trivial convenience for many clubs but previously unthinkable for one the size of Eibar – and a plan for 280 underground car park spaces, an official club shop and a restaurant has been discussed. In just two years the number of *socios*, of members, has even risen from 1,800 to 4,600.

Wonderfully, this none-too-salubrious valley town's football club is now a global entity. The benefits will be huge over the course of the next decade, and throughout the inevitable return to the *Segunda* at some stage.

This club has admitted its 'natural place' is in the third division. The clock may have struck 12 on Eibar's La Liga dream, but the glass slipper did not fit Elche's financial model; instead Eibar's 'sustainable' model is the one which wins the place for next season.

I'll end this journey with a lovely quote from Unai Eraso on why Eibar is both La Liga's mightiest and smallest club:

"Greatness does not come from being big," he says. "Greatness comes from doing big things even when small."

SD Eibar, a miniature giant of the game we love.